TUXEDO

An Open Approach to OLTP

TUXEDO

An Open Approach to OLTP

Fulvio Primatesta

Prentice Hall

London New York Toronto Sydney Tokyo Singapore
Madrid Mexico City Munich

First published 1995 by
Prentice Hall International (UK) Limited
Campus 400, Maylands Avenue
Hemel Hempstead
Hertfordshire, HP2 7EZ
A division of
Simon & Schuster International Group

Printed and bound in Great Britain

Library of Congress Cataloging-in-Publication Data

Available from the publisher

British Library Cataloguing in Publication Data

A catalogue record for this book is available from
the British Library

ISBN 0-13-101833-7

---

1 2 3 4 5   99 98 97 96 95

*To my father, Giulio, and
my brother, Roberto*

Contents

Contents

Contents

Preface

When I joined AT&T UNIX System Laboratories in 1990, my perception of on-line transaction processing (OLTP) was mainly based on my previous experience as a support engineer at Ing. C.Olivetti & C. This typically involved banging my head for several days on banking applications which for obscure reasons would refuse to behave. In my restricted English vocabulary, my definition of OLTP would have sounded something like "that thing about transactions that you do on big computers and big databases".

Like many, I had never heard of the TUXEDO System and I was actually surprised to see that AT&T did not just produce UNIX, but also a transaction processing (TP) monitor for UNIX environments. Although I had seen other TP monitors for UNIX, these were proprietary products and were never intended for use outside certain specific environments. The availability of a TP monitor from a company which provided technology to a large segment of the information technology (IT) industry seemed to me something particularly new in the area of OLTP. Moreover, this product was making available a set of capabilities for distributed computing that I had never seen implemented before.

After becoming involved in support and training for this product, I had the privilege to work in regular contact with the people in charge of its development. This gave me the opportunity to discover an entirely different world beyond the stereotyped definitions of OLTP. I soon became convinced that a lot of use can be made of the TUXEDO System in a changing IT industry.

I also had to realise, though, how difficult it can be to convey sufficient information and technical detail to the people who turn to this product for the first time. This is why the idea of a book came about. Thanks to a continuously growing interest in UNIX OLTP (and to some improvements in my English vocabulary), I was eventually able to undertake the adventure of writing this book.

Being the first book on this subject, I worked kind of blindfold as far as the amount of information and detail was concerned. Of course much more could be done and different approaches could be taken, but I hope I have been able to put together a reasonable mix of everything. I no longer work for AT&T UNIX System Laboratories (now Novell's), but I still believe that TUXEDO will play an increasingly important role in OLTP and distributed computing. If you are currently using the product or planning to, I hope this book will be useful reference material.

Finally, it is my personal belief that everyone should contribute to improving the living conditions on our planet. In a world where wars, grief, and misery are common facts of life, where ignorance, prejudice, and poverty dictate the fate of hundreds of millions of people, I think that widespread school education is the only basis for making people more tolerant. For this reason I decided to contribute all royalties from this book to the support of students in the developing countries. This is my modest contribution; by purchasing this book, this will be your contribution too.

Acknowledgements

Writing this book has been a challenging task all the way through, one which required an effort that I had probably underestimated (prefaces to books are full of good advice, but of course I did not believe that until I touched it with my own hand), but also one which certainly proved very rewarding on a personal and professional basis. I am fully aware of the fact that my efforts would have produced nothing if I didn't have the help and support of a number of people, to whom I owe a lot of gratitude.

First of all, I would like to thank Scott Orshan, Graeme Vetterlein, Julian Lomberg, Mark Carges, Terry Dwyer, and Ed Heeren for going through the unenviable task of reading my English, trying to make some sense out of it, and making valuable comments nevertheless. Working in the same office as me, Graeme and Julian had also the even less enviable privilege of listening to my spoken English. I hope this wasn't too painful for anyone. Thank you.

Thank you also to Rainer Lutz and Steve Pendergrast, who contributed some of the examples in the Appendix, and to Peter Lord and Agnieszka Wadowska-Rees, who helped me when I ran into troubles with xcip and troff.

For some time Daves Rossell and I considered the possibility of writing the book together, but timeframes and distance prevented it. Daves' support was nonetheless very important for me, as it helped me gain confidence at the very beginning of the project.

Many other people offered their help and support at several stages: Alan Brown, Amma Brown, Jennie Grimes, C.H. Hariharan, Bill Hartford, Bob

Mitze, Chris Papayianni, and Ed Saunders. Angela Greaves gave me the number of Prentice Hall; this mistake, plus the fact that she had her desk next to mine, forced her to be supportive ever since, especially during the lunch breaks.

I would like to thank Novell/USL, for allowing me to use the product's glossary and some diagrams from their training material. A big thank you goes also to Viki Williams, my editor, for giving me the opportunity to complete this task, to Ann Greenwood, for her suggestions about the layout of the book, and to the reviewers, for their valuable comments.

Finally, last but by no means least, a grateful kiss goes to my wife Kathryn, who was not my wife when this job started, and despite being forced to spend many weekends at home fixing my English, still agreed to marry me.

Brussels, January 1995

Introduction

The subject of on-line transaction processing (OLTP) has often generated a special interest within the information technology (IT) industry, probably because transactions have always been associated, in one way or another, with money. Whether a transaction is an actual money transfer, a change of seat reservation between flights, or an update of insurance premiums, whether one sees the transaction from a business or a technical point of view, the sequence of operations constituting a transaction mean money to the parties involved. The unsuccessful or inefficient handling of such operations, typically in the case of failures somewhere in the system, will no doubt have some financial implications for either the customer or the company.

Because of this special interest, transaction processing (TP) systems have often been seen as a world on their own. As a consequence, the specific technology they have introduced over the years has mostly been associated with certain types of business, for example banking, and with particular types of computers, mainly mainframes.

As a result of the growing interest in Open Systems, however, in recent years there has been increasing demand for UNIX® environments to make available the OLTP capabilities traditionally provided by mainframe systems. At the same time, growing emphasis on distributed computing has led to the need for transaction processing to address new types of requirements related to the exploitation of the very nature of Open Systems, i.e. the interoperability of the widest possible range of different hardware and software.

Within this framework, the TUXEDO® System (or, in short, TUXEDO) has gained a considerable reputation as one of the first products available to put together these industry requirements. Since a number of vendors brought it onto the market, it has generated increasing interest within traditional OLTP environments such as financial institutions, and among a variety of other environments, which have started considering OLTP capabilities for a more effective implementation of distributed applications.

Because of the inherent complexity of OLTP in distributed environments, a system like TUXEDO, designed to address multiple requirements of different nature, provides an array of features which reach beyond the scope of pure transaction processing. Therefore, a clear understanding of TUXEDO's features and the context in which they belong is important for a correct evaluation of this product at various levels, from management information systems (MIS) planning to application design and development. Yet, a clear understanding of TUXEDO's characteristics is made difficult by a number of different factors, which include the many angles from which the product can be approached, the new technology it brings, and the fact that it cannot really be compared on a one-to-one basis with mainframe TP monitors.

The purpose of this book therefore is to assist a variety of IT professionals with their understanding of TUXEDO and hopefully with some decision-making related to it. In order to achieve this, the book provides a set of guidelines within which the TUXEDO System can be observed and a comprehensive description of the product's architecture and capabilities.

This book will not cover the history of OLTP in any detail, since that would require an entire book in its own right. Equally, it will not examine any specific OLTP environments, nor will it compare TUXEDO with other OLTP monitors, since this approach would probably not have general validity. Instead, it will first examine the changes in the market which have led from mainframe OLTP to Open OLTP, and will then provide a description of TUXEDO in such a way that the reader can model any previous knowledge of OLTP or OLTP products into TUXEDO's framework. Hopefully this will make it possible to carry out an examination of the product in a sufficiently flexible way, outside the scope of predetermined classifications. This is the approach I have adopted for this book, and I very much hope that you will find it effective.

Who should be reading this book

Due to the relative novelty of the product, I have tried to design this book in a way that provides sufficient information to a number of categories of IT professionals. These categories include:

- MIS directors interested in acquiring a high-level understanding of the boundaries and benefits of TUXEDO, so that they may take decisions about the role of this product in their computing environment. Chapters 1, 2, and 8 are recommended in this case.

- Project managers interested in understanding the features of TUXEDO in detail, so that they may evaluate its ability to address and resolve their project's constraints. Chapters 1, 2, 3, and 8 should be read, and the high-level descriptions provided in Chapters 4, 5, 6, and 7.

- Application designers and developers who are interested in a full overview of the concepts and features of TUXEDO first from a high-level perspective, and then in more detail. Chapters 3-7, and, possibly 8, should be read in their entirety.

- People already familiar with the product but interested in different ways of looking at TUXEDO, or interested in clarifications of specific areas.

How the material is organised

Because it is designed to be used by different categories of people, this book covers more conceptual aspects than purely technical ones. The product and its features are put into context with respect to OLTP, distributed transaction processing (DTP), and more general distributed processing. Areas of interest and/or potential difficulty with respect to common knowledge are pointed out and emphasised. Examples are provided either to help with the clarification of concepts or to illustrate the usage or alternative usage of a particular feature. Wherever possible, however, examples do not refer to diagrams or illustrations, thus making reading more straightforward. For the same reason, I have tried to use a colloquial style, as if talking to the reader.

The material is organised in such a way that each chapter builds upon the contents of the previous ones, starting with the basic concepts and features and moving towards more specialised ones. When the "building" process is complete, a final chapter organised by topics provides a sort of "transversal" reading of the book, putting together ideas and features seen in the previous chapters. To permit a high-level reading of the book, descriptions of all features begin with a conceptual introduction, which can be read independently of the technical presentation. Chapter by chapter, the material is organised as follows:

- *Chapter 1* provides a brief introduction to OLTP and describes the changes in the industry that have led to a new definition of OLTP for open systems. This will help to set the proper framework within which the TUXEDO System must be observed.

- *Chapter 2* provides a general introduction to the TUXEDO System. Since the reader may have little or no previous knowledge of the product, it is presented from different perspectives. First, TUXEDO is presented in its role as software backplane for distributed computing. Here the emphasis is put on the integration of heterogeneous environments rather than directly on OLTP. Second, the relationship between TUXEDO and OLTP is discussed, as well as the requirements that must be addressed by an OLTP monitor for open systems. From this discussion, two different areas of computing are identified: distributed processing and distributed transaction processing. The specific requirements and the scope of both areas are presented. TUXEDO's basic philosophy for developing distributed applications is also introduced. Finally, comments are made about the most common reasons why TUXEDO is used in the marketplace.

- *Chapter 3* provides a detailed presentation of TUXEDO's client/server architecture. First, a high-level discussion about TUXEDO's representation of the client/server model in comparison with some traditional representations of such a model is presented. This is done by examining a couple of commonly accepted representations of the model and subsequently looking at how the presence of TUXEDO can alter the perceptions of clients and servers. Second, a detailed description of the main components of such an architecture is given, in particular application clients and servers. The application to transaction manager interface (ATMI) is also introduced, and a summary of all programming functions is provided. TUXEDO's internal implementation of the enhanced client/server model is presented, and information is provided about some of the internal administrative processes. Comments about the effectiveness of TUXEDO's architecture in relation to OLTP, DTP, and distributed processing conclude the chapter.

- *Chapter 4* examines the distributed processing features offered by the core component of TUXEDO, System/T. These features do not specifically relate to transaction management, as they constitute the more general basis for distributed computing in TUXEDO environments. The description of each feature concentrates on a set of different points, which include a conceptual introduction, a user's perspective, and additional information about the implementation. Information is provided on each feature, but the description is also put into the context of the requirements of an application. Comments are made about the importance of these features with respect to distributed processing, but not necessarily transaction processing. Meaning and usage of relevant programming interfaces and specific configuration requirements are also discussed.

- *Chapter 5* is dedicated to examining TUXEDO's capabilities in the area of transaction processing, and how these are implemented. The subjects described here include TUXEDO's DTP model, the XA interface, the two-phase commit, and a comparison between TUXEDO's DTP model and X/Open's. Emphasis is put on TUXEDO's role in DTP, on the role of resource managers, and on the features for programming transactions in a TUXEDO application. Meaning and usage of relevant programming and configuration requirements are also described.

- *Chapter 6* describes the general concept of administration in a TUXEDO environment. Information is provided about the role of the system administrator and system programmer, and procedures about the configuration of a TUXEDO application and its day-to-day administration are presented. The tools for configuration and administration are described here.

- *Chapter 7* examines those features and capabilities which are often provided as extensions and add-ons to the core product. Descriptions follow the same structure as that of the distributed processing features in Chapter 4, where a conceptual introduction is followed by a user's perspective and by comments about the implementation. In general, more considerations are provided, due to the wider implications that each of these extensions has. The extensions presented here include System/WS, System/HOST, System/Q, and System/DOMAINS.

- *Chapter 8* discusses some of the topics that are frequently the subject of interest in distributed applications and OLTP environments. The purpose of this chapter is to provide the reader, within a single section, with a collection of issues that require a transversal reading of the book. Attention is focused on understanding the reasons why the topic is relevant in TUXEDO's context, and how TUXEDO relates to it. Some of these subjects might already have been mentioned and perhaps partially addressed in previous sections, but here they can be seen from a different perspective and in a more complete form. These topics include business modelling, high application availability, migration towards TUXEDO, and a few comments on how to decide whether TUXEDO is suitable for a certain environment.

- For those who cannot resist looking into the code, *Appendix A* provides a brief case study. Examples of one client and one server in different programming languages are presented, as is a configuration file. Finally, *Appendix B* provides a list of platforms on which the TUXEDO System is available.

1. On-Line Transaction Processing

If we look back at the history of mankind, we will probably find that transactions have always been common facts of life, at least since humans started developing a type of society based on the exchange of goods. The Neanderthal man, exchanging his club for a dozen dinosaur teeth with his friend in the cave, was happily unaware that one day this action would have led to his descendants using complicated systems for making sure that one received exactly twelve teeth and not just eleven. Still, he was sowing the seeds for what, some years later, would become one of the most sophisticated areas of computing and, funnily enough, the reason for writing this book. For both these consequences, I personally haven't been able to decide if I am grateful to him or if I'll hate the man for the rest of my life; perhaps you will shortly have a strong opinion, especially as far as the latter is concerned.

Anyway, we do not need to go such a long way back and put the blame on this fellow. The subject of on-line transaction processing (OLTP) is much more a product of our times, and if someone must be blamed, it is probably the inventor of computer systems. The availability of such systems has led over the years to an increasing demand for features which would allow computers to execute transactions in a reliable and efficient manner; these features have gradually evolved into complete products, the so-called transaction processing monitors (TP monitors, or even TPMSs), and through the deployment of such products, OLTP has assumed its own identity as an independent branch of computing.

Since the TUXEDO System is very much associated with OLTP, it is important that before we start the examination of this product, we have at least a brief look at what is commonly intended as OLTP, and that we present the changes that have in recent years justified the introduction of new techniques and new systems.

1.1 OLTP

To present the characteristics of OLTP, the first step is to examine what makes transaction processing (TP) different from other types of computer processing, and this can be made easier by looking first at the actual nature of transactions.

From a business perspective, a transaction is an operation that modifies some of the business elements in such a way that the modifications are consistent with one another. A money transfer modifies the status of two bank accounts in a way that while one account is debited by a certain amount, the other is credited with the same amount. A change of flight reservation modifies the available number of seats on different flights, in a way that one more seat is available on one flight and one less is available on the other. As far as the business is concerned, a transaction is a single operation, the execution of which is either possible or impossible.

From a computing point of view, on the contrary, a transaction is typically made up of a sequence of operations, all of which have to be executed in order for the whole transaction to succeed. To complicate matters, the sequence of operations that constitute a transaction can be seen differently depending on what level of software we consider. At an application level, for example, a money transfer would probably consist of a withdrawal from one account and a deposit into another account; a change of flight reservation would consist of a cancellation on one flight and a reservation on another. At a database level, though, the same operations will correspond to a different sequence of actions, probably updates to multiple data records. A money transfer could consist of the update of a record containing the debit account, the update of a record containing the credit account, and, possibly, the update of a record containing the number of transfers performed, say, during the day. A change of flight reservation could involve the update of the list of free seats on two different flights, and, possibly, the update of records about the availability of, say, non-smoking seats on each flight.

Of course we could go into other levels of detail: file system, disk drive, and so on. Whatever the level, one important characteristic is that the computing operations which constitute a transaction could somehow be interrupted and possibly never completed, thus creating a mismatch between the business definition and the actual execution of the transaction. The main task of OLTP is to guarantee that the business definition of a transaction is maintained across the sequence of computing operations corresponding to it, no matter how technically complicated, and that either all operations are executed or none is.

Because this type of capability is not normally made available by operating systems, special systems must be used in order to enhance the computing environment with the sufficient degree of resilience and recovery required for an on-line handling of transactions, and to guarantee the expected level of operation integrity.

The need for operation and data integrity is the most evident difference between OLTP and other types of computing, but it is not the only characteristic. Because of the complexity of transactions, OLTP for example requires application control and central administration of many different components; due to the typically large number of users of OLTP systems, it puts strong emphasis on performance, efficiency, reliability, and flexibility; finally, because of the nature of the businesses addressed by OLTP environments, it usually requires high application availability.

In general, OLTP has become a branch of computing specifically aimed at addressing a certain set of requirements, which can be summarised as follows:

- *Operation integrity*: The sequence of operations corresponding to a transaction must match the business definition of the transaction, and they must therefore be guaranteed to either all succeed, or all fail.

- *Data integrity*: The sequence of data updates corresponding to a transaction must also match the business definition of the transaction, and they too must therefore be guaranteed either to all succeed, or all fail.

- *Application control*: The different components of an OLTP application must be under the control of the system, so that central administration is possible.

- *Performance management*: The system must be able to optimise the usage of communication facilities, resources, processes, and to handle situations which can have an impact on the overall performance, such as peak hours.

- *Continuous operation*: The application and its components must be available continuously, or their unavailability must at least be reduced as much as possible.

- *Graceful degradation*: The system should never totally fail. No matter how serious the failures are, at least portions of the system should stay up.

- *Quick recovery*: When problems arise, the system must be restored to a sufficient level of effectiveness and consistency in the shortest possible time.

1.2 Proprietary OLTP

Due to these special requirements, TP monitors have traditionally been "special" systems, highly specialised products specifically used for OLTP. Also, due to the types of capabilities they had to provide, typically complex and expensive from a processing point of view, TP monitors have been available mainly on mainframe systems, the only computing environment for quite some time to have sufficient power to perform such operations for a large number of users. Because of the costs related to the purchase or rental of mainframes, the main users of TP monitors have usually been either financial institutions like banks, or high-volume, high-availability environments like insurance companies or airlines.

Apart from various different features provided by different products, which we will not discuss here, a common characteristic for mainframe TP monitors has been the high degree of integration between the operating system, the data handling systems, and the TP monitor itself (Figure 1).

These components would be strictly integrated in order to achieve better results, but because of this they would also be almost impossible to split apart. As a consequence, another characteristic associated with mainframe TP monitors has been the fact that whatever the choice made for a TP system, it would also be strictly linked to a specific operating system, data handling system, and, most probably, to a specific hardware product line. The decision or the need to change software or hardware, or the attempt to integrate other components, would basically mean replacing the whole environment, and often the entire application.

Despite this potential drawback however, mainframe environments have provided over the years the most popular and widespread OLTP technology, to the extent that the number of users of OLTP systems on mainframes today is probably in the order of several millions.

Alongside the mainstream mainframe OLTP, characterised by high initial investments and high running costs, cheaper versions of OLTP have been made available in recent years on minicomputers. In response to the requirements of certain market niches, or in order to create opportunities, many computer manufacturers have developed TP monitors for environments which do not need the full power of a mainframe system. A small branch of a bank, for example, could have a TP system on a local minicomputer for local operations, and a link to a central mainframe system for access to corporate data. Like mainframe TP monitors, however, these other systems have also usually required much the same degree of integration between the various components, thus making them proprietary solutions just as much as the others.

For the same market niches, an alternative approach has been introduced,

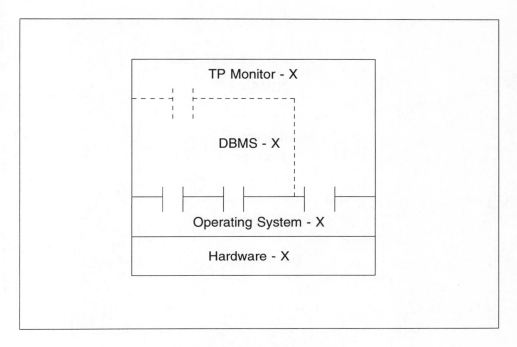

Figure 1. Mainframe OLTP

in even more recent years, by database management systems (DBMSs). These products have evolved from the pure provision of data-storing facilities to the provision of more sophisticated distributed operations, high-availability features, and administrative control. Being separate from the operating system, and being available on different platforms, very often UNIX platforms, DBMSs have constituted a more open approach to OLTP, thus introducing a new dimension for OLTP on minicomputers (Figure 2). The availability of standards in the area of database interfaces, typically SQL, has also contributed to improving the situation and making UNIX a possible platform for OLTP.

To this day, the features made available by DBMSs have constituted the main step towards the diffusion of OLTP in those environments that were trying to move away from proprietary systems. Unfortunately, though, they haven't provided a real open alternative to mainframe OLTP; if the problem with proprietary TP monitors was their applicability to one specific vendor's platform, the problem with DBMSs has been their applicability to one specific DBMS environment. Moreover, DBMS technology on minicomputers has not really been able to match the types of performance obtainable on

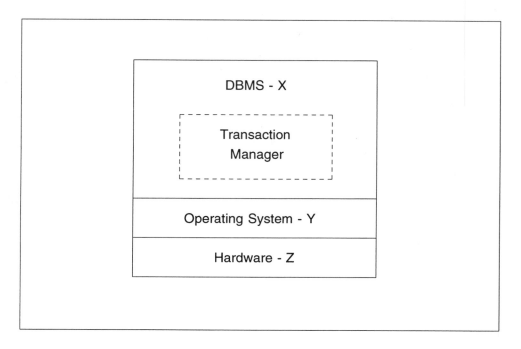

Figure 2. DBMS OLTP

mainframe systems, thus leaving the latter as the only real source of high-performance and high-volume OLTP. For several years the combination of these factors prevented the establishment of UNIX environments as a viable alternative to mainframe environments for the provision of general OLTP.

1.3 Open OLTP

If this was the situation until not very long ago, several changes have taken place in the information technology (IT) industry in a relatively short time:

- Technology has provided more power in small systems, making minicomputers more and more suitable for high-volume activities. Networking has become more and more reliable. Hard disks have become smaller but more capable. Mainframes are no longer the only answer for achieving high performance or for storing large volumes of data.

- Hardware and software investments have grown to a point where companies cannot afford to replace their computing environments completely. The phasing out of certain components and the acquisition of new ones must be planned as a gradual process over the years. Interoperability has become the main requirement, and distributed computing has become the vehicle for achieving this.

- There is now a wider range of businesses interested in OLTP. With a more demanding base of users, with the need to move ahead and provide better services, many businesses have started considering features which help enhance the performance, flexibility, robustness, and reliability of their computer systems.

- Standards have been developed for many aspects of computing including transaction processing, and the industry has accepted that standards are the only viable solution to interoperability.

- Open systems have become a more and more appealing choice for both users and manufacturers. Users have recognised the potential benefits of being able to shop around for individual components of their computing environment, while manufacturers have seen the potential benefits of competing in all environments with anybody else already operating in such environments.

- The attitude and expectations of users have changed in relation to their hardware and software suppliers. If the attitude towards suppliers was, "I need to achieve certain goals; what will I have to buy from you?", now it is rather, "I need to achieve certain goals, I want to preserve certain investments; what can you offer me that the others cannot?".

The combination of the above has led to the need for a new generation of OLTP monitors, and, in many ways it has changed the whole definition of OLTP, as well as adding a degree of complexity to the subject. With open systems, the "building blocks" for OLTP are now the same as those for other general purpose computing - different hardware, software, graphical interfaces, databases, PCs, etc. As a result, a new concept of Open OLTP is replacing that of proprietary, mainframe-based OLTP (Figure 3).

The main requirement for Open OLTP is the ability to guarantee the same degree of effectiveness and reliability as mainframe OLTP over a more complex and differentiated environment, like the one constituted by different hardware and software components from different vendors; at the same time, its main challenge is to be able to cope with the higher degree of flexibility provided by a wider choice of components.

Within this new context, the function of an OLTP monitor is not just to guarantee the successful execution of a transactional application, but also to

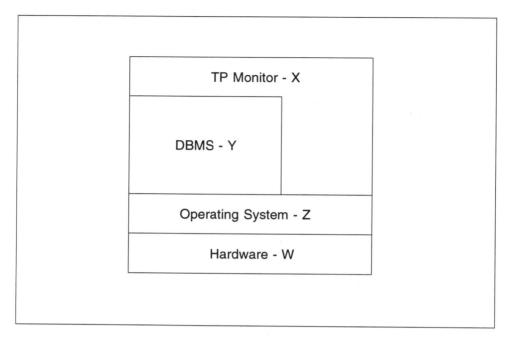

Figure 3. Open OLTP

make available these capabilities in a completely heterogeneous environment while making it appear as an homogeneous one. In a closed environment, a TP monitor was supposed to provide transactional control over a specific system by taking advantage of the consistent set of features provided by such a system. In an open environment, a TP monitor must provide transactional control over a number of different platforms from different vendors, and at the same time take advantage of the transactional capabilities that certain components might already offer, e.g. database systems.

The presence of standards has also started playing a crucial role, and in the last few years a lot of work has been done specifically in the transaction processing area. Leveraging some of the work done for UNIX OLTP products like TUXEDO, organisations like X/Open® have defined a standard framework for distributed transaction processing (DTP), and the market can now rely on products compliant to these standards.

In general, the new concept of Open OLTP (or UNIX OLTP, which is virtually a synonymous term), goes beyond the pure concept of transaction processing as a vehicle for satisfying requirements of consistency, reliability, performance, efficiency, etc. It also encompasses computer interconnection, resources interconnection, process communication, and standards.

Besides those listed earlier, which are clearly still applicable, the new requirements for Open OLTP monitors include:

- *Vendor independence*: Users must have the freedom to choose the components of their computing environment based on their needs.

- *Application portability*: Applications must be portable across platforms, and application development must be consistent across systems.

- *Location transparency*: Elements of the application must be able to access other components without knowing their location beforehand.

- *Connectivity*: Different computing environments must be interconnected and interoperated.

- *Scalability*: Applications must be split into modules that can be dynamically added or removed, and the system must allow machines with different computing power.

- *Reconfigurability*: Applications must be allowed to change in order to better adapt to the changes in the business environment.

- *Extensibility*: Applications must be allowed to encompass new systems as the need to distribute processing power changes.

- *Security*: Applications require both user authentication (who can use the system) and service authorisation (what they can do), in order to be able to protect the business resources.

This is the context in which today's TP monitors must measure themselves, and this is the context which the TUXEDO System has helped create and for which it was developed.

2. The TUXEDO System

In most existing literature, the TUXEDO System is defined as a transaction processing monitor for UNIX environments. The implied meaning of this definition is that of a product that allows the implementation of OLTP applications across a set of different UNIX or UNIX-like systems, with the possible integration of non-UNIX systems like PCs, workstations, and mainframes.

The identification of TUXEDO as an OLTP monitor for UNIX environments is widely accepted and usually appropriate. However, as a definition, it is not sufficient by itself for providing a clear, unambiguous understanding of the relationship between such a system and OLTP. This is not just because the concept of OLTP monitors for UNIX environments as opposed to OLTP monitors for mainframe environments is still relatively new, but also, as we said in Chapter 1, because as a result of the expansion of open systems and the availability of standards for both transaction processing and distributed computing, the very concept of OLTP for UNIX environments has actually changed.

In addition, a definition of TUXEDO which purely emphasised transaction processing aspects would be somewhat inaccurate and restrictive, as it would overlook a number of non TP-related properties which contribute equally to the effectiveness of this product in distributed environments. In fact, these properties are such that not only can they be used along with the transactional capabilities of the system, but they can also be used outside the scope of pure transaction processing in a more general fashion.

Therefore, as a first step, before we start our examination of TUXEDO's architecture and features, it is important that we take a look at what the TUXEDO System really is. The purpose of this chapter is to clarify how TUXEDO relates to OLTP, to present alternative definitions from different perspectives, and to discuss why the industry is increasingly interested in it. This will hopefully provide a more accurate and complete characterisation of the system and will set the correct framework for examining its features. Before doing this, though, let's first look at the history of the product and at the way it is structured.

2.1 Brief historical notes

Although the TUXEDO System has gained in popularity only relatively recently, it does in fact date back to 1978, when AT&T Bell Laboratories started developing a UNIX-based transactional system named UNITS, to be used in the AT&T telecommunication business.[1] The system had two components, TUX (Transactions for UNIX) and DUX (Database for UNIX), and, although limited in comparison with the present system, it already implemented most of the architectural solutions available with the existing product. These included the client/server model, the name server structure, and features such as load balancing and prioritisation of operations. The database component, DUX, supported a version of dynamic SQL which was later adopted by X/Open as the reference SQL interface.

This system was initially deployed in several departments of AT&T, and in the mid-eighties was enhanced with the introduction of DTP. This enhancement allowed the TUX component to coordinate transactions between multiple instances of the DUX component. At that point the name for TUX was changed to TUXEDO, an acronym for transactions for UNIX extended for distributed operations.[2] Because the name for the entire system, UNITS, was too close to UNIX and therefore a potential source of confusion (!), the name TUXEDO was adopted to identify the whole system, while the components were renamed as System/T and System/D. At that stage the product was named TUXEDO 3.0, which then evolved to TUXEDO 4.0 and started receiving more widespread market attention. With the addition of internationalisation features, the product became TUXEDO 4.1 at the turning

---

1. The fact that TUXEDO was developed by the same company which developed UNIX, and the fact that it has many years of parallel development with this system, are the keys to understanding TUXEDO's particular suitability for UNIX environments. At a time when UNIX is gaining importance in the commercial market, TUXEDO implements a number of architectural solutions specifically developed for taking advantage of UNIX characteristics. In addition, while providing compatibility with a number of existing UNIX platforms, it is also set to integrate further enhancements, for example OSF's distributed computing environment (DCE™).

2. Those of you who thought the name derived from a certain elegance of the product or its smart cut will be disappointed here, I'm afraid.

of 1990. At that time the communication interface between System/T and System/D for distributed transaction coordination was proposed by AT&T and adopted by X/Open as the reference interface between transaction managers and resource managers in the X/Open DTP model, under the name of X/Open XA. At around the same time, in 1991, the division of AT&T which developed UNIX and TUXEDO became an independent company under the name of UNIX System Laboratories (USL).

The addition of the Workstation, Host, and Queue extensions, plus the implementation of additional features for System/T, produced the present product named "The TUXEDO 4.2 Enterprise Transaction Processing System". This name emphasises the specific intention to integrate, within the same product, the three tiers of enterprise computing: the user level (desktop PC or workstation), the departmental level (UNIX mini), and the corporate level (mainframe). At the same time, two portions of TUXEDO's application to transaction manager interface (ATMI) have been accepted by X/Open as reference interfaces in the DTP model under the name of X/Open TX and X/Open XATMI.

In 1993, USL was acquired by Novell, and, as a result, the TUXEDO System is now a product developed and owned by Novell Inc. Novell licenses the source code of the product to many OEMs, and directly sells binary versions for the most popular UNIX and PC platforms. The latest additions to the product include the Domains extension. This is part of TUXEDO 5.0.

Since it constitutes the basis for the TUXEDO-based Systems commonly available today in the market, the TUXEDO 4.2 Enterprise Transaction Processing System is the subject of this book. The Domains extension is also included. TUXEDO 4.0 and TUXEDO 4.1 are functional subsets of TUXEDO 4.2, and for the common functionalities all considerations made for TUXEDO 4.2 apply to the previous releases as well. If you are already familiar with any of these previous releases, it will be sufficiently easy to identify which considerations are not applicable. If you are not, it is unlikely that you will have to become, since the vast majority of the current TUXEDO products are based on TUXEDO 4.2.

2.2 Product composition

When considering the TUXEDO System, it is important to realise that the system is in fact a collection of several components, as presented in Figure 4. These are:

- System/T (/T), the component that implements the distributed processing and distributed transaction processing capabilities of the system. This component provides a framework for developing and

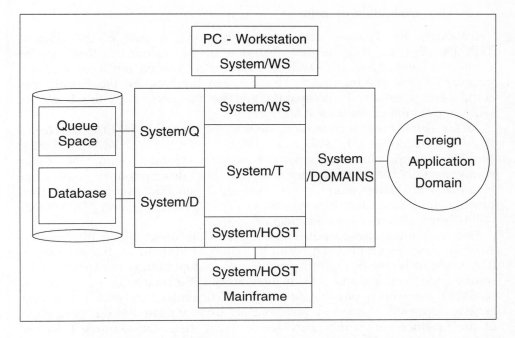

Figure 4. Components of the TUXEDO System

executing client/server applications, a set of programming interfaces, and a set of tools to monitor and administer the execution of such applications.

- System/D (/D), the product's native DBMS subsystem.

- System/WS (/WS), the extension that provides PCs and workstations which do not have System/T on board with the same programming interface and the same functionality as native System/T application clients.

- System/HOST (/HOST), the extension that allows foreign host services to be requested from within a System/T-based application using the same programming interface used for requesting native System/T services.

- System/Q (/Q), the extension that provides TUXEDO applications with the possibility of storing service requests into recoverable queues on disk for delayed or batch execution.

- System/DOMAINS (/DOMAINS), the extension that allows a TUXEDO application domain to request services from, and to provide services to, another application domain.

Although the database component, System/D, is part of the original TUXEDO System, it is in fact just one of the resources[3] that can be connected with System/T, and, in practice, it is often replaced by other popular DBMSs like Informix®, Oracle®, and Ingres®. For this reason, this component is usually kept separate, and for the purpose of this book we will not describe its features at all.

As far as this book is concerned, we will use the term TUXEDO to refer to the combination of /T, /WS, and /HOST. /Q and /DOMAINS, which provide specific features, are not usually covered with the other components. Unless otherwise specified, the description of individual features will relate uniquely to System/T, as this provides the core functionality. Considerations specific to /WS, /HOST, /Q, and /DOMAINS will be presented in a separate chapter.

Finally, it must also be noted that the product presented in this book is what is sometimes called the "vanilla" TUXEDO System, i.e. the product as it is made available by Novell prior to the customisations implemented by source code licensees and system integrators. The reason for this is that it wouldn't have been possible to cover all customisations with a fair and general approach. Also, customisations are usually related to the integration of the product with application development tools, for example Informix 4GL®, or with OLTP application generators like Magna X®. These types of customisations relate more to the look of the product than to the substance, which in pure TUXEDO terms is virtually the same for all implementations.

2.3 A high-level approach: software backplane

With the very basic background provided in the previous pages, let's start our introduction to the TUXEDO System from a high-level perspective. From a general point of view, TUXEDO can be presented as a suite of products that make available a set of standard programming interfaces for creating distributed applications capable of running transparently across a network of different machines. TUXEDO hides the systems' differences through a common programming interface, so it can be seen as a software backplane under which you can integrate different hardware, software, and resources.

---

3. Since we haven't given a definition of resource so far, and won't be giving one until much later, we can for the moment associate the idea of a resource with a database, and that of a resource manager with a DBMS.

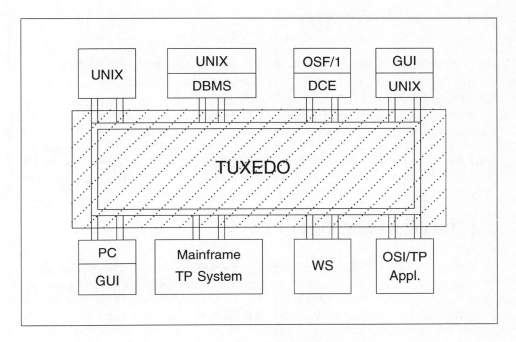

Figure 5. Software backplane

To use a metaphor taken from the world of electrical appliances, TUXEDO can be seen as a sort of "universal plug adaptor", which enables appliances which have different plugs, voltages, etc. to "plug" into the same circuit (Figure 5). Another definition quite often used is that of "middleware", i.e. software which sits in between an application and the different underlaying systems, and makes up for the differences between what the application wants to see and what the systems really are.

The elements which can be "plugged" into the backplane are many of the components of enterprise computing environments:

• minicomputers running different flavours of the UNIX system, or other UNIX-like systems like OSF/1®

• desktop PCs or workstations running popular operating systems such as MS-DOS®, MS-Windows®, OS/2®, and Apple Macintosh®

• mainframe TP systems, typically MVS™/CICS™

• widely used relational DBMSs, such as Informix, Oracle, Ingres, Unify®, and Ally™.

15

- popular graphical interfaces

- growing OLTP standards such as X/Open's DTP and OSI-TP®

- emerging distributed computing environments such as OSF's DCE.

This initial way of presenting TUXEDO takes the emphasis out of any OLTP considerations and focusses the attention more on the high-level role that the system can play in enterprise computing, especially as far as the interoperation of proprietary and open systems is concerned. This approach provides a definition of the boundaries within which TUXEDO operates. and helps with the appreciation of the characteristics of openness of the system. Suitably enough, it also prepares the ground for a few considerations which can be used to clarify its relationship with OLTP.

2.4 TUXEDO and OLTP

A definition of TUXEDO as a software backplane presents the product as the "glue" which holds together a number of different entities within the same application, or, in other words, as the software which allows the integration of different components, typically resident in different locations, under the same programming interface. However, in relation to transaction processing, what sort of applications are we considering once we have "plugged" all or a subset of these elements together? As far as transactions are concerned, applications which integrate the elements mentioned above could do one of the following:

- *No transactions at all:* Applications like these would typically make use of distribution capabilities either for making services available to remote users, for example printing services, or for splitting the execution of separate portions of the application across multiple machines, for instance to support a higher number of users. An example of such an application could be an image-processing system over a network of small UNIX machines (Figure 6). Given the high CPU and memory requirements for graphical computation, the processing could be split into partial steps, each being executed in parallel on different machines. A program dedicated to the display would receive the result of the partial computations and draw the picture on the system where the terminal is attached. Because of the absence of transactional requirements, this type of application does not qualify for OLTP, as it belongs more to the realm of pure distributed processing.

- *Transactions involving one resource on one machine at a time:* This second case represents the most popular case of OLTP. A number of users on

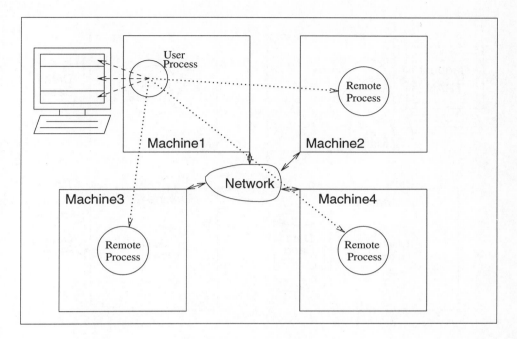

Figure 6. No transactions

different machines execute transactions that involve one single resource, typically a database, on a mainframe or a dedicated mini. Because it is executed where the resource resides, i.e. it is local to the resource, this type of transaction is referred to as a *local* transaction (Figure 7). An example could be a credit card application, in which the database with all the credit card accounts is located somewhere on a central system. When a request for a new credit card is submitted from any one of the involved organisations, the verification and all the work is done remotely on such system. This is the style of applications traditionally built with mainframes or pure DBMS.

- *Transactions involving more than one resource at a time, possibly on more than one machine:* This case is another example of OLTP, in which a number of users on different machines execute transactions that involve more than one resource on more than one machine. Because this case is specifically characterised by transactions spanning multiple resources and/or machines, this type of transaction processing is more commonly identified as DTP. In this framework transactions are usually referred to as *distributed* or *global* transactions (Figure 8). Although this case is not

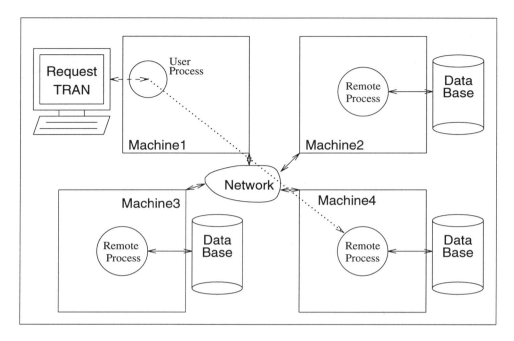

Figure 7. Local transactions

unknown in mainframe environments (e.g. transactions spanning two different CICS regions), this situation is likely to become more frequent in distributed UNIX environments. A typical example here could be a banking application in which all branches have their own local data in a local database and operations like money transfers are executed on-line between branches.

Despite some obvious differences in requirements, it is quite possible to accept that all three cases might benefit from the use of a kind of software capable of hiding system differences, allowing development of applications independently of the actual operating system, and providing central monitoring. We already said that TUXEDO provides precisely these capabilities, so the question is simply to which of these applications it is applicable?

Well, perhaps a little surprisingly for a product purely defined as an OLTP monitor, TUXEDO can be effectively used for all three types of application, including those which do not have transactional requirements. In this respect, therefore, a better definition for TUXEDO would be that of monitor for distributed applications, as it provides the framework for

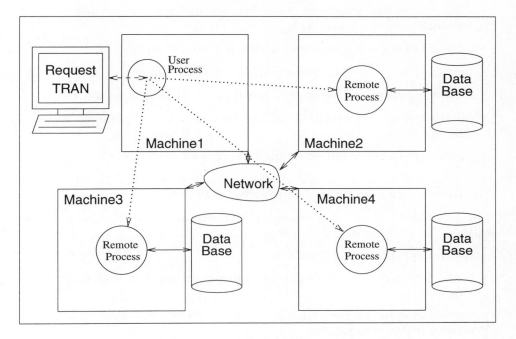

Figure 8. Global transactions

developing and monitoring distributed applications independent of any OLTP considerations. This definition is not in conflict with that of an OLTP monitor (actually the two assume the same meaning when we consider distributed applications with transactional requirements), but it is more general and implies a set of capabilities which live outside the scope of transaction processing.

2.4.1 Distributed processing

To clarify what these capabilities are, let's consider the first two types of applications mentioned earlier (no transactions and local transactions). There are several general characteristics that we could identify in relation to both applications:

- users located on different machines
- different data representation on different machines (e.g. with or without byte swapping)

- different visual interfaces available to different users (e.g. ASCII terminals versus X/Terminals)

- different networking implementations (e.g. socket versus TLI)

- remote access to data or to portions of the application

- location of data or of portions of the application variable in time

- different power of execution of different hardware, operating systems, database systems

- parallelism of execution on multiple processors

- availability of part or all of the application dependent on various business conditions or hardware/software availability.

In relation to these characteristics, the requirements that need to be satisfied can be summarised as follows:

- common programming interfaces

- possibility to access all application components regardless of their actual location

- optimisation of the use of hardware and software resources, in order to achieve better performance

- dynamic adjustment of the hardware/software configuration

- improvement of application availability.

In order to satisfy these requirements, the role of an application monitor is to allow different degrees of "distant" or "tele" processing, or, as we would say in more fashionable terms, distributed processing. Even in the second case, where local transactions are considered, coordination of transactions is not a particular requirement for the application monitor because this task can be left to the actual manager of the resource, typically the DBMS. The important aspect in both cases is the efficient and effective delivery of requests and responses, but not the actual control of transactions. When considered separately, these capabilities can be defined with the name of Tele-Processing, and in this respect TUXEDO is sometimes defined in the literature as a Tele-Processing Monitor.

More specifically, TUXEDO allows the same application to be executed by users located on different types of machines. Each user can have his/her own screen interface, and the data corresponding to such interface can be represented with common predefined data types. For accessing the various components, the application can make use of a common programming interface, either TUXEDO's native ATMI, or its X/Open's counterpart, the

XATMI.

The system looks after the transmission of data across different implementations of networking and across different types of machines in such a way that differences in the data representation and in the networking implementation are not noticed by the application. It allows access to local or remote portions of the application in a way which is transparent to the programming, i.e. it provides location transparency. As a result of this, it also allows dynamic relocation of portions of the application in such a way that the programming is not affected.

TUXEDO allows applications to take into account the different power of execution of the various machines, operating systems, and databases, by defining load factors and performing load balancing among the set of operations available. In addition, it allows the selection of priorities for the execution of such operations. Portions of the application can be executed in parallel on different processors in order to achieve better performance, or conversely, operations can be sequentialised when the resources suffer from too a high degree of parallel access.

The TUXEDO software keeps on monitoring the execution of all components of the application and dynamically performs corrective actions in order for the application to execute more efficiently or with less interruptions. It also allows external intervention from an administrator, to perform corrections or changes to the application when conditions so require.

Because these capabilities exist outside the scope of transaction processing, the evolution of a TUXEDO-based application can move through different stages while its structure, architecture, and implementation are only marginally affected by the changes. This allows a more flexible implementation of migration policies, and a greater adaptation to changing transactional requirements, for example from local transaction control to global transaction control, within the same architecture and structure and with maximum degree of code reuse.

2.4.2 Distributed transaction processing

If we consider the third type of distributed application mentioned earlier, we can identify other characteristics besides those described in the previous section:

- different resources, or multiple instances of the same resource, involved in the same transaction (e.g. an Informix and an Oracle database)

- different types of connection to different resources (e.g. via libraries versus via connection to a server)

21

- different types of access to different resources (e.g. SQL versus C-ISAM)

- different recovery facilities for different resources.

In this case, besides those mentioned earlier, there are other requirements that need to be satisfied:

- consistent definition of global transactions

- transparent access to the various subcomponents of the transaction

- transparent coordination of the transaction components

- ACIDity.[4]

These are the areas that in this case need to be specifically addressed by an application monitor. Each individual component of the global transaction will not in general have information about the others, so each individual resource manager cannot intervene at that level. The application monitor is the only part of the whole system which can access all the individual components of the global transaction, and therefore is the only one which can coordinate them. When this is the case, the DTP capabilities of TUXEDO are taken into consideration, and, because of this, we can properly define the system as a DTP monitor.

TUXEDO allows an application to define global transactions in a consistent way, by providing a uniform programming interface for defining the transaction's boundaries; this is possible either via TUXEDO's native ATMI, or via its X/Open counterpart, the TX interface. Once the boundaries are defined, the system allows different resources (e.g. databases and ISAM files), or different types of the same resource (e.g. two different databases) or multiple instances of the same resource (e.g. two Informix databases), to be involved in the same transaction; with the assistance of its distributed processing capabilities, it allows partial components of the transaction to be hosted on different machines and operating systems.

TUXEDO provides global transaction control by implementing a two-phase commit algorithm, under which each resource manager involved in the global transaction will commit or abort the relevant portion of the transaction depending on the decision taken by TUXEDO. The communication between TUXEDO and each resource manager is implemented through the standard X/Open XA interface, thus allowing different resources to communicate with TUXEDO in a consistent way.

---

4. ACIDity is a term used to identify four properties usually associated to OLTP: atomicity, consistency, isolation, durability. See Chapter 5 for a better definition.

TUXEDO initiates any necessary recovery procedure for transactions which cannot complete, due to failures of some parts of the system. In doing so, it guarantees that the ACID properties are satisfied for the global transaction.

2.4.3 Some considerations

The definition of the case where an application performs local transactions as a case of distributed processing instead of transaction processing may seem a little inconsistent with the definition of TUXEDO as an OLTP monitor. However, this should not generate confusion as far the relationship between TUXEDO and OLTP is concerned. If an application based on TUXEDO contains elements of OLTP, then TUXEDO can still be seen as an OLTP monitor. This is not the same as saying that whenever an application has transactional requirements the TUXEDO System is requested to make use of its transaction processing capabilities. These need only be used for the third type of application, when DTP and global transactions are involved. In the other cases distributed processing is sufficient.

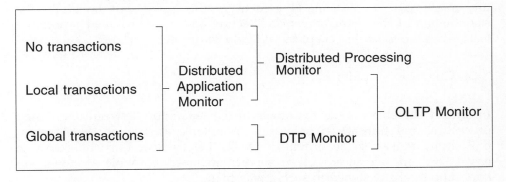

Figure 9. Summary of possible definitions for the TUXEDO System

A summary of the possible approaches and ways of defining this product is given in Figure 9. In general, TUXEDO should be seen as a monitor for distributed applications. This encompasses all three types of application presented before. When applications do not have DTP requirements, TUXEDO makes use of capabilities which relate to distributed processing, and it can be seen as a distributed processing monitor. This includes the case where the only type of transaction processing is local to one resource. When DTP requirements are present, TUXEDO can be seen as a DTP monitor. This only applies to applications which execute global transactions. Whenever transaction processing is present, TUXEDO can be seen as an OLTP monitor;

this involves both local and global transaction processing. Of course, all these definitions are mainly theoretical, and in practice tend to blend together.

Another aspect which might seem theoretical is the separation of TUXEDO's capabilities into distributed processing and DTP. This separation might be seen as a step for appreciating the degree of generality of the system, but it may also seem a little exaggerated, because, after all, most OLTP systems do provide distributed processing capabilities not strictly related to pure transaction control. However, what is sometimes not immediately evident is that the complete separation between distributed processing and DTP constitutes one of the key differences between TUXEDO and other OLTP or DBMS systems. These may have elements of distributed processing integrated with TP and/or DTP, but none of these elements exists on its own.

Furthermore, this separation is the key element that enables TUXEDO to fulfil its role as an open TP monitor, through which Open OLTP and Open DTP can be implemented. It is interesting to note that X/Open have adopted TUXEDO's model as the base for their DTP model, in recognition of the degree of openness achievable through this approach. A justification for this might not be particularly evident at this point, but hopefully the examination of the client/server architecture and the distributed processing features in the following chapters will help clarify it.

2.4.4 Client/server philosophy

In order to be able to take advantage of the separation between distributed processing and transaction processing, a suitable application development philosophy must also be provided. In TUXEDO's case, this philosophy is based on an enhanced client/server architecture, which allows an application to be designed in such a way that:

- individual tasks or operations are defined as services

- services are offered by application servers

- servers can be replicated and distributed across the network

- services are requested by application clients

- clients can request services by name regardless of their actual location

- services and servers are centrally monitored and dynamically administered

- clients or servers define the boundaries of transactions

- transactions can span multiple servers, resources, and machines.

This philosophy allows a high degree of separation among the application components, and yet a strict integration of them through application interfaces and central administration; as such, it is simple to use and effective at the same time. In general, it provides a framework within which distributed applications can be developed and maintained, and allows the degree of modularity, performance, scalability, and reliability required by today's Open OLTP. Because of its importance in TUXEDO's framework, the details of the client/server architecture are examined in more detail in Chapter 3.

In addition to an application development philosophy, TUXEDO provides a set of commodity tools for generating clients and servers from the source code, and for generating other components of the application, such as request buffers. Moreover, because the client/server architecture lends itself well to 4GL and CASE development, tools are beginning to be provided by various vendors, thus making the TUXEDO System a complete application development environment.

2.5 The industry and TUXEDO

Having examined some of the possible perspectives from which it can be observed and having introduced its main characteristics, it is probably useful to complete this introduction with a closer look at the main reasons why the industry is interested in the TUXEDO System. Hopefully, this will help translate into real terms the various theoretical aspects discussed so far.

As we have seen, TUXEDO's pure transactional capabilities play a role only in the case of DTP, and in several cases they may not even be required. Although it is expected that DTP will become increasingly common in future OLTP, it is also true that other areas of Open OLTP are, and will probably remain, significantly more important than pure DTP. DTP capabilities are offered today by virtually all TP monitors available for Open OLTP (e.g. Transarc's Encina™ or NCR's TopEnd®), so DTP is more like a necessary but not sufficient feature for all products in this area. Implementation of DTP features is one of the reasons why TUXEDO is becoming a building block in distributed environments, but is neither the only nor the main reason why companies today choose TUXEDO for their business.

Bearing in mind that TUXEDO is in fact more like a monitor for distributed applications, most of its capabilities such as data-dependent routing, load balancing, and network independence, to name but a few, are beneficial for any type of general distributed computing. These features were studied and developed for Open OLTP frameworks, but provide specific answers to general problems and requirements of distributed processing on UNIX systems and help provide the additional flexibility requested by distributed applications in open systems environments.

Consequently, the reasons why TUXEDO is considered for Open OLTP are related to a number of aspects of distributed processing which are directly intertwined with OLTP. Possibly in order of importance, these reasons can be summarised as follows:

- integration of different hardware, software, resources

- performance

- availability on existing software

- introduction of new technology

- migration and evolution

- standards

- access to multiple data stores.

The rest of this section is dedicated to examining these reasons in greater detail. If you are not interested in this market approach to TUXEDO, and wish to go straight into the implementation of the system, you can skip the rest of this chapter and turn to Chapter 3.

2.5.1 Integration of different hardware, software, resources

The TUXEDO System is available on over 25 different platforms; these include many of the most popular UNIX or UNIX-like systems on CISC or RISC processors, but also other operating systems such as MS-DOS, MS-WINDOWS, OS/2, and Apple Macintosh, through the use of System/WS (see Appendix B). On all these platforms, TUXEDO provides a consistent programming interface, network implementation independence, and data representation independence, thus hiding operating system and hardware differences from the application level. Its availability on all these platforms is a significant advantage for many companies. Because of the gradual acquisition of hardware, companies find themselves with a range of different systems that are difficult to interoperate to a full extent in a single application. In this respect, TUXEDO is in a unique position. Having been endorsed by many hardware manufacturers, and having been ported on just about all the most widespread platforms, it is not linked to a specific manufacturer or product line, as many other products in this area are.

TUXEDO cannot only be used to put together within a single application the different types of software/hardware one might already have, but also to add new software/hardware as it becomes available, without having to modify the architecture of the application to compensate for the differences. Moreover, because it links together different systems, it also offers the possibility of accessing the different types of resources available on the different systems. Since the application servers reside where the resource resides, suitable interfaces can be used to communicate with the resource. At the same time, since the application clients reside where the user resides, the user's preferred interface can be used to handle the data in input and output. This makes it possible to develop applications which provide the same user interface while accessing different types of resources, or conversely, to have different user interfaces while accessing the same resource.

Resources can be databases, but they can also be other software/hardware components of a distributed environment, ISAM files, queues on disk, printers, removable media, even entire applications. TUXEDO services are not restricted to just SQL code, but can use any other interface with any other environment. In all cases, TUXEDO's task is to handle the communication between the various entities of the application efficiently. In general, in a TUXEDO application you can "plug in" different new components as soon as they are available, and if new resources are XA-compliant, they can also be involved in distributed transactions.

2.5.2 Performance

A significant number of benchmarking tests, conducted on different software and hardware platforms with different DBMSs, have shown that the use of TUXEDO for OLTP applications produces significant improvements in terms of cost per transactions per second (cost per TPS). If I remember well, at one point USL was able to claim that most of the top ten results obtained with the TPC-A benchmark had been obtained with a TUXEDO-based system. This is mainly due to the fact that TUXEDO's client/server architecture allows for reduced data traffic on the network, a reduced number of concurrent accessers to resources, e.g. DBMS servers, and reduced idle time for the application processes.

Better performance is of course another critical factor for many companies. In response to customers' demands, companies are often pressurised to increase the speed of their existing applications. In other cases, they are requested to support a larger number of users without affecting the response time. Both situations can typically be improved by increasing the performance of the existing systems, and not necessarily by purchasing more powerful hardware. The savings made on the hardware alone can often pay for the adoption of TUXEDO and the restructuring of the existing applications.

2.5.3 Availability on existing software

TUXEDO is available today on a wide number of software/hardware platforms, and this makes it applicable to a wide number of existing environments. Because of this, companies can use TUXEDO to develop or re-engineer their applications on existing systems without having to upgrade their software or hardware. This is an important reason by itself, but all the more important if you consider the situation with some of the other UNIX TP monitors, for example those based on OSF's DCE and therefore totally dependent on its availability.

TUXEDO can be integrated with DCE but doesn't require it. This makes a distinctive business difference for many companies. Firstly, they are not forced to buy into a complete suite of distributed computing tools which they might not need. Secondly, TUXEDO-based environments do not suffer from some potentially risky assumptions made by the suppliers of DCE-based monitors. These assumptions can be summarised as follows: DCE will be a stable component on most UNIX environments; DCE is suitable for OLTP. This is, for example, the case of Transarc's Encina™ and IBM's CICS/6000™.

Both these assumptions are still regarded by large sections of the industry as unproven and possibly over-optimistic. Despite the fact that DCE is a very effective model for distributed computing and that many manufacturers have pledged their commitment to provide it on their platforms, it also has associated costs, both in terms of software and in terms of resource requirements (memory, hard disk, maintenance, etc.). Of course it is expected that technology will reduce these costs in the years to come, but in the meantime, a number of business environments are finding it difficult to afford the price of these additional layers of software for implementing an application which can be implemented on available software platforms under other environments like TUXEDO.

Moreover, although DCE is very effective for distributed computing, its implementation is still seen as not yet mature for OLTP, which has very specific requirements in terms of performance. The existence of separate layers of software for the provision of a comprehensive approach to distributed computing may result in slower execution and may put constraints on the way operations are executed. The combination of these might prove unacceptable for UNIX OLTP applications, and, significantly, no benchmarking results are available for the moment to demonstrate that this is not a concern for DCE-based monitors. Although certain features of DCE will be improved, it is not clear today if DCE-based monitors will be able to meet OLTP requirements with cost-effectiveness. On the contrary, this is not a concern for TUXEDO-based applications, since results are already available to demonstrate that high performance can be achieved at low costs.

Finally, because both DCE and DCE-based TP monitors are very new technology, they are affected by the concern that accompanies all new products, i.e. that it might take quite some time before the integration of all these components is completely reliable. As these are early stages for both types of environment, there are a number of companies which feel they cannot afford to wait until a more mature stage is reached. On the contrary, TUXEDO has already had a number of years of deployment in commercial applications, especially within AT&T, which has greatly helped stabilise the product.

2.5.4 Innovation

In terms of new technology, the TUXEDO System does not merely provide XA-compliance and other features related to the standards for DTP. It also introduces a consistent implementation of an enhanced client/server model, which is recognised as a type of architecture well suited for distributed environments.

This is another appealing factor for companies who need to use the flexibility of a distributed environment without being tied into a fixed implementation. A fixed architecture is often the situation with other UNIX TP monitors, which, being UNIX implementations of existing mainframe TP monitors, offer direct programming compatibility and migration, but deny the degrees of flexibility obtainable through a more free client/server architecture.

2.5.5 Migration and evolution

TUXEDO gives the possibility of accessing from within a UNIX-based application programs running on a mainframe system, for example programs running under MVS/CICS. This is possible through the use of the same programming interface used to access native TUXEDO services, and for this reason, companies moving from mainframe environments to UNIX can undertake the migration in steps, according to their own timeframes and budgets.

Because the application interface for requesting services off a mainframe is identical to the one for requesting application services in a native System/T environment, application clients can be developed once for all and do not have to be modified when a service is moved from the mainframe to the UNIX system. This reduces the costs of migration, and allows to preserve existing investments for as long as business conditions so require or dictate.

Thanks to a modular architecture, TUXEDO allows not just migration from mainframes to UNIX systems, but also evolution from single to multiple UNIX systems, or from UNIX OLTP applications with no DTP requirements to ones with such requirements. This again can be done according to the company's timeframes and without rearchitecturing the code of the existing TUXEDO components of the application. In this respect, TUXEDO allows continuity of application development and maintenance across different platforms and timeframes.

2.5.6 Standards

TUXEDO's code is based on several industry standards and as such is inherently portable to many systems. TUXEDO is compliant with the X/Open DTP model, and Novell/USL have repeatedly given assurance that significant additions to such model will be incorporated in the system. This assurance is valid not only for the components defined by the X/Open DTP model but also for other aspects of TP, such as those defined by OSI/TP, and for other aspects of distributed computing, such as those defined by OSF's DCE.

Adopting TUXEDO as the base technology for distributed applications is seen by companies as a guarantee that enhancements to transaction processing and to distributed processing technology will be available within a consistent framework and through consistent programming interfaces and tools.

2.5.7 Access to multiple data stores

Because of its integration capabilities, TUXEDO helps put together different systems within the same application. Through the use of data-dependent routing, TUXEDO allows service requests to be directed to different systems, where the data relevant to a particular request are located.

Data do not have to be stored in the same type of database, or indeed in a database at all. Because each system can run its own servers for local data access, the data accessible from within a single application do not have to be of the same type or on the same system. This offers a much higher degree of flexibility than that offered by, say, DBMS systems, which have distributed data access capabilities, but only applicable to the data handled by the DBMS itself.

In most cases, data are accessed and possibly updated, only on one site at a time. When simultaneous updates at multiple sites is a business requirement, and the resources involved are XA-compliant, TUXEDO can not only provide access to data, but also transaction coordination. All of this is important for the growing number of companies which base their business on the availability of data in many forms and from many types of data stores.

2.6 Summary

Although the TUXEDO System has enjoyed relatively recent popularity, it goes back a number of years, and it has evolved through a number of milestones such as the development of dynamic SQL, the XA interface, the ATMI, all of them later adopted by X/Open in its standard DTP model.

From a high-level point of view, TUXEDO can be seen as a software backplane with which different operating systems, hardware, and resources can be connected and interoperated. From an application point of view, it can be seen as the provider of a client/server model for distributed environments. From a development perspective, it can be seen as the provider of an architecture suitable for 3GL, 4GL, and CASE development.

In general, TUXEDO can be seen as an OLTP monitor for Open OLTP, and, as such, it addresses requirements of both distributed computing and distributed transaction processing. TUXEDO's capabilities can be split into distributed processing and DTP, and, because of this separation, the system can best be defined as a monitor for distributed applications with transactional capabilities.

The separation between distributed processing and transaction processing is one of the main differences between this system and mainframe OLTP monitors or DBMSs. The combination of distributed processing and DTP constitutes the basis for Open OLTP and Open DTP.

The reasons why the industry is interested in this product are not only related to DTP, but also to other factors to do with general distributed computing. These include its availability on a large number of platforms, its ability to integrate multiple components of enterprise computing, its use for improving the performance of distributed applications, its relationship with standards, and, finally, its help for the provision of a framework for consistent migration and evolution.

3. Architecture

In Chapter 2 we mentioned the fact that TUXEDO's architecture is based on a client/server model, and that TUXEDO-based applications are made up of client and server processes which communicate with one another via the TUXEDO software.

This way of presenting TUXEDO was adequate from a general point of view, but it needs now to be explained in more detail. Experience suggests that this is one of the initial causes of difficulty and potential misunderstanding for the people who turn to this product for the first time. A clear understanding of TUXEDO's architecture is fundamental for appreciating what the product can offer in terms of design, development, administration, and, of course, transaction processing. Equally, a good appreciation of TUXEDO's client/server model helps with the understanding of how it integrates with other software products, for example DBMSs.

The purpose of this chapter is therefore to set the boundaries of TUXEDO's architecture and to present its components. If you are already confident of the exact meaning of the term "client/server" in a TUXEDO environment, you might want to skip the next two sections. If you have any doubts, then the content of these sections will hopefully provide clarification.

3.1 The client/server architecture

Despite its frequent use, and sometimes, abuse, the term "client/server" is more like a buzz word than an actual, agreed upon definition. Client/server is used to indicate a wide variety of different situations, which often have in common only the fact that certain entities, called *clients*, do not perform certain actions by themselves, but rather request other entities, called *servers*, to perform these actions (*services*) on their behalf. In colloquial terms, often the term client indicates a PC and server a minicomputer or a mainframe system. In general, even within the boundaries of specific areas, such as OLTP, client/server can still be perceived to have different meanings, depending on the different software components that interact with one another.

What follows is by no means an extensive discussion about the client/server model in OLTP environments, nor is it an attempt to provide a formal definition of it. It is rather an examination of a couple of common client/server configurations, in which in the absence of a more specific definition we can identify different ways of perceiving such a type of architecture.

The examples are taken from an environment such as a traditional DBMS application for UNIX systems. Since DBMS systems provide a common background to many IT professionals, and since DBMS applications constitute significant examples of currently implemented OLTP solutions in the UNIX market, the chosen framework should provide a sufficiently popular and well-understood environment.

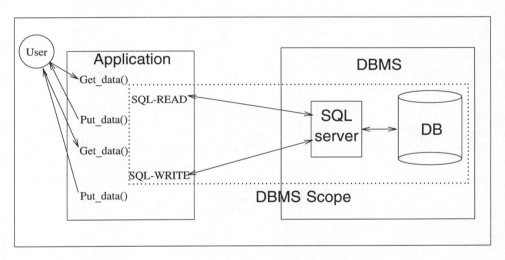

Figure 10. DBMS application on a single machine

Figure 10 represents an abstraction of a DBMS application on a single machine. A DBMS system is available on the machine to provide the data storing/retrieving logic. Applications, usually one instance of the same executable program per user, include code for handling both the interaction with the end user (terminal input and output) and the interaction logic with the database (through the use of SQL statements). The actual execution of the SQL statements is provided by an SQL server, to which a particular instance of the application is connected.

In this configuration, the application requests the execution of database work from a separate entity, the DBMS engine. Because of its role of "requester", the application is referred to as the *client*. The SQL server and the underlying software for data provide the services requested by the application, i.e. the execution of the database operations. Because of their role as service providers, they are referred to as the *server* environment. In this representation of the client/server model, the emphasis is put on the distinction between the application (client) and the database engine (server). This is quite a popular representation of a client/server architecture.

The benefits of this approach include the fact that the actual database management is kept outside the scope of the application, so that different applications can access the same database without having to worry about the others. Also, unlike early DBMS applications, client applications are no longer monolithic objects which need to carry around all the relevant software. Therefore, memory requirements for the application are smaller.

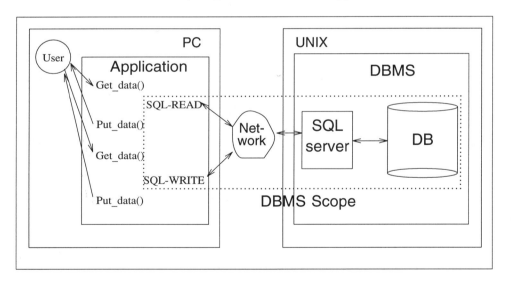

Figure 11. A DBMS application over a network

The above model lends itself well to distribution. Taking advantage of the distributed (client/server) capabilities of many DBMSs, which allow, for instance, remote execution of SQL operations over a network, the same application can be moved onto a different machine, perhaps a PC or a workstation (Figure 11).

In such a configuration, the actual PC or workstation would request remote execution of database work, and it would therefore be identified as the *client*. The machine where the database engine resides, usually a bigger machine, would be defined as the *server*. From one point of view, there is no real difference between this model and the previous one, because the emphasis is still on the distinction between the application and the database server, only in this case they reside on different machines; there is a one-to-one correspondence between the PC and the application (client), and between the big machine and the database engine (server). From another point of view, though, the latter model is more general, because the PC can at different times be a client of different servers, possibly through the use of different applications. Similarly, the big machine can provide different server environments, probably used by different applications. This is a second and even more common representation of a client/server architecture.

The benefits of this configuration, besides those already described for the single-machine configuration, include the fact that the terminal interaction is now handled by the PC. This reduces the load on the server machine, the main purpose of which is to provide data management. Higher numbers of users can be supported. At the same time the DBMS handles internally the remote execution of SQL statements, in a way which is transparent to the application. Finally, geographically remote users can execute the same application as the local or native ones.

Additional aspects must be noted though in both configurations. For example, the actual client/server functionality is provided internally by the DBMS (indicated by DBMS scope). This puts implicit constraints on the operations that can benefit from this architecture. Basically, only when database "services" are requested can the application benefit from this client/server implementation. An application wishing to perform other operations (no SQL), or needing to access different resources (no SQL or different SQL), would have to code the different logic in some other inconsistent style. Moreover, the distributed configuration in Figure 11 is based on an implementation of the client/server architecture which uses a technique known as *data shipping*, where, for each execution of an SQL statement, data are moved from one machine to the other. This is a potential obstacle for large OLTP applications on UNIX environments, as a lot of network traffic might be generated. Although DBMS vendors have started addressing these issues, for example through stored procedures, the current perception is still that this type of architecture requires a significant amount of network traffic.

In the light of the above aspects (and again, this is not a comprehensive discussion of all the possible relevant aspects), a TP monitor like TUXEDO can provide both significant enhancements and ways around the potential limitations. This is achieved through the implementation of an enhanced client/server model, as described in the next section.

3.2 TUXEDO's client/server architecture

With reference to Figure 10 (single machine), let's see where the TUXEDO System comes into the picture, and how its presence may affect our perception of clients and servers (Figure 12).

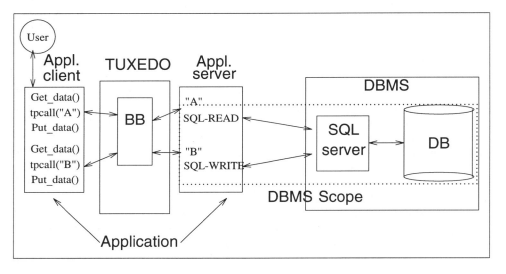

Figure 12. TUXEDO and a DBMS application on a single machine

On the right-hand side of the diagram, nothing has changed. The DBMS, its client/server implementation, and its benefits, are still there. Equally, the scope of the DBMS is still the same, i.e. the execution of SQL statements is handled internally by the DBMS system; TUXEDO has not affected it. What TUXEDO has affected, though, is the application. The entity that we used to identify as the client is now split into two separate components: an *application client* and an *application server*.

The application client handles the interaction with the user (terminal input and output) and does not contain SQL code. The portion of the original application which used to perform (to request, in fact) database work has become a specialised application server. It provides a set of database operations under a unique name (*services*, "A" or "B" in the example). The application client, through the use of TUXEDO and its internal structures, for example the Bulletin Board (BB), requests such services simply by invoking their name.

From the DBMS point of view the application server is still a client application and the SQL server is still the server. The two overlapping perspectives from which the application can be seen must not be confused. When talking about TUXEDO, only the left-hand side of Figure 12 must be kept in mind. TUXEDO's client/server architecture applies uniquely to the application. The emphasis is put on the fact that the application is split into client processes (dealing with the user) and server processes (dealing with a resource). This is valid regardless of the actual implementation of the resource access method, which might be based on another client/server architecture. Therefore, from this moment on and unless stated otherwise, we will refer to the term client/server in the sense specified above, and we will define a TUXEDO application client simply as a client, and a TUXEDO application server simply as a server.

3.3 Why enhanced?

Having defined TUXEDO's boundaries as far as the client/server architecture is concerned, let's discuss the impact of such an architecture on the two configurations considered so far, and the enhancements that TUXEDO brings into the models.

Going back to Figure 12, it can be seen that there is now a complete decoupling between the application client and the application server. Clients and servers have a completely independent life, which means, for instance, that there is no need to have a one-to-one correspondence between clients and servers. While a client is handling the terminal input/output, a server can execute operations on behalf of another client. Because the user interaction time is usually much longer than the execution of database update, a smaller number of servers can support a higher number of clients. The addition of one user to the system has a limited impact in terms of memory requirements, as the client program does not carry around, for example, the DBMS libraries. This allows a higher number of users to be supported on the same machine. Also, the services don't necessarily have to perform database operations; as far as the client is concerned, services are any set of operations identified by a name. In this way, the architecture is more general.

The TUXEDO System handles all the communication between clients and servers through the use of a name server, the so-called Bulletin Board, which keeps information about what server provides which service. In addition, the TUXEDO System provides other features such as administration, load balancing, prioritisation, and of course, transaction coordination. The ability to provide these additional, more general, capabilities is the reason why TUXEDO's client/server architecture is defined as "enhanced".

If we now consider the distributed DBMS application in Figure 11, the impact of TUXEDO is even more evident. Because the application is now split into clients and servers, the clients can be executed on PCs while the servers still reside on the machine where the data are located (Figure 13).

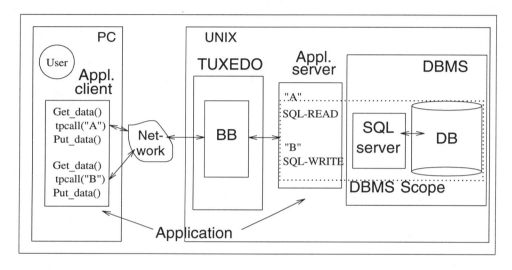

Figure 13. A distributed application with TUXEDO and a DBMS (1)

This has a significant impact on the execution of the application, because little data have to be transmitted across the network. The client simply requests the execution of a service; the service is carried out where the data are and only the final result is passed back to the client. This technique is often known as *function shipping* (the whole set of operations is shipped, once and for all, near the resource), and constitutes a key factor for meeting the performance requirements of OLTP environments.

Within this architecture, the same client can request other services on other machines, possibly database operations on different databases, perhaps under different operating systems. The client can use a consistent programming interface to access all sorts of services, and servers can use the same consistent interface to reply to clients.

The TUXEDO System looks after the communication between clients and servers in a way which is transparent to the application, not just in terms of networking, but also in terms of location. Clients don't have to know where a particular server resides, TUXEDO will find out for the client which server can best serve its request, for example through the use of data-dependent routing. And if a client requests database operations on different machines, TUXEDO may look after the coordination of any transactional requirements.

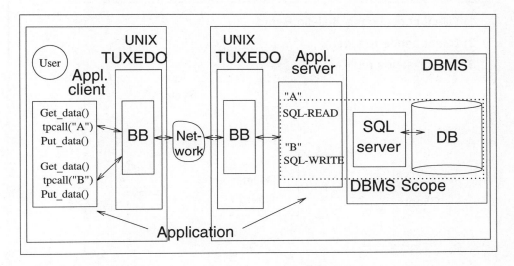

Figure 14. A distributed application with TUXEDO and a DBMS (2)

In the configuration provided in Figure 13, the TUXEDO software (System/T and the name server) is available on the machine where the DBMS resides, and the client is connected to the System/T environment via System/WS (not indicated in the picture). In other distributed environments, the System/T software might be available on multiple machines (Figure 14). Clients running on the same machine as System/T ("native" clients, in TUXEDO terminology), will still access the same services in the same fashion. This allows the mixing of "native" UNIX users and PC users within the same application environment, while keeping the application servers near to the resource with which they interact.

3.4 Main components of the TUXEDO System

If we consider the model presented in the previous section, we can identify some components of TUXEDO's client/server architecture: application clients, application servers, and a name server structure, the Bulletin Board.

In fact, to understand better what components constitute TUXEDO's architecture, let's have a closer look at what lays between clients and servers, i.e. at what we have represented as a box named System/T. A more precise representation is given in Figure 15.

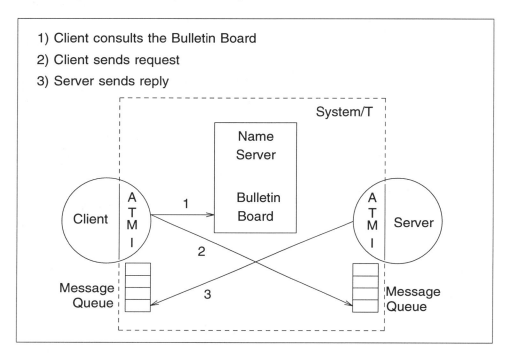

Figure 15. TUXEDO's architecture

The box that was represented as a separate element between clients and servers stretches in fact to these processes as well. To make use of the TUXEDO System, clients and servers are linked to TUXEDO's ATMI libraries (the application to transaction manager interface) and are assigned message queues. Through these, they have access to the information provided in the Bulletin Board, and can exchange messages.

The information in the Bulletin Board allows the client to identify a queue to which it can send a request. The information contained in the request allows the server to identify the queue to which it must send a reply. The ATMI functions perform the sending and receipt of messages to and from the queues. Following is a more detailed description of each one of these components. If you are not interested in further detail, you might want to skip the rest of this section and probably the following one. A few more comments about TUXEDO's architecture in relation to OLTP are provided towards the end of the chapter, in Section 3.6.

3.4.1 Application clients

In the TUXEDO System, clients are processes which typically perform a repeated sequence of operations; they gather input from the end-user terminal or workstation, send service requests and data to server processes, receive the result of the service execution, and display the service output to the end-user. Clients may also establish connections with servers, send initial data to a service, display partial results, gather new input, send additional data to the connected service, as many times as required by the application.

In neither case is there a need for a client to access directly the resources upon which the service must be executed, and its structure will in general look like the one presented in Figure 16. The client is the point of contact with the end-user, and this means that when the latter enters a program to perform operations within the system, the process invoked is ultimately a client process. The term "front-end process" is another way to describe the client.

The first task the client carries out is to register itself with the TUXEDO application, which basically consists in the allocation of an entry in the Bulletin Board so that the system is aware of its existence. At this point a message queue is also automatically created, and, if necessary, user authentication is performed. This action is executed once at the beginning, and from that moment on the client has access to the services provided by the application.

After registration, the next step for the client is to determine all the specific information it needs to perform the desired operation. This typically implies the display of an input mask and the collection of some data from the user. Once this information is obtained, the client packages the data into a format known to the server process and suitable for transmission. At this point it can actually send a service request to the server for processing.

After the request is sent, the client will typically wait for the reply. This will typically contain information about the outcome of the service request. If the request was for an operation, a small acknowledgement may be the only information returned to the client. If the service request was a query for information, there will be a new, enlarged buffer returned in place of the one sent.

In order to obtain sufficient information for the end user, the act of sending/receiving might be repeated several times, either in connection to

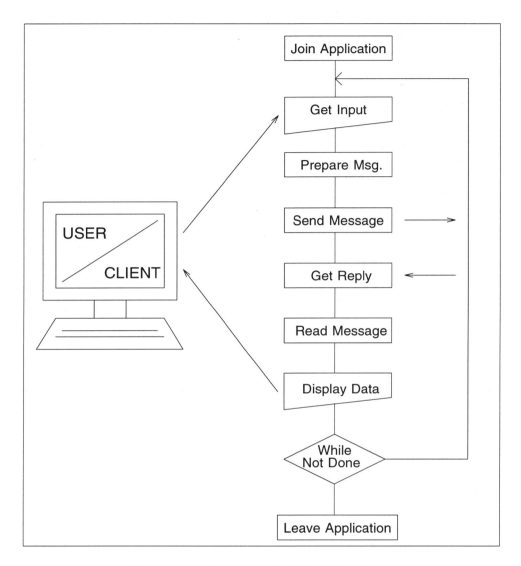

Figure 16. Structure of a TUXEDO client

the same server, or with different servers. Upon receipt of each individual reply, the return buffer is checked to evaluate the outcome of the service request, and, when sufficient information is obtained, this is displayed to the end user in the expected format.

At the end of the session, i.e. when the user disconnects from the application, the client unregisters from the Bulletin Board, removes its message queue, and terminates.

3.4.2 Application servers

Server processes perform a repeated sequence of operations as well. Typically, they receive a service request, execute the service, and return the outcome of the operation to the client. Application servers have the following properties:

- They are processes which continually accept requests and dispatch them to application routines, called services, for processing. It is the service routines which, for example, access DBMS resources.

- They are unavailable for processing until the current request is finished, and there is no system support for maintaining state information. While processing a request, however, a server can exchange messages and data with the originator of the request.

- They may advertise many services, and one service may be advertised by many servers.

- They may act as clients and make service requests or connection requests to other servers.

The typical structure of a TUXEDO server is presented in Figure 17. The server is the point of contact to the resource to be accessed in the overall system. For example, a server could be the point of contact for a database and would therefore make the queries and modifications to it. To perform in this capacity, the server needs to open, i.e. register with, the database manager when it starts up. To complete its initialisation, the server advertises a number of service functions to the overall system, so that client processes will know where to send service requests.

Once these two steps are complete, the server can go into a perpetual loop of receiving requests, processing them, and sending back the replies. Receiving requests involves reading the message queue and dequeueing a service request. Processing the requests involves examining the contents of the request buffer, performing action on the basis of the information contained in the request, and returning a reply buffer with all necessary information about the outcome of the service execution. Intermediate messages may be exchanged with the requester, but no other requests would be served at the same time.

When the administrator of the application decides to shut down a server,

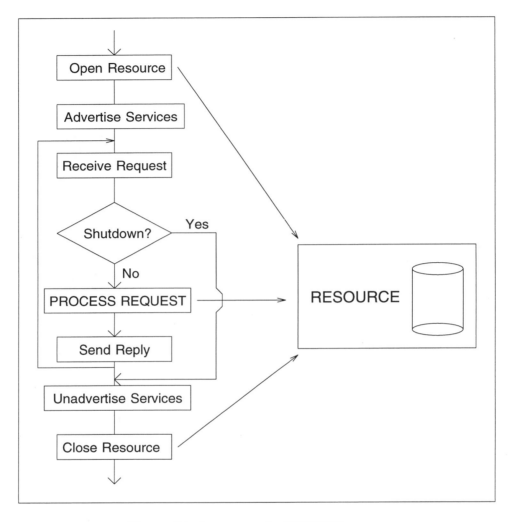

Figure 17. Structure of a TUXEDO server

a shutdown request is sent to the server. At that point, it will unadvertise its services, serve the requests still in its queue, close its connection with the resource, and terminate.

It must be noted that whilst clients must be programmed in order to perform all actions described earlier, servers perform most of the described actions automatically. Programmers need only to code the service routines, i.e. the application-dependent operations. Advertising services, reading requests, and sending replies, are operations provided by a main program to which application-dependent service routines are linked.

3.4.3 The ATMI

The ATMI (application to transaction manager interace) is the TUXEDO API. It includes a set of application primitives for communicating with the TUXEDO software and, through it, performing the following operations:

- Join/leave the application

- Manage request buffers

- Request services

- Return responses to service requesters

- Advertise/unadvertise services

- Establish connections and exchange messages

- Define and manage transactions

- Send and receive unsolicited messages

- Set priorities of service request

- Enqueue and dequeue requests in permanent queues.

The ATMI includes about 30 functions and is available in 3GL languages such as C and COBOL or, via abstractions, in different 4GL languages. Several DBMS vendors, for example Informix and Ally, provide 4GL tools to generate TUXEDO applications that integrate with their specific DBMS. CASE tools are also available. TUXEDO's ATMI is also supported by programming environments like VisualBasic® and is available for shell programming via the Windowing Korn Shell®.

Depending on the chosen language, the functions will obviously have a different syntax and a different look. For example, the function for requesting a service could be any one of those presented in Figure 18.

For the purpose of this book, we will use a "C-like" abstraction, since this is the most immediate in terms of syntax. Such abstraction will only mention the function name and, at times, some of the parameters involved, but never the full C syntax. With reference to the example above, the function will be presented as *tpcall()*, or, in some examples, as *tpcall(SERVICE,data)*. The meaning and usage of the ATMI functions will be described in Chapters 4, 5, 6, and 7, but a summary might be useful here.

Function *tpchkauth()* is used to determine the level of authentication

---

Synchronous service request: tpcall()

- C:

  ret = tpcall("MYSERV",(char *)ibuf,ilen,(char **)&obuf,&olen,flags)

- COBOL:

  MOVE "MYSERV" TO SERVICE-NAME.

  CALL "TPCALL " USING TPSVCDEF-REC

                     ITPTYPE-REC

                     IDATA-REC

                     OTPTYPE-REC

                     ODATA-REC

                     TPSTATUS-REC.

- ACCELL/4GL$^{®}$:

  EXTERN BOOL FUNCTION MYSERV (param1, RESULT result1)

  MYSERV (param, result)

Figure 18. Examples of TUXEDO service requests in different languages

needed to join an application. Function *tpinit()* connects a client to the application and function *tpterm()* disconnects it from the application.

Functions *tpalloc()*, *tprealloc()*, *tpfree()*, and *tptypes()* are used to create, resize, free, and check communication buffers. The ATMI makes available four different types of buffers, which provide a suitable framework for data exchange between clients and servers.

Asynchronous service requests, in which the client can perform other work while waiting for a reply, are initiated with the *tpacall()* function; the response is received by *tpgetrply()* or it is cancelled by *tpcancel()*. The *tpcall()* function bundles the two into a single function call to provide synchronous service requests.

The priority associated to a service request can be obtained with *tpgprio()* and changed with *tpsprio()*.

Conversations are established with *tpconnect()*; data are sent using *tpsend()* and received using *tprecv()*. Disconnections may be requested with *tpdiscon()*.

Services can send replies with *tpreturn()*, or forward the request to another service with *tpforward()*. Services can be dynamically advertised and unadvertised through the use of *tpadvertise()* and *tpunadvertise()*.

Unsolicited messages can be sent with *tpbroadcast()* and received with *tpchkunsol()*. The function for processing unsolicited messages can be set with *tpsetunsol()*. Servers can send unsolicited messages using *tpnotify()*.

Transactions can be begun, committed, and aborted with *tpbegin()*, *tpcommit*, *tpabort()*. Function *tpscmt()* can be used to determine at what point the result of the two-phase commit algorithm must be returned to the application. To find out if the process is in transaction mode, *tpgetlev()* may be used. Functions *tpopen()* and *tpclose()* can be used to open and close resources which support the XA interface.

In the event of an error during an ATMI call, a global variable *tperrno* is set. Function *tpstrerror()* can be used to get a string describing the error. Some data structures, representing the input parameters to a server and the identity of a client, are also part of the ATMI.

The ATMI has been the subject of attention from X/Open and most of these functions have been adopted, either directly or with minor modifications as standard interfaces n X/Open's DTP model under the name of X/Open TX and X/Open XATMI. The TX and XATMI interfaces are also supported by the TUXEDO software, and can be used or mixed with the native ATMI functions. More specific information about these is provided in Chapter 5.

3.4.4 Message queues

The queues to which messages are sent are UNIX System V queues (or equivalent structures for non UNIX System V systems). UNIX queues are particularly suitable for the purpose of the TUXEDO System because they are separate from clients and servers, and support dequeuing policies other than FIFO. They provide an efficient means of communication for unrelated processes, because their names are not part of the UNIX file system, their descriptors are independent of any process, and they do not need opening/closing.

Because these queues are in memory, they allow for good performance, but are not particularly suitable for batch processing or any form of delayed processing. This particular functionality is provided through another type of queue, which is provided as an extension package (see System/Q in Chapter 7).

3.4.5 The Bulletin Board

The Bulletin Board is the core component of TUXEDO's client/server implementation. It is a segment of shared memory which provides the name serving function for the entire application, i.e. it maps names to addresses.

Being a structure in memory, it allows for fast access. All application processes use it both to communicate with each other and to register data about occurring events.

The Bulletin Board is created by a TUXEDO administrative process when the application is started, and it is filled from information contained in a TUXEDO configuration file on disk (Figure 19). The Bulletin Board's internal structure comprises data structures grouped together into tables (not to be confused with DBMS tables). The tables contain information about the application clients, servers, services, transactions, etc.

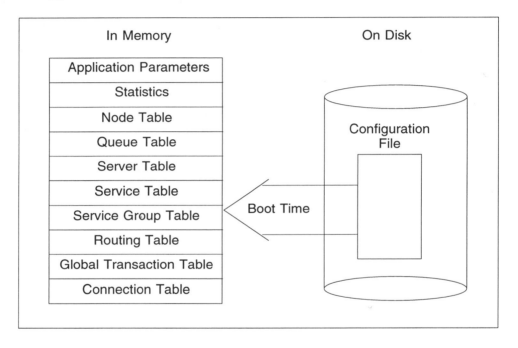

Figure 19. Structure of the Bulletin Board

To get access to the Bulletin Board, clients and servers attach to it. Once a process is attached to it, the Bulletin Board becomes part of the process's address space, thus guaranteeing fast access. If necessary, protection of the information in the Bulletin Board against unintentional corruption can be obtained by keeping the Bulletin Board in the process's address space only during the execution of ATMI functions and not during the execution of application code.

The Bulletin Board is propagated at application boot time to all machines running System/T (Figure 20), and part of the information contained in it is

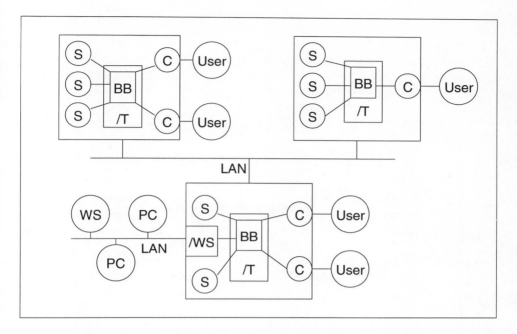

Figure 20. The Bulletin Board in a TUXEDO application

updated across all the machines whenever changes occur. For example, when a new server is booted, this information is registered in all Bulletin Boards, so that all clients on all machines can make requests to it. In addition to mapping names to addresses, the Bulletin Board keeps statistics for the implementation of load balancing, and to allow the administrator to perform dynamic tuning of the application.

3.5 Other components of the TUXEDO System

Besides the components described in the previous section, which constitute the main elements of TUXEDO's client/server architecture, there are internal elements and other components which make everything fit together. These are typically a set of internal processes which look after the execution of certain operations, and a set of administrative tools.

A representation of these components is provided in Figure 21. Internal administrative processes exchange information with each other, and via the information found in the Bulletin Board, monitor the execution of the application. They also perform duties on behalf of the administrator, who

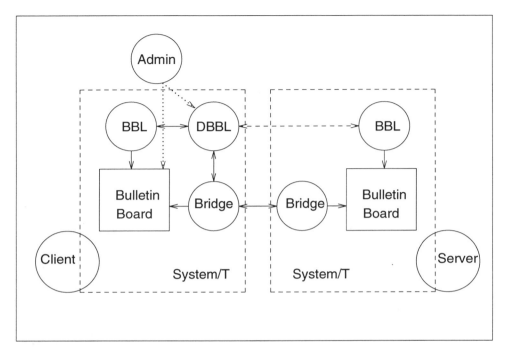

Figure 21. Internal elements of TUXEDO's architecture

interacts with them via administrative tools. In general, their tasks include:

- Boot of remote components of the application
- Message transmission across the network
- Consistency and availability checking
- Coordination of the two-phase commit
- Process restart and resource cleaning.

The role and functionality of these processes is described in some more detail in the next few pages. Again, you might want to skip the rest of this section if you are not interested in further details. The actual identity of some processes, for example those for coordinating the two-phase commit, will not be introduced here but at a later stage when describing relevant functionalities; when this is done, it will be made clear which of these processes are.

3.5.1 The Bulletin Board Liaison process

The Bulletin Board Liaison process (BBL) is the administrative process associated to the Bulletin Board. At specified intervals, the BBL carries out certain administrative processing, which includes:

- Timing out blocked processes

- Timing out transactions

- Cleaning and restarting dead processes.

The BBL serves administrative requests from the administrator and ensures that no other processes are still active on the machine when the application is shut down.

3.5.2 The Distinguished Bulletin Board Liaison process

The Distinguished Bulletin Board Liaison process (DBBL) is the first process to be booted in a networked TUXEDO application. Its initial task is to send a copy of the Bulletin Board to the remote BBLs as soon as they are started. When the boot sequence is complete, the DBBL keeps on working in the background to check the status of all the machines in the configuration. In the case of network failures, the DBBL sends a new copy of the Bulletin Board to the remote BBL as soon as the connection is re-established.

Other tasks include the coordination of global updates to the Bulletin Board when changes in the application occur. Finally, it makes sure that all processes have been shut down when the administrator requests a complete shutdown of the application.

3.5.3 The BRIDGE process

The BRIDGE process is an administrative server, the main purpose of which is to transfer messages on behalf of other processes from the local machine to the other sites in the application and viceversa. This process handles the transmission of messages to and from other machines by managing a set of virtual circuits. Each System/T machine in the network has one BRIDGE.

The BRIDGE accesses the network via the TUXEDO network library, a TUXEDO-provided library which hides the differences between different networking implementations.

Figure 22 presents the structure of the TUXEDO network library as used by the BRIDGE and other TUXEDO processes. These processes perform

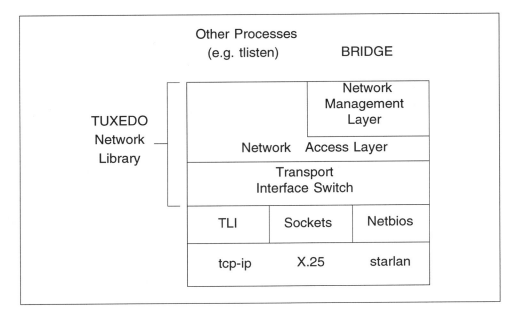

Figure 22. TUXEDO's networking library

network operations through a network access layer, which provides a set of abstractions of network operations (message send and receive) independent of the actual network provider. The BRIDGE uses in fact an additional network management layer for managing the open connections.

These functions, through the use of a transport interface switch, access the provider-dependent functions, and through these, the actual network. This also means that different networking implementations on different machines can communicate with one another. The transport interface switch currently supports the TLI, sockets and netbios interfaces. Because of this structure, the introduction of a new transport provider or new networking is confined to a well-isolated set of functions, and neither the code of TUXEDO's internal processes, nor that of the application, has to be modified.

3.5.4 Administrative tools and commands

The TUXEDO System provides a set of tools for the application administrator to enable him/her to perform various operations. These operations include:

- Creating a configuration file for the application

- Booting/shutting down the application

- Runtime administration

- Dynamic reconfiguration.

We won't go in any further details about these; a much more specific description of such tools in relation to the administrative operations is provided in Chapter 6.

3.6 Considerations with respect to OLTP

With reference to the previous sections where we have described both the impact of TUXEDO's architecture on traditional DBMS applications and the actual components of such architecture, let's now look at how this architecture addresses the requirements of OLTP environments, generic distributed computing environments, and specific DTP environments.

As mentioned earlier, *OLTP environments* are identified in general by specific characteristics: a large number of users who frequently perform a relatively small set of operations; a large number of fairly short interactions with a database; large shared databases. In order to evaluate the impact of TUXEDO's architecture, the important factors to be considered here are the number of users and the number of interactions. Because it has many users, an OLTP system must make sure that the addition of others has a minimal impact on the efficiency of the application. Also, because there are many interactions, such a system must make sure that they are as fast as possible and that throughput is maximised.

In the architecture described above, clients do not carry around code to access the resource, so they require smaller executables. They can run in less memory, and the network traffic they generate is restricted to service requests and replies, which is usually less than that generated by SQL statements. The addition of users has therefore a minimal impact on application efficiency.

Equally, application servers are specialised processes which do not need to carry around libraries for user interface, for example libraries for graphics. Moreover, because they do not correspond to clients on a one-to-one basis, they can handle multiple clients and in doing so they can sequentialise and prioritise requests. This reduces the number of simultaneous accessers for the resource, thus increasing the general efficiency of the DBMS, as it does not have to cope with too many simultaneous locks. On average, the same number of requests can be executed in less time. Also, thanks to prioritisation, those requests that have to be executed first are in fact

53

executed in less than average time. Overall, the length of interactions is minimised and the application throughput maximised.

Generic distributed computing is identified by other characteristics: the interoperation of different hardware, software, and networking. The important factors are compatibility, integration, modularity, and scalability. Because there might be many different hardware and software components, a system must make sure that the application doesn't need to be adapted in order to cope with these different components, and similarly, it must make sure that systems can be added or removed in a way which is transparent to the application.

In TUXEDO's architecture, clients and servers communicate with each other via a common API (the ATMI), which exists on many platforms, both UNIX and PC. The TUXEDO software hides hardware and software differences, so, in this respect, compatibility and integration are provided.

Clients and servers have a totally independent life, so modularity is provided too. Services can be added, removed, and moved to other machines without the clients having to know. The scalability is enhanced because clients and servers can be moved to other machines as new ones are added to the configuration.

DTP is identified by yet other characteristics, which refer to the involvement of different resources within the same transaction. The important factor here is the transmission of transaction information to the resources involved, and the coordination of such resources within the transaction.

In TUXEDO's architecture, different servers can be located on different machines and access different resources. Clients can request different services within the same transaction, while the TUXEDO software keeps track of the correspondence between servers and transactions in the Bulletin Board. Through the use of the information stored in the Bulletin Board, TUXEDO can coordinate all the resources involved in the transaction and implement a two-phase commit.

In terms of *application development*, this architecture allows clients and servers to be developed independently and possibly at different stages. New servers can be developed and later added to the application, possibly without even having to modify the clients. New user interfaces can be built without having to modify the servers. Especially during the application development phase, errors in the clients do not affect the execution of servers and vice versa. All of this concurs to make application development and maintenance more flexible and efficient.

3.7 Summary

In this chapter, we have examined the idea and the concepts behind TUXEDO's implementation of a client/server architecture. Client/server architectures can be interpreted in different ways depending on what is identified as client and server. TUXEDO's client/server architecture is mainly based on the separation of an application into client components, which deal with the end user and request the execution of services, and server components, which deal with a resource (e.g. a database) and execute a set of operations with it.

The architecture with which resource access is implemented is not relevant to the definition of clients and servers as far as TUXEDO is concerned. Resource access could just as well be implemented in a client/server fashion, but this must not be confused with TUXEDO's own definition of clients and servers.

Besides application clients and servers, other components of TUXEDO's client/server architecture include the Bulletin Board, the ATMI, message queues, and administrative processes, tools and commands. Through its client/server architecture, TUXEDO implements enhancements and features which address the requirements of OLTP environments, generic distributed applications, and DTP. The same enhancements and features contribute to efficient and reliable application development.

4. Distributed Processing

When we introduced the relationship between TUXEDO and OLTP in Chapter 2, a logical separation was identified between the capabilities related to distributed processing and those more specifically related to distributed transaction processing. That separation was necessary to emphasise the existence of two different sets of features, which can co-exist but do not always have to be related to one another. Following this separation, let's start our examination of TUXEDO's capabilities from the features related to distributed processing. Because these have general validity within and outside the scope of OLTP, a separate examination is also useful to address a number of individual issues, to discuss their generic function in distributed computing, and, finally, to prepare the ground for the TP-related considerations in Chapter 5.

TUXEDO's distributed processing features address the general differences found in distributed, heterogeneous environments, differences that applications must try and resolve in a consistent and effective way. First, we will examine the features which allow different components of the application to communicate with one another, that is, the communication paradigms between clients and servers and their related message types; second, those features used to achieve better performance, higher flexibility, and a consistent behaviour across networks of heterogeneous computers. These include load balancing, prioritisation, data-dependent routing, and unsolicited notification; finally, the features which can be used for implementing different layers of security over such types of environments.

All features presented here relate to System/T and are available on UNIX or UNIX-like systems used as backbones for the application. In Chapter 7 the same features will be addressed from the perspective of System/WS, System/HOST, System/Q, and System/DOMAINS. Where appropriate, differences with respect to what seen in this chapter will be pointed out.

4.1 Client/server communication

As presented in Chapter 3, one of the key characteristics of the TUXEDO System is the separation of applications into client and server processes; the clients handle the interaction with the user and request services, whilst the servers handle the interaction with the resource and execute services.

Being separate processes, possibly on different machines and different operating systems, clients and servers must be able to communicate with one another in a way independent of the characteristics of individual systems and of the communication facilities (e.g. remote procedure calls). Due to the absence of standards in this area, at least until very recently, TUXEDO makes available a set of communication paradigms and data buffers which can be used regardless of the underlaying communication facilities provided by the systems. The fact that the communication is controlled by TUXEDO has also several side-benefits. By handling the communication between clients and servers, TUXEDO can assist processes with the transmission of requests and replies, with the delivery of messages and data, and with the execution of operations such as load balancing, data-dependent routing, and prioritisation. All of this contributes to the implementation of the enhanced client/server architecture presented in Chapter 3.

At programming level, the communication between clients and servers occurs through the use of a set of ATMI functions for interprocess communication and buffer handling, and is implemented according to one of two paradigms, *RPC-like* and *conversational*. The RPC-like paradigm is so called because it resembles the UNIX remote procedure call (RPC) mechanism, in which a procedure (a service, in our case) can be invoked and executed on a remote system. The Conversational paradigm, on the contrary, implies a more involved exchange of messages between the client and the server.

Although these communication methods have been developed specifically within and for TUXEDO, in recent years there has been a growing recognition of the need for standards in this area. In this respect, TUXEDO's communication paradigms have been the basis for some of the work carried out by X/Open, and have been adopted as standard communication paradigms between applications and communication resource managers. We will say more about this in Chapter 5, where we will examine the whole X/Open's DTP model. If you are already familiar with it, it might be worth mentioning here that this is the work related to X/Open's XATMI.

4.1.1 The RPC-like paradigm

The RPC-like paradigm is identified by the fact that a client makes service request ("calls" the service) and subsequently receives the result of the entire service's execution.[5] While the service is being executed, the client doesn't have information about what is going on in the service and no access to partial results. When the service completes, the server communicates the success or failure of the requested operation, and, if necessary, final data. This behaviour is very similar to that of traditional remote procedure calls in UNIX environments. In TUXEDO's case, however, services are only logically remote, since they might actually reside on the same machine as the client. In fact they are "remote" in the sense that they cannot be accessed via a direct function call, but only through a request mechanism.

Another difference with respect to traditional RPC is that there are in fact two possibilities for the handling of replies. Clients can either decide to request a service and wait until the reply arrives (*synchronous request*), or to request a service, do useful work while the service is being executed, and then read the reply at a later stage (*asynchronous request*). The reasons why we decide to use one type or the other is entirely application-dependent, but, in general synchronous requests are easier to program, while asynchronous requests offer the possibility of a more efficient use of the client's execution time. In particular, the work done while waiting for a reply can include making other service requests, thus increasing the parallelism of execution of services, especially if the different requests are routed to different machines.

Synchronous or asynchronous requests are used when the client doesn't need to have access to partial results of the service's execution, and when the service can complete its tasks by making use of the data passed along with the request. When this is not the case, a conversational paradigm may be more appropriate, as we will see in the next section.

---

5. In fact clients are not the only processes that can request services; servers can sometimes behave like clients and in turn request other services for the execution of subportions of the operation. In the case of a bank transfer for example, the service TRANSFER might request service WITHDRAWAL on one machine and service DEPOSIT on another, thus acting as a client. In order to keep the language easy, we will keep on using the term client/server with an implied meaning for the term client as either real client or server acting like one.

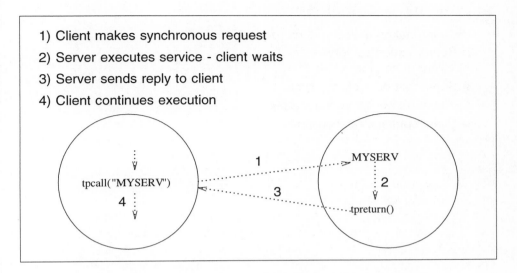

1) Client makes synchronous request

2) Server executes service - client waits

3) Server sends reply to client

4) Client continues execution

Figure 23. RPC-like paradigm - Synchronous request

4.1.1.1 Usage

The use of synchronous or asynchronous communication between clients and servers depends on the use of dedicated functions provided by TUXEDO's ATMI libraries. The following is a description of the main aspects related to the use of these functions. As was said in Chapter 3, we will only use an abstraction of the functions instead of the real functions in a real programming language. Also, not all parameters to the functions will be shown, but only those relevant to the discussion.

A process wishing to make a synchronous service request must use function *tpcall()* (Figure 23). This function receives as parameters the name of the service which needs to be executed, an input buffer, an output buffer (possibly the same as the input buffer), and a set of flags to determine the behaviour in case of particular blocking conditions, such as the impossibility of sending the request because the destination queue is full.

The process does not need to know what server offers the service, or where the server is located. If there is more than one server capable of serving the request, TUXEDO will make a choice based on criteria like data-dependent routing or load balancing. In the absence of any criteria, it will simply send the request to the first available server. A request is represented by a message containing the name of the service, the input buffer, and information about the identity of the requester.

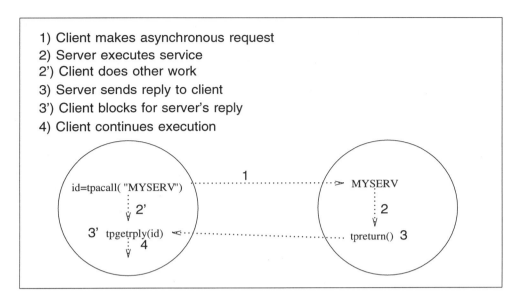

1) Client makes asynchronous request
2) Server executes service
2') Client does other work
3) Server sends reply to client
3') Client blocks for server's reply
4) Client continues execution

Figure 24. RPC-like paradigm - Asynchronous request

Once the message has been sent, tpcall() waits for the reply from the server to come, and then compiles the data received into the specified output buffer. If desired, TUXEDO can verify that the data passed back and forth are of a predefined type, or it can notify the requester if a timeout has expired without receiving a reply. If these conditions are verified, tpcall() returns a failure, and if a late reply arrives, it is silently discarded. Normally tpcall() will receive the reply in time, and the client will receive back the control after the server has executed the request.

Instead of tpcall(), a client wishing to make an asynchronous request uses function *tpacall()* (Figure 24). This is very similar to tpcall() (i.e. it receives as parameters the service name, an input buffer, and flags; it performs load balancing, data-dependent routing, etc.), but after sending the message it returns the control to the client. The client is provided with a call identifier (a "handle"), so that it can later identify the reply corresponding to that call. After receiving the handle, the client is free to do other work, possibly to request other services.

A client can have up to 50 outstanding requests at any time, and can read the incoming replies through the use of function *tpgetrply()* (Figure 25). This function is passed a handle and a buffer in which to receive the data passed back from the server. If a reply associated to the handle is available, it returns it to the client. If it is not available, the function can be instructed to either wait indefinitely until the reply arrives, or to wait for a certain amount of time, or to return immediately thus allowing other work to be done. Depending upon the setting of a certain flag, tpgetrply() can also be instructed to read the first available reply instead of a specific one, and to return information about the handle to which the reply corresponds.

If the client wishes to cancel an asynchronous request (it can't do it in the case of a synchronous request because it won't get the control back until that request is terminated), it can use the function *tpcancel()*. This function marks the specified handle as invalid, so that the corresponding reply will be silently ignored. It must be noted, though, that cancelling a request means that the client is no longer interested in the reply, but it does not prevent a server from executing the request (it might in fact already be under way, or even terminated). Its usage should therefore be limited either to those calls that the user knows will never be executed (for example, because the system on which the server resides has crashed), or to those calls for which it might not be so important to get to know if they did execute or not (for example, print on a remote printer). In these circumstances, cancelling the request allows to free one of the 50 available handles that would not be released otherwise. It is probably worth anticipating here that tpcancel() is not allowed during a global transaction, since this would cause the system to lose track of the all components involved in the transaction, thus causing potential inconsistency across the different data stores.

After a request is sent, a server will at a certain point read it from the queue and dispatch it to the corresponding service function. The service carries out all necessary operations (which may include other service requests), and, at the end, it communicates the outcome of the execution through the use of the function *tpreturn()*. This function sends to the originator of the request a message containing information about success or failure, and if successful, any data the service may have provided in a return buffer. The return buffer is passed as a parameter to the function, and can be the same as the one received from the client.

After sending a reply with tpreturn(), the server re-enters its main loop and reads another request from its request queue. Under certain circumstances, typically when some critical events occur during the execution of the service (for example, the detection of some type of corruption in the database), the application can instruct tpreturn() to return a failure to the client and to make the server stop, to avoid further problems (for example, corrupting the database even further). When this happens, TUXEDO reads the outstanding requests from the queue and sends a message to each requester, to communicate the impossibility to execute the service.

As an alternative to sending a reply to the client, a service can forward

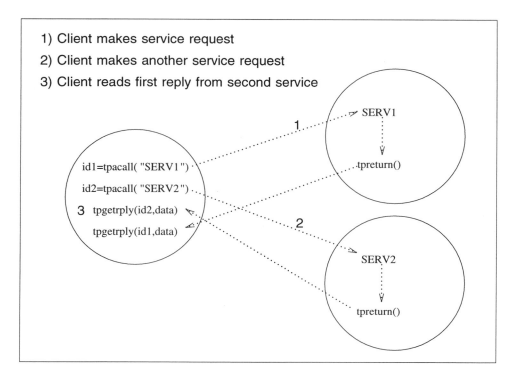

1) Client makes service request

2) Client makes another service request

3) Client reads first reply from second service

SERV1

id1=tpacall("SERV1")

id2=tpacall("SERV2")

3 tpgetrply(id2,data)

tpgetrply(id1,data)

.tpreturn()

SERV2

tpreturn()

Figure 25. RPC-like paradigm - Example of asynchronous requests

the current request to another server for additional processing using the function *tpforward()* (Figure 26). This function behaves very much like tpcall() (i.e. it uses a service name and an input buffer, performs load balancing, data-dependent routing, etc.), but it internally informs TUXEDO about the fact that any replies will have to be sent to the initial requester and not to the process which is forwarding the request. After forwarding a request, the server is free to read and serve another request while the current one is taken over by the new server. When the new server terminates the execution, it can either forward the call to another server, or execute a tpreturn(), which will automatically reply to the originator of the request. The server which receives a forwarded request serves it as if it was a direct service request, i.e. the service doesn't have to use special code for executing a forwarded service. Also, there is no limit to forwarding so long as a server eventually returns a reply to the client within an acceptable timeframe, i.e. before timeouts expire for the client waiting for the reply.

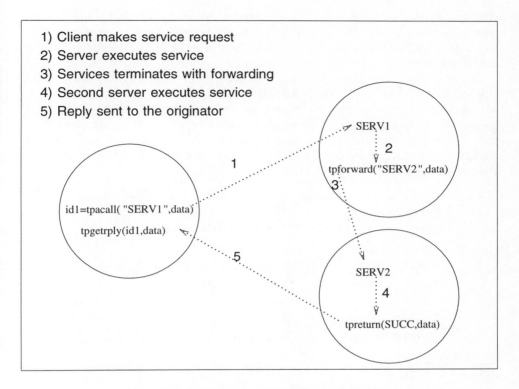

1) Client makes service request
2) Server executes service
3) Services terminates with forwarding
4) Second server executes service
5) Reply sent to the originator

Figure 26. RPC-like paradigm - Forwarding

4.1.1.2 *Implementation*

When a request is made, tpcall() or tpacall() consult the Bulletin Board to find out which server can best serve the request. After doing this, they compile the information in a message and send it to the server. If the server is not located on the same machine as the client, these functions send the message to the local BRIDGE process; this sends the message to the BRIDGE of the machine where the server resides; finally, the BRIDGE local to the server enqueues the message in the server's request queue.

Working in synchronous mode, tpcall() will then wait for the reply to arrive, and will not give control back to the application until either the reply comes or a timeout expires. tpacall() will, on the contrary, return immediately to the application.

When tpgetrply() is invoked, the function scans the reply queue and returns the reply corresponding to the given handle, if the reply is already in the queue. When a special flag is specified (TPGETANY), tpgetrply()

reads the first available reply and returns information about the handle corresponding to the call. tpgetreply() reads only one reply at a time (i.e. the read of all outstanding replies must be done through successive calls to this function).

On the server side, the information found in the request is compiled into a predefined structure (TPSVCINFO - figure 27) before executing the service. The function corresponding to the service receives the TPSVCINFO structure as an input parameter, and, through it, gains access to the data passed by the client. This include application data, the client's identity, and security information. On the basis of this information the service can then perform the set of operation it is meant to.

```
struct TPSVCINFO   {
        char      name[32]          ]─  Service name invoked
        char      *data             ]─  Request data
        long      len;              ]─  Request data length
        long      flags;            ]─  Service attributes
        int       cd;               ]─  Connection descriptor (conversations only)
        long      appkey;           ]─  Authentication key
        CLIENTID  cltid;            ]─  Id for unsolicited notification
};
```

Figure 27. The TPSVCINFO structure

When the service terminates, tpreturn() is passed a success/failure flag, a buffer containing the data to be sent to the client, and, optionally, a code to distinguish between different types of success or failure. This numeric code - rcode - is made available to the client by tpgetreply() through the setting of a global variable, tpurcode. If the client is on the same machine as the server, tpreturn() sends the reply directly to it. If not, it sends it to the local BRIDGE. As a last operation, tpreturn() returns to the server's main, which then goes and read another request.

If the service terminates with tpforward(), it must specify a new service name and all the necessary data. tpforward() manipulates the information in the message so that any reply will then be sent to the originator of the request. It also ensures that the a service doesn't forward a request to itself, in order to prevent infinite loops. If tpforward() fails, TUXEDO notifies the client about the failure so that it doesn't hang waiting for a reply which will never come.

4.1.2 Conversational paradigm

The conversational paradigm is identified by the fact that instead of simply requesting a service, the client connects to a service (with a server offering such service, in fact), and then exchanges with it a sequence of messages. The connection between clients and servers is logical, in the sense that TUXEDO maintains information about the identity of the two processes and about the machines on which they reside, but the processes do not need to know where their counterpart is located and how messages are actually transmitted. Also, the connection doesn't involve physical network connections if the two processes are on different machines. Until the connection is in place, the server is "dedicated" to the client and does not read requests from other clients. Thanks to this behaviour, a conversational server can maintain state information about the client across successive messages, unlike an RPC-like server which will not keep track of the client's identity and data across successive requests.

The possibility of clients and servers exchanging information is useful both for clients to drive the execution of the service via intermediate decisions, and for servers to communicate results in multiple steps. The reason why we decide to use this paradigm instead of the RPC-like is mainly application dependent, but in general, conversations give clients more control over the execution of the service. If necessary, conversations and RPC-like requests can be mixed in any order. This would be the case, for instance, when a client estabilishes a connection with a server, receives intermediate data, uses such data in an RPC-like service request, and then uses the reply from the RPC-like request to take the decision about the next step to perform with the connected server.

Conversations occur in a half-duplex fashion, in the sense that the two processes involved can at any one time either only receive or only send messages. An equivalent definition is *polarised* communication (as, for example, in OSI/TP terminology). The direction of the conversation can only be changed by the process in control of the connection, i.e. the one which is in send mode at that time. This is done by communicating to the receiver that it will now put itself in receive mode (the typical "pass" in the walky-talky). A change in direction can occur as many times as necessary. Disconnection can occur either in an orderly manner, when the connected server sends the last message ("over"), or in a disorderly manner, when either the client drops the connection, or the server terminates the service before completing the expected sequence of message exchange with the client.

4.1.2.1 Usage

A process wishing to estabilish a connection with a conversational server must use the function *tpconnect()*. Similar to tpacall(), this function receives as parameters the name of the service with which the client wants to communicate, a data buffer, and a set of flags for specifying the initial direction of the conversation and for determining the behaviour in case of blocking conditions. The process doesn't have to know where the service is located, and tpconnect() applies the same techniques as tpacall() (data-dependent routing, load balancing) for both selecting the appropriate server and for sending the initial message.

When tpconnect() returns, the connection has been established, and the process requesting the connection is provided with a connection descriptor. This will be used for all subsequent messages exchanged with the same server. Each process can have up to 10 conversations open simultaneously and therefore 10 different connection descriptors to deal with. A connected server can, in turn, have up to 10 different conversations with other servers, and/or request services in RPC-like fashion.

The process in control of the conversation can send messages using function *tpsend()*. This function sends a data buffer in correspondence to the conversation identified by a certain connection descriptor. If the sending process is the client, the connection descriptor is the one made available by tpconnect(). If the sending process is the server, the connection descriptor is the one made available in the TPSVCINFO structure, in field *cd*. Along with the message, tpsend() can specify that the direction of the conversation must change. This is done by communicating an *event*. Events are particular conditions of the conversation, and are set either explicitly by clients and servers for communicating situations like a change of direction or successful termination, or internally by TUXEDO for communicating the occurrence of disconnections.

At the other end of the connection, the process receives messages using function *tprecv()*. This is somewhat similar to tpgetrply(), with the difference that it reads a message in correspondence to a connection descriptor instead of a handle. tprecv() returns in a buffer the first available message in the process's queue, and, if an event has occurred, it sets a global variable (tperrno) to a special value. The type of event is compiled into one of its parameters.

Once the exchange of information has taken place through any number of calls to tpsend()/tprecv(), the connected server can terminate the conversation by sending a final message. This is done through the use of tpreturn(), like in the RPC-like case. The server should call tpreturn() when in control of the conversation; the connecting process should be in tprecv(). This constitutes an *orderly* disconnection procedure, in which tprecv() is

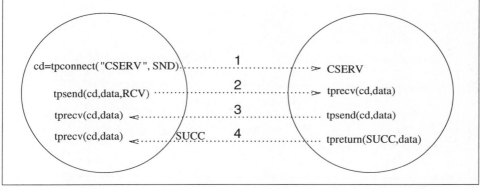

1) Client establishes connection and keeps control

2) Client sends another message and gives up control

3) Server sends message and keeps control

4) Server orderly disconnects by returning final message

Figure 28. Conversational paradigm - Orderly disconnection

passed a final message and an event describing the success or failure of the service (Figure 28). Unlike RPC-like servers, conversational servers cannot terminate their involvement in a conversation by forwarding it to another server, i.e., the use of tpforward() is forbidden for conversational servers. Once the connection is dropped in an orderly fashion, there is no need for the client to perform any other actions.

If the client wants to drop the connection before receiving the final message from the server, it can use function *tpdiscon()*. This will cause a *disorderly* disconnection because it will not give the server the possibility to successfully send the final message. The server will be informed of the disconnection at the next operation (tpsend(), tprecv(), or tpreturn()), through an event describing that a disconnection took place. The only thing the server will be able to do at that point is to tpreturn() without success (Figure 29).

Servers are not allowed to use tpdiscon(), but can still perform a disorderly disconnection by executing tpreturn() when not in control of the conversation. The client will be informed of the disconnection at the next operation (tpsend(), tprecv(), or tpdiscon()), through an event describing how the server disconnected (with success or failure), i.e. if the server called

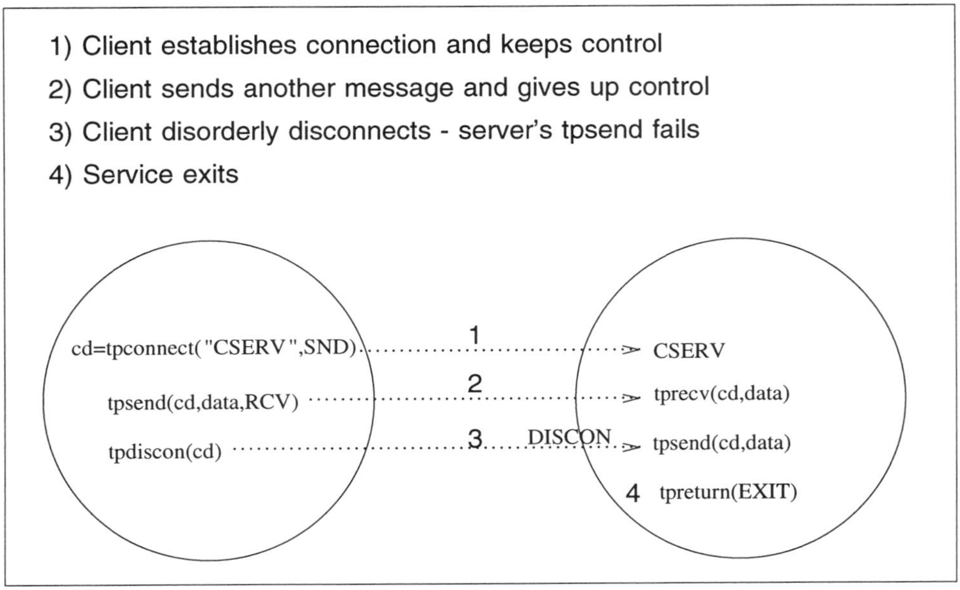

1) Client establishes connection and keeps control

2) Client sends another message and gives up control

3) Client disorderly disconnects - server's tpsend fails

4) Service exits

Figure 29. Conversational paradigm - Disorderly disconnection - Client

tpreturn() with TPSUCCESS or TPFAIL (Figure 30).

4.1.2.2 Implementation

Because conversational services tend to have an execution time longer than RPC-like ones (this is not always the case, but in general they are "reserved" to clients and therefore will be typically unavailable to other users until the client wishes so), it is important that new connection requests find free servers. To guarantee this, a conversational server reading a connection request when there are no other free servers will create a new free instance, up to a configurable maximum number.

In order to establish the connection, tpconnect() first verifies that the service is actually offered by conversational servers; this is because by default servers are assumed to be used in RPC-like fashion, and therefore conversational servers must be explicitly defined as such in the configuration. If the servers offering the service accept connection requests, tpconnect() consults the Bulletin Board to apply decision criteria like data-dependent routing, and, if the server is remote, it uses the BRIDGE to send messages.

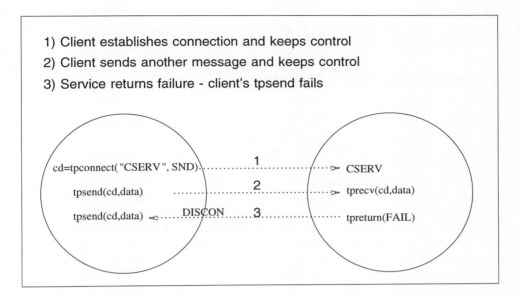

1) Client establishes connection and keeps control

2) Client sends another message and keeps control

3) Service returns failure - client's tpsend fails

Figure 30. Conversational paradigm - Disorderly disconnection - Server

Once a connection is established, TUXEDO keeps sufficient information about the connected processes so that it can look after all open connections and handle the cases when connections get interrupted by network or machine failures. In such cases, TUXEDO will clean up the relevant entries and will communicate the failure to the process at the active end of the connection.

tpsend() and tprecv() send and receive messages by reading information about the connection in the Bulletin Board. As far as the event handling is concerned, when an event occurs TUXEDO sets the tperrno variable to a special value (TPEEVENT), and makes the event available in parameter revent. This implementation is not the most intuitive, since tperrno is the generic error variable set by all ATMI functions and setting it in the case of conversational events (change of direction, disconnection, etc.) basically means that events are treated by TUXEDO as errors. This makes the error-handling procedures for conversational ATMI look overly complicated, as they must check for real errors as opposed to events.

If a connection terminates in an orderly fashion, TUXEDO discards all relevant information both at the server's and at the client's side. If a connection terminates in a disorderly fashion, TUXEDO finds out what happened in the Bulletin Board, silently discards late messages, and communicates a disconnection event to the process at the active and of the connection. It is probably worth mentioning here that whenever a disorderly disconnection occurs during a global transaction, the TUXEDO software makes sure that the transaction is aborted.

4.2 Communication buffers

As we have seen, clients and servers communicate with one another through the use of functions like tpacall(), tpconnect(), tpreturn(), etc. All these functions compile the necessary information in a message. For example, tpacall() compiles in a message the name of the requested service, the data, and the identity of the client, and then sends it to the destination process. This is done in a way transparent to the programming, in the sense that clients and servers do not have to worry about the format of the message and its actual transmission. TUXEDO performs the transmission through the use of the message sending facilities available with the system kernel (typically IPC and networking).

Although the data portion of the message might be null, in most cases clients and servers will have to transmit a certain amount of specific information along with the request. For example, in the case of a request for a service for opening a bank account, the client will have to communicate information such as the branch in which the account must be opened and the initial amount, while the server will have to return the number of the newly opened account.

All TUXEDO application processes provide data to the communication functions in *communication buffers*. These are private to each process and are allocated for the specific purpose of transmitting or receiving data. The allocation and handling of communication buffers is performed through the use of dedicated ATMI functions, which allow for allocation, reallocation and freeing of such buffers. As a result of the allocation of a buffer, an application process has an area in which to store the data it needs to transmit or receive. From an internal perspective, the allocation of these buffers does more than just allocate a certain data area, it actually creates an entire message buffer in which the communication functions can store additional information such as the sender's identity. The application code, however, only has access to the data portion of such messages.

TUXEDO's ATMI functions for buffers also provide for the definition of the type of data which will be stored in the buffer. By default, TUXEDO supports four different types of data in the communication buffers, and for this reason they are usually defined as "typed buffers", in the sense that each type is used to represent and manipulate different types of data in a different fashion. If necessary, TUXEDO can be customised with the addition of application-specific buffer types.

4.2.1 Buffer types

The use of communication buffers relates to the definition of information about the type of data to be handled, and to the use of the ATMI functions for allocating and handling such buffers.

The four default types of buffer that can be allocated by a TUXEDO process are:

- *String*: This type represents an array of characters that terminates with the NULL character (Figure 31).

- *Carray*: This type represents an undefined sequence of bytes of a specified length. This is the typical case of bitmaps where any character, including the NULL character, could be a valid sequence of bits (Figure 31).

STRING:

   "Any sequence of characters terminated by \0"

CARRAY:

   "Any sequence of, say, 30 bytes"

Figure 31. Buffer types: string and carray

- *View*: This type represents data structures that the application may want to transmit in their entirety, typically C structures or COBOL records. Because there will usually be many different structures or records to be used for communication, this type of buffer requires the definition of subtypes, where the subtype is actually the name of the particular C structure or COBOL record.

  All structures used for communication must be described in the so-called "view description files", according to a TUXEDO-defined syntax. From the description files, proper include files or copy files can be generated through the use of dedicated tools (viewc(1) or CBLVIEWC(1)). These tools, for example viewc in Figure 32, also create binary representations of the structures, used at runtime by the communication functions for the implementation of data-dependent routing.

- *FML* (field manipulation language): this is a TUXEDO-defined type of buffers, in which each buffer is made up of a certain number of fields, in a variable order. Each field carries its own identifier, an occurrence

71

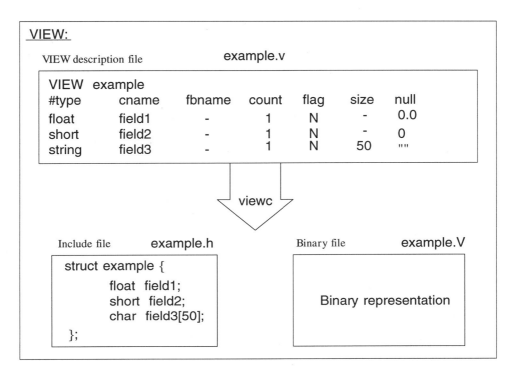

Figure 32. Buffer types: views

number, and, if necessary, a length indicator. Through the use of these fields, the structure of the buffer can be created at runtime, thus allowing a greater degree of flexibility for both the content of the buffer and the type of data.

The use of FML buffers requires that all the possible fields are listed in files called *field tables*, and that each field is assigned a *field-id*. Through the use of command mkfldhdr(1), include files are created. These describe the correspondence between field names and field-ids (Figure 33). The created files are used by the application, whilst the field tables are used at runtime by the communication functions for the implementation of data-dependent routing.

Once the fields are defined, the application can decide at runtime which fields must be inserted in each FML buffer and, of course, which values the fields have at that time. It is possible to insert in the same buffer more than one occurrence of the same field, in any order. The fields can be of seven different types (char, short, long, double, float,

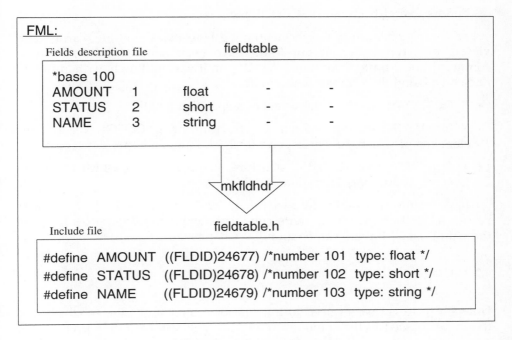

Figure 33. Buffer types: FML

string, and carray). To enter, modify, or extract fields in an FML buffer, TUXEDO provides a set of manipulation functions belonging to a subsystem called field manipulation language. This subsystem provides a TUXEDO-specific data entry system, mainly used in conjunction with System/D. Since this subsystem is only available on UNIX platforms, and more appealing front-end systems can be found on the market, TUXEDO's data entry system will not be described in this book.

If the application needs to use views and FMLs together, it is possible to assign, in each view description file, a correspondence between the elements of the view structure and FML fields. When this correspondence is available, it is possible to use FML functions to move the content of an FML buffer into a view buffer and viceversa, thus allowing greater flexibility in buffer handling.

A limitation for FML buffers is that these cannot be used in COBOL, since the syntax does not allow for the use of pointers to data areas, which are necessary for changing the structure of the buffer at runtime. Applications which have COBOL clients or servers can still communicate with C clients or servers which use FML buffers by converting their buffers to and from views (COBOL records).

For completeness, it is worth mentioning here that the string, carray, and view buffer types (i.e. all but FML) have been adopted by X/Open as communication buffers for the XATMI primitives, although with different names and slightly different definitions:

- *X_OCTET*: An array of characters of a specified length.

- *X_COMMON*: A non nested C structure or a COBOL record, the elements of which can correspond to short, long, and char data types.

- *X_C_TYPE*: A non nested C structure, the elements of which can be of type int, short, long, char, float, double.

These buffer types can be used along with, or instead of, TUXEDO's native ATMI buffers. Some more comments about the differences between these and native buffers can be found in Chapter 5.

4.2.2 Usage

Unless a process doesn't need to transmit or receive any data, in which case the buffer passed to the communication functions can be null, a process will have first to allocate buffers. This is done through the use of the function *tpalloc()*. This function is given the type of the buffer to be allocated, the length, and, in the case of views, the name of the view to be allocated (the buffer's *subtype*). It returns a pointer to the data area of the allocated message.

A buffer can be reused for successive messages so long as the data stays within the initial length and is of the same type as the one specified when the buffer was allocated. If necessary, buffers can be enlarged using the function *tprealloc()*, or, alternatively, released using the function *tpfree()* and allocated again using tpalloc(). Each process can allocate as many buffers as necessary, but it must be noted that incremental allocations without corresponding freeing could lead to memory problems. This could become a serious problem for a client, but even more so for a server, given its looping nature.

The buffer passed to tpgetrply() or tprecv() must also have been allocated prior its use with these functions. However, if the size is not sufficient to contain the received data, TUXEDO reallocates it automatically and returns information about the new size to the application. The buffer passed to tpreturn() or tpforward() can either be the one received from the client (in which case it doesn't need to be allocated), or any other buffer the service allocated (in which case TUXEDO will free it automatically after sending the

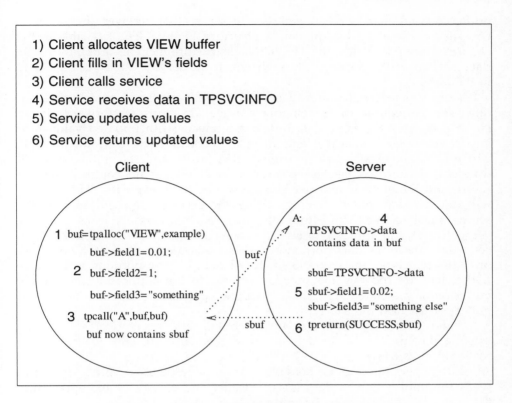

1) Client allocates VIEW buffer
2) Client fills in VIEW's fields
3) Client calls service
4) Service receives data in TPSVCINFO
5) Service updates values
6) Service returns updated values

Client   Server

1 buf=tpalloc("VIEW",example)   A: 4
                                     TPSVCINFO->data
   buf->field1=0.01;   buf   contains data in buf
2   buf->field2=1;   sbuf=TPSVCINFO->data
   buf->field3="something"   5 sbuf->field1=0.02;
                                   sbuf->field3="something else"
3   tpcall("A",buf,buf)   tpreturn(SUCCESS,sbuf)
   buf now contains sbuf   sbuf   6

Figure 34. Use of ATMI and buffers: example

message). For applications which use different types of buffers, the function *tptypes()* can be used to identify which type of buffers are being handled.

An example of usage of buffers is presented in Figure 34. The client allocates a VIEW buffer (1), the one presented in Figure 32, then fills in its fields (2). The client then makes a service call, specifying that the same buffer must be used for the returned data (3). The service receives the buffer in the data field of structure TPSVCINFO (4), modifies its contents (5), then returns the modified data to the client (6).

4.2.3 Implementation

When tpalloc() is called, a sufficient area is allocated in memory to contain the data and a set of control structures. These control structures store information about the message itself and about the type of buffer. If the buffer is used in a service request, the server that receives the message compiles the received information in structure TPSVCINFO, available to the service. Among its fields, the TPSVCINFO structure includes a pointer to the data portion of the message, through which the service can access the data in the message.

Besides the received buffer, a service can allocate additional buffers for other service requests or for temporary usage. On return (or forward), it can either pass back the same data buffer it received (with updated values), or any other buffer it allocated and filled in. TUXEDO will transmit the data and will automatically free the transmitted buffer and the input buffer (if different). It does so because the service will not regain control after the return and therefore would not be able to free them explicitly. However, it will not free any other auxiliary buffer the service allocated, so it is the service's task to free them before returning, to avoid memory leaks.

tpgetrply() and tprecv() receive the message in an internal buffer, then copy the data in the data portion of the user-allocated buffer. If the data are of a different type, the operation will fail with a corresponding error code. If the data are too big, the function returns to the application its internal buffer (which is big enough) and reuses the application buffer as its internal buffer for the next message.

tprealloc() increases the size of the buffer but won't decrease it. The existing data in the buffer are left untouched and are still available after reallocation. tpfree() simply releases the memory reserved for the message. After this operation it is not possible to restore the released buffer. tptypes() reads the information in the message header and returns to the application the type and, if applicable, the subtype.

4.3 Load balancing

A fairly typical scenario in distributed environments, especially in OLTP environments, is given by a large number of users who more or less simultaneously execute operations on one of the machines in the network. Users might be local to or remote from the machine where the operation is executed, and the operation itself might be split into different suboperations, possibly executed on other machines.

The user who requests the operation is not aware of how expensive this is in terms of resource occupation, network traffic, etc., nor is he/she interested in how many other users are requesting the same or similar operations at the same time. The user is simply interested in having the operation performed as quickly as possible, regardless of where it is executed or how. On the other hand, however, many users acting simultaneously generate a heavy workload on several systems components.

If the available resources are not efficiently used, this will typically result in significant degradation of performance, especially from the user's perspective.

When operations can be performed on more than one machine, or by more than one process on the same machine, it is desirable that the workload generated by all user's requests is evenly spread across all the possible processes, so that the usage of resources is optimised and the case where one process is overloaded while an equivalent one is idle is minimised. This contributes to the effectiveness of the system and helps improve the overall performance of the application. Unfortunately, in environments that integrate many different components within the same operation, the definition itself of workload is not consistent, let alone the balancing of it. The operating system, the database, the network, etc., all suffer from heavy workload, but for none of them is there an easy way to identify the type of workload and and balance it with one another.

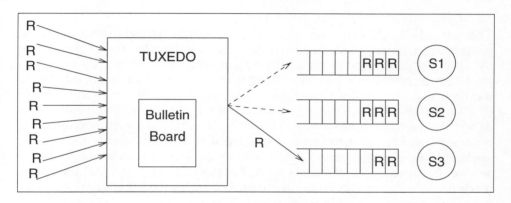

Figure 35. Load balancing

The use of TUXEDO's load balancing can prove an effective and direct solution to this problem. In a TUXEDO environment, a user request corresponds to a service request, whilst the process that performs the operations corresponds to the application server. TUXEDO has control over such entities, and by maintaining sufficient information, it can balance service requests among all the application servers that can execute them (Figure 35).

If requests are balanced among all servers, then the individual operations against the resources are also balanced. For example, a DBMS does not know how many SQL operations are being requested of one database server as opposed to another, and therefore it cannot balance that type of workload. However, if the service requests are balanced, then the SQL operations executed by the services are also balanced among different database servers, making their usage more efficient. Also, the balancing of service requests helps with the balancing, if not the minimisation, of the network traffic.

TUXEDO performs load balancing on the basis of a load factor assigned to each service. This factor is a numeric value usually specified at configuration time by the application administrator. It corresponds to an estimate of the service execution time with respect to the execution time of the other services. Depending on whether TUXEDO (System/T) is located on one or more machines, the system performs different load balancing algorithms, real-time, or round robin. Both algorithms have the purpose to send incoming requests to the least-loaded servers.

4.3.1 Usage

The use of TUXEDO's load balancing is usually straightforward, as no programming is required. Load balancing is activated by the administrator by setting a parameter in the configuration, and, if necessary, by assigning load factors to the services. The assignment of load factors is not strictly required because TUXEDO assigns by default a load factor to all services (the same for all). However, because different services will typically have different execution times, better efficiency is achieved by providing more differentiated values. It must also be noted that different values are not just applicable to different services, but also to different instances of the same service. If, for example, the same service is available on a fast and on a slow machine, its relative execution time with respect to the other services might vary significantly depending on where it is executed. By setting different load factors for the different instances of such service, a more effective behaviour can be obtained.

To set effective load factors, it is necessary to have an estimate of each service's execution time. One way of doing this is to call a timing function at the beginning and end of the service and printing the difference. This requires, however, the addition of code for this specific purpose. To avoid this, it is possible to configure the application servers in such a way that they keep statistics about the execution time of each service. Through the use of a tool provided by the TUXEDO environment (txrpt(1)), it is then possible to print a table of the average execution time of each service over a certain period of time (for example, during the period of beta testing). By selecting a reference service and assigning it a load factor of, say, 100, all other services can be assigned load factors depending on how much faster or slower they executed. This value can then be specified in the configuration file, or, if the application is already deployed in a production environment, it can be assigned at runtime through the use of the administrative tools. In the latter case, runtime and dynamic tuning can be performed in order to find the most effective factors.

When services are executed on multiple machines, a load-balancing algorithm purely related to the service's execution time might not always be sufficiently effective, because it would not take into account the time needed for sending the request to another machine. If the network time is not negligible with respect to the service's execution time (for instance, in the case of slow lines), the administrator can define a global network load factor, which is added automatically to the service's load if the service is on a remote machine. This guarantees that a local server is always more likely to be chosen, unless it is loaded much more than a remote server.

4.3.2 Implementation

Load balancing is implemented via two different algorithms, depending on whether there is just one System/T machine involved or more than one. In the first case, a real-time algorithm is performed, whilst in the second case, a weighted round-robin technique is used. Both algorithms are based on workload information kept in the Bulletin Board for all request queues.

4.3.2.1 *Real-time load balancing*

This technique is used when only one System/T machine is involved, i.e. when only one Bulletin Board is available for the entire application (this is called SHM mode in TUXEDO terms). The real-time algorithm is based on exact statistics kept for each queue in the Bulletin Board. When a request is sent to a server, the load in its queue is increased by the load factor corresponding to the requested service. When the server reads the request, the load in its queue is decremented by the load factor corresponding to the request dequeued. This means that at any moment the workload in all servers' queues reflect the actual workload on each server.

Based on the workload in the queue, requests are sent to the queue which is least loaded at that time. If two servers have the same workload, the request will be sent to either one, for instance the first found.

An example of real-time load balancing is presented in Figure 36. Three servers (S1, S2, and S3), running on the same machine, offer three services with different load factors (A, B, and C). The Bulletin Board stores information about the work enqueued in the server queues, and all queues start with zero load when the requests start arriving at time T0 (in fact, an

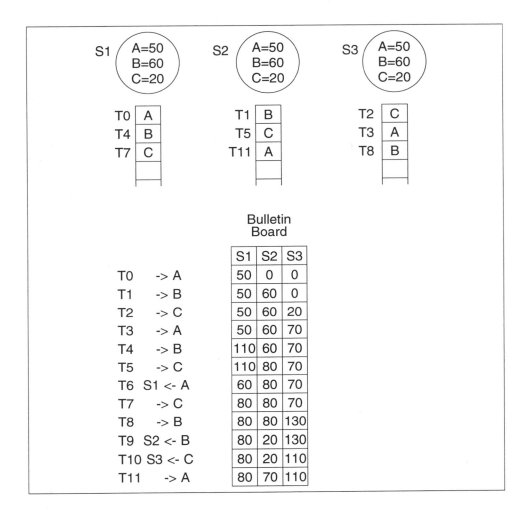

Figure 36. Real-time load balancing

initial workload equal to zero can always be assumed; when a new server is started, all other workload values are zeroed so that the algorithm can start with a clean situation).

The example shows how requests are distributed among the servers, and how the least-loaded queue is selected for the next request. At time T0, a request for service A arrives; this is sent to the queue of server S1 as all queues are empty and the one associated to S1 is the first found. In the Bulletin Board, the load factor of service A (50) is stored in correspondence of the queue of server S1. At time T1, a request for service B arrives; this time it is sent to server S2 because it is the first among those with the least load. Again, the load factor (60) is added to the corresponding entry in the Bulletin Board. Because S1 hasn't read the request yet, the value in its entry in the Bulletin Board is still 50. The same applies for all subsequent requests until time T6.

At time T6, when server S1 reads the request (the example assumes that servers won't start reading requests immediately, perhaps because they were already executing a request at time T0), the load in its queue is decremented. Because of this, the next request (for service C at time T7) is sent to S1 since it is the one with less work enqueued. The request at time T8 is sent to server S3, and, finally, after S2 and S3 read from their queue, the last request at time T11 is sent to server S2. Every time, the server with least load in its queue is chosen.

At the end of the interval of time considered (T0 to T11), this example would also appear to demonstrate that all servers have received the same amount of work. Although true, this is totally incidental. Had the requests been spaced over a longer interval, thus giving more time to the servers to complete their services, the first server would have probably received more. This behaviour is correct. The goal of this algorithm is to select the best server at a certain time, not the one with the best history.

4.3.2.2 *Round-robin load balancing*

This technique is implemented when there are multiple System/T machines in the configuration, i.e. multiple Bulletin Boards replicated on the different machines (this is called MP mode in TUXEDO terms). In such a case, the real-time algorithm where the workload in each queue is dynamically incremented and decremented would be impractical, since the workload statistics would have to be propagated at all times to all Bulletin Boards, which would probably take more time than actually executing the requests.

The round-robin algorithm is based on the statistics that each machine can maintain individually, i.e. the workload generated by the requests originating from it. Whenever a request originates from the machine, either from a native client, or a /WS client (via the workstation handler), or a server acting like a client, the load corresponding to the requested service is recorded in the local Bulletin Board in correspondence of the queue, local, or remote, to which the request was sent. This value is never decremented and therefore it represents the history of that queue as far as the machine is concerned. A successive request for the same service will then be sent to the queue which has got the best history, i.e. for which this machine has generated fewest requests.

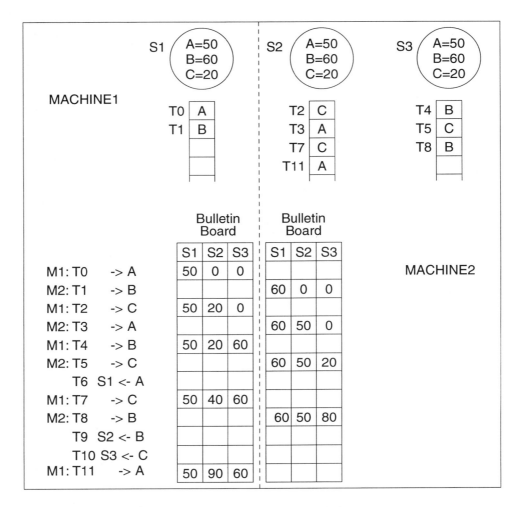

Figure 37. Round-robin load balancing

By using the local history of each queue, every machine performs a (weighted) round-robin load balancing, and because all other machines use the same technique, a global round robin is obtained for the whole application. This does not guarantee that at a certain time the best choice is made, but that over an interval of time all servers, regardless of where they reside, will have received (more or less) the same amount of work. Practical experience suggests that this type of load balancing is quite effective, and from an efficiency point of view, it is a reasonable compromise between the optimal algorithm and what is possible to implement over a network of different machines which cannot share the same information.

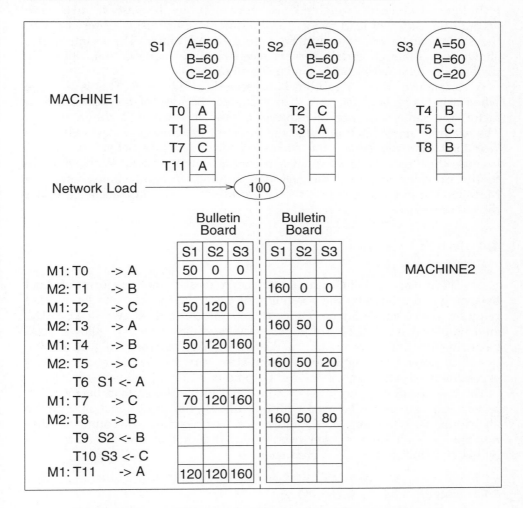

Figure 38. Round-robin load balancing with network load

An example of round-robin load balancing is presented in Figure 37. The same three servers as in the real-time example are now located on two machines. There are two copies of the Bulletin Board and requests come from both machines. In this example, requests come in the same order as the previous example, but from both machines alternately. The example shows how each machine keeps a private history of the load generated, and how requests from each machine are sent using a weighted round-robin technique. The term "weighted" is more accurate because it takes into account the different load factors for the different services; if all services had the same load factor, it would be a pure round robin. The example also shows that although certain servers received more requests than others, in the end the total workload is similar for all of them.

A variation of these algorithm is presented in Figure 38. This is the case when a network load factor is also provided. Because of the network load factor, the same sequence of requests is now handled in a different way. The example shows that although the server on Machine 1 has actually more workload than the others, the clients on Machine 1 are better off with it, because their requests do not have to cross a slow network. With reference to the previous example, the last two requests from Machine 1 stay on Machine 1 instead of crossing the network, which is a better choice under the circumstances.

4.4 MSSQ

In addition to the balancing of service requests, another form of load balancing is provided by the possibility of having more than one server read requests from a single queue (Figure 39). This technique, known in TUXEDO environments as MSSQ (multiple servers single queue), allows load balancing on the same queue, in the sense that the workload put on the queue is spread among a set of equivalent servers. While one server is executing a service, another one can become free to read the next request.

The use of MSSQ is not directly connected to the use of load balancing of service requests (it can be used with or without), but in conjunction with the algorithms seen before, MSSQ allows for best service turnaround because not only are all queues used evenly, but requests in the queues have a higher probability of being served soon.

4.4.1 Usage

As with load balancing, the usage of MSSQ is usually straightforward, as no additional programming is required. The way to set it for a certain group of servers is to assign, in the configuration file, a logical name to one server's queue, then repeat the same name for the the other servers. This will make all servers with the same queue name read from the same queue. It is advisable, though, to define private reply queues for each server, so as to avoid the case where one server picks up a reply directed to another server.

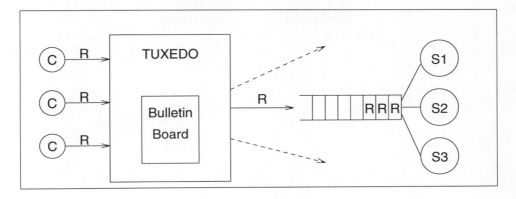

Figure 39. Multiple servers single queue

If this is the case, the server puts the message back in the queue, but this is inefficient and does not guarantee that the server waiting for the reply will ever get it in a reasonable timeframe.

Any number of servers may read from the same queue, but the optimal number is in general determined by two factors: the ability of the application to keep the queue sufficiently full, so that when a server is free it will immediately find a new request to serve, but also the ability to not fill it up completely, since this would cause other inefficiencies such as timeouts when trying to enqueue requests.

4.4.2 Implementation

The implementation of MSSQ sets is simply constituted by the fact that all the servers in the MSSQ attach to the same queue when they start up, and therefore share the same queue entry in the Bulletin Board. The only constraint is that all servers must actually be the same executable program, and must offer the same services. This implies that when a service is advertised/unadvertised by one server in a MSSQ, all the others will do the same in order to avoid inconsistencies. This is taken care of by TUXEDO and by the relevant ATMI functions (see dynamic advertisement in Chapter 6).

When MSSQ is used in conjunction with load balancing of service requests, the workload associated to the queue is divided by the number of servers, and the resulting value is used in the algorithms. An example is presented in Figure 40. Although there is a higher workload in the queue associated to the MSSQ (220), the next request will still be sent to it because

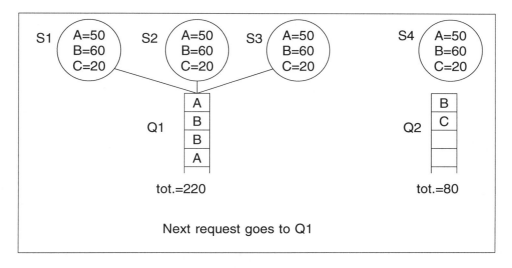

Figure 40. Load balancing plus MSSQ

the workload for each server (220/3) is less than the one for the other queue (80).

4.5 Prioritisation

While load balancing is an important factor in distributed applications for making effective use of all available resources and as a result achieving better performance, it does not specify in what order operations should be executed once they have been evenly spread across all possible processes. Operations from the same user will typically have to be executed in a predefined sequence, but this is not the case between unrelated operations from unrelated users.

A fair and acceptable procedure is to have operations performed in sequence according to the order in which they have been requested by the users. However, this is effective only when all types of operations have the same importance from business perspective. In reality this is not always the case, and when the business has different types of priorities, load balancing alone might not be sufficient to make important operations be carried out within the required timeframes. A typical example is that of banking services. If a number of users request a balance of account and one executes a deposit, it makes business sense to have the inquiries executed at a lower priority than the deposit, regardless of whether these operations were requested slightly before it.

To take care of these situations, all services in a TUXEDO application are assigned a priority level. This is basically a numeric value which describes the priority of execution of a certain service with respect to the others. In the previous example, the deposit operation could have a priority level of 50, whilst the inquiry could have a level of 30.

By default, all services are assigned the same priority, but this can be changed in the configuration of each service, and also at runtime for each individual service request. When a client makes a request, the priority associated to the service is sent along with the message. When servers read requests, they dequeue them in priority order, thus guaranteeing that those requests which have higher priority are executed first. An example of this is presented in Figure 41.

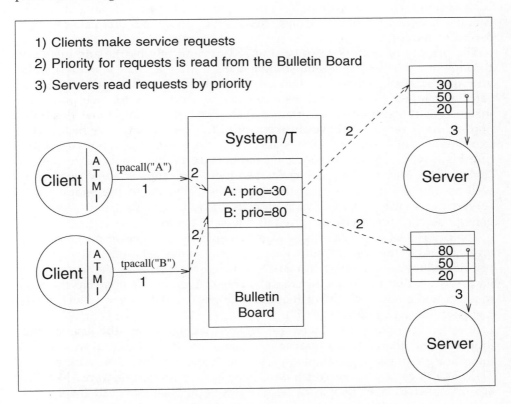

Figure 41. Prioritisation of service requests

If the use of load balancing makes it possible to reduce the average queue time for requests, the use of prioritisation makes sure that more important requests have an even shorter queue time. This helps with the actual user's perception of faster execution and allows for a more flexible business modelling within the application.

4.5.1 Usage

The use of TUXEDO's prioritisation is usually straightforward, since in most cases no programming is required. Programming priorities is typically only used when the application needs a particularly flexible definition of priorities.

In the configuration file, a special parameter (PRIO) can be defined for each service. This has a default value of 50, but it can be changed to any number between 1 and 100. Unless dynamically modified, this value is used for every request made for the service.

The priority of a service can be changed dynamically by the administrator through the use of the administrative tools. After a change made by the administrator, all requests for that service will use the new value. The value can be changed either for all instances of the service, or for one particular instance of the service in a certain server. This allows additional flexibility and allows a service to have different priorities depending on which server executes it. Let's assume, for instance, that there are two types of servers offering, say, a service for enquiring the balance of an account. One type of server offers only enquiry services whilst the other offers enquiry services as well as others (e.g. deposit). If the request is delivered to the enquiry-only server, the service is served at normal priority; if it is routed to the more general server, the service is served at a lower priority.

The priority of a service can be also dynamically changed at programming level through the use of function *tpsprio()*, which sets the value of the priority of the next request to a specific value regardless of the service and its priority value in the configuration. This change applies only to the next request, while any subsequent requests will use the configured value, unless tpsprio() is used again (Figure 42).

It must be noted that there are no restrictions about the use of this function, and therefore an application client can abuse this feature and set the priority of its requests always to the highest value. The reason why TUXEDO doesn't impose constraints here is very simple; features like this are provided to help people develop effective applications, but there is no general rule applicable to decide what is or is not a sensible usage. If the environment is such that people use features in a way not sensible, there is very little that the system could do anyway. On the contrary, restricting its use would impose constraints on a higher number of environments in which

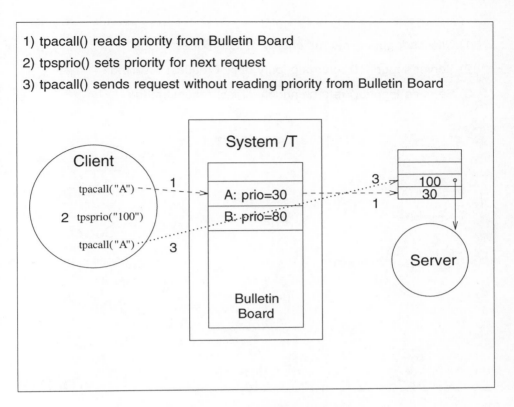

1) tpacall() reads priority from Bulletin Board

2) tpsprio() sets priority for next request

3) tpacall() sends request without reading priority from Bulletin Board

Figure 42. tpsprio() - example

such problems do not exist.

A reason why one might want to increase the priority of a request could be to provide a better service in certain rare circumstances. If, for example, the service for the balance of account is being requested by the managing director of the bank, we might want to give him/her a better treatment. Another reason could be to allow a better tuning of the service requests. In the case of a money transfer, for example, implemented as one call to withdrawal and one to deposit, the priority for these two service requests might be set higher so that they are served before other individual requests for deposit or withdrawal. In this way, the requester of the transfer is not penalised by having to wait once for the transfer request and then for the other two subrequests.

For an application client to obtain the priority value of the last request, function *tpgprio()* can be used. The same function can be used in the service

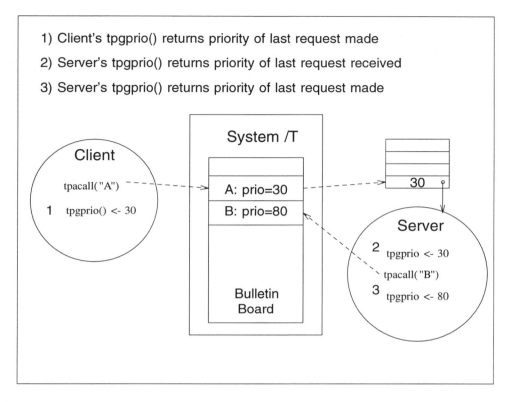

1) Client's tpgprio() returns priority of last request made

2) Server's tpgprio() returns priority of last request received

3) Server's tpgprio() returns priority of last request made

Figure 43. tpgprio() - example

code to obtain either the priority with which the service was called, or, if the service makes a service request, the priority of the request made (Figure 43).

4.5.2 Implementation

The priority value for each service is stored in the Bulletin Board along with the service's information. When tpacall() looks into the Bulletin Board and decides to what server the request must go, it reads the priority value associated to the chosen service, and sends it along with the message.

Servers normally dequeue requests by priority. To prevent starvation of very low priority requests, one request out of ten is dequeued in FIFO order. This is a very simple implementation, and of course it is possible to create fictitious cases where this algorithm does not work so effectively.

However, this behaviour is in general efficient because it's not expensive in terms of processing, and constitutes a good compromise between efficiency and effectiveness.

When the administrator changes the priority value for a service, the new value is stored in the Bulletin Board, so that the new value applies from that moment. When the client changes the priority with tpsprio(), it sets a flag indicating that the next request must not read the value from the Bulletin Board, but use the value set by the function, stored in a global variable. When tpacall() or tpcall() send the request, they check for the flag; if set, they take the value of the global variable, then reset the flag so that the next request will read again from the Bulletin Board unless tpsprio() is used again.

4.6 Data-dependent routing

One of the benefits of distributed environments is that the handling of operations can be split among different machines. For example, print requests can be directed to different printers, perhaps to the one which is least loaded at any one time. In many cases, however, while the operations are logically the same, the data handled by these operations are different. In a banking environment, for instance, a deposit is always the same type of operation, but each individual deposit will have to be executed on the machine where the specific account is held.

For distributed applications, understanding where an individual operation must be performed can be an expensive problem, because specific information must be stored in the programs. This often involves knowing in advance about the possible processes, machines and even the name of the executable program or the machine's network address. In a network of heterogeneous machines, PCs, etc., this can prove a nightmare, not just for the setup, but also for the administration and maintenance. If one machine is replaced, if a new program is added, the application has to be modified accordingly, potentially causing a lot of disruption. In environments where high availability is critical, this becomes unacceptable.

In a TUXEDO application, some help is given by a feature called data-dependent routing. This is actually quite a powerful capability which can make the life of many developers of distributed applications a lot easier. The idea is quite simple; when a service request is made, TUXEDO looks into the data buffer and, according to configurable criteria, routes the request to the group of servers which is associated to a certain value of a certain field in the buffer. In the case of a bank application, for example, assuming that each branch keeps local data about accounts, a request to open an account could be routed according to the value of the branch-id specified in the request. In such a case, TUXEDO will read the current value of the field and will match it against a set of possible values specified in the configuration file. It will then send the request to the group of servers associated with the matching value, on the appropriate machine in the right branch.

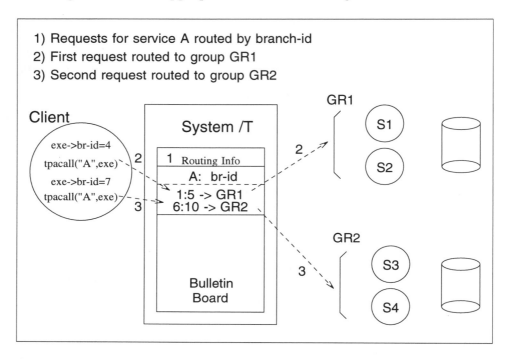

Figure 44. Example of data-dependent routing

An example of this capability is presented in Figure 44. The client assigns a value to the branch-id field of a buffer, say a VIEW buffer, then makes a service request. tpacall() finds in the Bulletin Board that when making a request to service "A", a routing by branch-id must be performed. In the routing table, it finds that for values of the field between 1 and 5 the request must be sent to group GR1. The same request with a value of 7 for the same field would on the contrary make tpacall() send the request to group GR2.

Because of this technique, the application will simply request the general operation (open account) and fill in the current value for the branch-id, while TUXEDO will take care of the routing. This is useful, not just because the application doesn't have to take care of it explicitly, thus making development and maintenance easier, but also because changes that occur in the configuration do not affect the application. If a machine is replaced,

TUXEDO will take care of routing requests, regardless of the new machine's name and network address. If a new server or a new machine is added, TUXEDO will take care to include these new entities in the routing. Even if the data on one machine are then split to two machines, TUXEDO can take care of these changes. Changes occur only in TUXEDO's configuration, not in the application's code.

In addition, because routing applies to groups of servers and not to machines, high availability requirements can also be addressed. If, due to the failure of one machine, the application servers on that machine have to be migrated to another one, TUXEDO can keep on routing requests to those servers, even if the machine is no longer the same. This occurs at runtime, without the application having to be stopped, restarted, or modified.

4.6.1 Usage

Like load balancing and prioritisation, the use of data-dependent routing does not require programming. It only requires a definition of the routing criteria in the configuration file. All routing criteria for the application are described in a dedicated section of the configuration file, where routing criteria are defined by service (i.e. each time a service is requested, the associated criterion applies).

```
*ROUTING
br-id         FIELD=br_id
              BUFTYPE="VIEW:exe"
              RANGES="1-5:GR1,
                  6-10:GR2,
                  *:*"
```

Figure 45. Example of a routing criterion

Although more information about this is presented in Chapter 6, an example of a routing criterion is presented in Figure 45. Each criterion is described in the form of values or ranges of values associated to a group of servers. The values or ranges are matched against the value of a single field. A current limitation is that no logic expressions are allowed.

4.6.2 Implementation

The routing criteria are static (defined at configuration time) and stored in each Bulletin Board. When tpacall() (or tpconnect()) looks into the Bulletin Board, it reads in the data buffer the field corresponding to the one specified in the criterion, and matches its value against the specified values. The request is then sent to the first available server in the matching group, or, if load balancing is turned on, to the least-loaded server in that group. The behaviour of data-dependent routing in conjunction with load balancing is presented in Figure 46. Data-dependent routing is first applied, then load balancing.

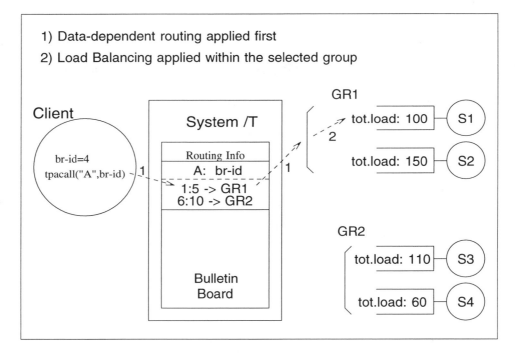

Figure 46. Data-dependent routing and load balancing

In order to find the right field in the buffer, i.e. its offset within the buffer, tpacall()/tpconnect() use either the view description file in case of VIEW buffers, or the field-id in case of FML buffers. To do this, these functions access the directories where the description files are (VIEWDIR or FIELDTBLDIR) and read the necessary files (VIEWFILES or FIELDTBL).

4.7 Unsolicited messages

Complex applications, like OLTP applications, usually need to implement methods for communicating and handling the occurrence of asynchronous or unexpected events, in order to allow a higher degree of reliability. This is often achieved by integrating specific operating system capabilities within the application (for example, the electronic mailing system). Such an approach, however, brings in a number of inevitable complications in terms of programming, flexibility, and compatibility, especially when the application spans different operating systems.

Within a TUXEDO application, unsolicited notification represents a method for communicating asynchronous information outside the usual resquest/response protocol. This asyncronous information can be directed to all users, for example a broadcast message that the system will undergo maintenance work in 15 minutes for 1 hour, or to an individual user, for example a warning that the requested service can no longer be executed without an authorisation code.

Unsolicited (out-of-band) messages can be sent both by the administrator through the use of the administrative tools, or by application clients and servers through the use of dedicated ATMI primitives. The recipients of such messages are the application clients, which handle them by choosing a message handling method (ignore or accept), and setting a customisable message handling function.

TUXEDO's implementation of unsolicited notification provides an application with the possibility to model within its own programming boundaries both the logic with which asynchronous or unexpected events must be communicated, and the logic with which they must be dealt with. This results in increased flexibility and portability for the application, as it allows for a uniform implementation across different machines and operating systems.

4.7.1 Usage

The use of unsolicited messages in a TUXEDO environment relates to three different areas: the choice of the handling method, the use of the message handler, and the use of the ATMI functions for sending and receiving such messages.

4.7.1.1 The handling method

Each application client selects the desired handling method by setting relevant flags in the *TPINIT* buffer when the client first registers with TUXEDO. The possible methods are:

- Ignore all unsolicited messages

- Receive unsolicited messages via ATMI functions

- Receive unsolicited messages via signals.

If the client chooses to ignore unsolicited messages, all such messages sent to the client will be silently discarded by the TUXEDO software.

If the client chooses the ATMI method for accepting unsolicited messages, all ATMI functions invoked by the client will check for the existence of unsolicited messages before executing their actual task. For example, function tpgetrply() will first check for unsolicited messages in the client's queue, pass them to the message handling function, then read an actual reply message. The checking for unsolicited messages is performed by all ATMI functions through a call to the function *tpchkunsol()* which is an ATMI function itself. This also makes it possible for the client's code to check for unsolicited messages at any time, without having to wait until another ATMI function is used. If unsolicited messages exist in the queue, tpchkunsol() will pass all of them one by one to the message handler.

If the client chooses the signal method, then the client will be sent a signal whenever an unsolicited message is sent to its queue. A TUXEDO-provided signal handler, linked to the client, will then pass the message to the message handler. Unlike the ATMI method, which is available to all clients (System/T and System/WS), this method is limited to native System/T clients which have the same ID as the owner of the application (usually the administrator). Although this might appear a strong limitation, signalling can be effectively used for those applications in which the clients are started automatically when the terminals are switched on (i.e. users don't go through the login program), as they can all be assigned the same user ID. This method makes the clients receive an unsolicited message as soon as it gets into the queue, whereas the ATMI method makes the client receive it when the next ATMI function is called.

4.7.1.2 *The message handler*

Unsolicited messages are passed to the handler for processing. This requires each client to set a message handling function, which provides the handling logic appropriate for the application. The setting of the message handler is done through the use of the function *tpsetunsol()* and is typically done soon after joining the application (i.e. soon after the client has called the function tpinit()).

The message-handling function is client-specific, and is in fact a subroutine of the client itself. This allows, for instance, direct communication of events with the client's main program through the use of global variables. If this function is not provided, a NULL function is provided by TUXEDO.

A simple handler could just dump the message in a file, but more complicated situations can be handled. For example, the administrator could broadcast the message that the system is going down in 5 minutes. The handler could display a pop-up mask with the message and set a global variable, say "mustexit". If the client's main program checks the variable "mustexit", for instance after every ATMI calls, then it can perform a termination routine to close up everything automatically and cleanly when shutdown is imminent.

Because it is a portion of the client's code, the message handler is linked with the ATMI libraries, and therefore it can use ATMI functions. However, not all ATMI functions can be used within a message handler. Typically, only the functions for handling messages (tpalloc(), tprealloc(), tpfree(), tptypes()) can be used.

4.7.1.3 *Sending unsolicited messages*

Clients and servers can send unsolicited messages through the use of function *tpbroadcast()* (Figure 47). Messages can be sent to all clients in the application, but it is also possible to restrict the scope of the function by specifying a user name, a client name, a machine name, or any combination of the three. Messages can be of any type (string, FML, etc.). If this function returns a failure, the message will have been sent to no one. If it succeeds, there is still the possibility that certain processes will not receive the message, for example because of network or machine failures. Unlike the case of the communication paradigms described in Section 4.1, the sender is not notified of this failure. Note though, that unsolicited messages are not meant to be a fully reliable communication paradigm like the others. Again, the reason for this implementation relates to the need to find an acceptable compromise between effectiveness and efficiency.

In addition to broadcasting, servers can also send specific out-of-band messages to the client for which they are executing a service through the use of function *tpnotify()*. This function can be used, for example, to send the user information not regularly passed in the reply buffer, or to implement a synchronisation mechanism between the client and the server outside the scope of tpgetreply(). For example, this is useful when the client issues a sequence of asynchronous calls which can have a very variable execution time. In such a case, the client continues doing work and relies upon the servers to be notified that a reply has been sent. Alternative usage includes

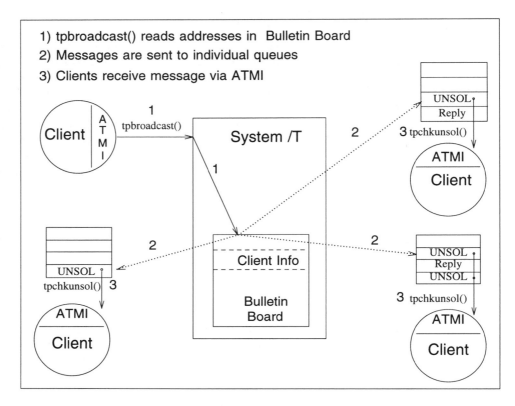

1) tpbroadcast() reads addresses in Bulletin Board
2) Messages are sent to individual queues
3) Clients receive message via ATMI

Figure 47. Unsolicited notification - message broadcasting

the notification of errors which require particular attention from the operator, besides the handling done by the application itself.

4.7.2 Implementation

When the client sets the message handler, the address of the function to be called is recorded in a variable function pointer. tpchkunsol() will use the pointer to call the function when necessary.

As far as receiving unsolicited messages is concerned, if the ATMI method is chosen, each ATMI function will call tpchkunsol(). This function checks for unsolicited messages in the queue and calls the handler with the message as a parameter. At the handler's return, tpchkunsol() will either find another unsolicited message, or will return. This means that at tpchkunsol()'s return, all unsolicited messages in the queue will have been handled. The same happens if tpchkunsol() is called directly by the client's code.

If the signal method is chosen, TUXEDO will send a signal to the client after enqueuing the message. The TUXEDO signal handler linked to the client will then handle the signal by calling tpchkunsol() on behalf of the client. Because UNIX processes can only send signals to processes that have its same user ID, only clients directly started by the same user who started the application (usually the administrator) can receive unsolicited messages with this method.

4.8 Security

With an increasing number of activities performed on computer systems, and with an increasing number of users who have access to computer systems, the subject of security has become more and more critical for many computer environments. This is even more true in distributed environments, where users are not just local to one system and therefore under some form of direct control from the system administrator (assuming this helps), but also remote and possibly unknown.

Of course security in computer environments is not a new subject, but because it usually means different things to different environments, for a long time it has been treated almost on a case by case basis, with specific features being implemented "ad hoc" by the various computer manufacturers and systems vendors.

Generally speaking, security is intended as a set of features provided by various layers of software for guaranteeing that either unauthorised users don't get access to certain systems (and, of course, the data stored on them), or that authorised users can access only the portions of the system they are supposed to. The more complex the environment, the more sophisticated the level of security which needs to be implemented, which is usually a combination of the following:

- *Authentication*: The set of security features aimed at guaranteeing that a user who requests access to a system or application has an identity known to the system and is allowed to do so.

- *Authorisation*: The set of security features aimed at guaranteeing that an authenticated user is entitled to execute the operations he is requesting. A typical feature in this respect is given by *access control lists*, which verify the user's identity against the set of users allowed to execute the operation.

- *Data encryption*: A security feature aimed at hiding the real content of messages or data from users who are not allowed to have access to them.

- *Auditing*: A security feature aimed at registering the user's identity and the type of operations a user does during an authorised or unauthorised working session.

Although the problem of security is general and applicable to single-machine applications as well as to generic distributed environments, in distributed OLTP environments it has particular relevance because of the importance of the operations usually performed in such environments. This is even more so in open OLTP environments, where a wide range of different software layers, typically independent of each other (e.g. operating systems, resource managers, networking), are integrated in a single application.

The UNIX operating system does not by itself provide sophisticated security features; it only provides a type of authentication via the login-password mechanism, and a type of authorisation via the read-write-execute permissions on files, programs, and memory structures. Databases add forms of authentication and authorisation at data level. When more sophisticated security features are required, add-on packages are usually available from software vendors, either to provide full compliance to specific definitions like the C2 or B1 levels from the American Department of Defence, or to provide individual features like encryption. Standards are being put forward for security, and certain environments like OSF's DCE have started providing a common definition for a number of these features, which are expected to be more widely adopted and used as time passes.

In order to have secure applications (at least from the software point of view - we all know that software is only one of the building blocks for security, much depends on the control that the environment can provide over both the authorised and unauthorised users), these features need to be mixed together, and in an heterogeneous environment it is desirable that this can be done in a consistent way.

To make up for the lack of security in normal UNIX environments, and at least until standard security features begin to find wide use in the industry, the TUXEDO system provides its own implementation of security. This can be integrated consistently within a TUXEDO-based distributed application regardless of the underlaying differences between the involved systems. TUXEDO's implementation of security is based on three incremental levels, which can be used, depending on the needs of the specific environment, to build some of the security features listed above.

The first level is based on the standard UNIX permissions, to login into the system, execute the client's program, and register in TUXEDO's Bulletin Board. This level of security is based on the UNIX identity of the user, and is usually not satisfactory for distributed environments.

The second level is provided by an application password set by the application administrator and which all application clients must know when attempting to register in TUXEDO's Bulletin Board. If authentication services are available on the system, for instance MIT's Kerberos, TUXEDO suppliers can replace the application password control with such services. In Kerberos's case, the application password is replaced by the user's credentials for obtaining a ticket and a session key from Kerberos's authentication service.

The third level is provided by an application-defined authentication server, and is invoked after the application password is verified. This server validates other information depending on specific application criteria. Application clients must know which type of information must be provided, and the correct values to match the authentication criteria. If this is successful, the application authentication server assigns the client a hidden application key, which the TUXEDO software will pass to the application servers every time the client makes a request. This allows application servers to validate the client's identity on an individual basis and to perform a selective control over service execution based on the identity of the client.

If an encryption package is available on the system, the TUXEDO libraries for buffer (message) handling can be enhanced with the integration of encryption routines in the pre- and post-send operations. Secure administration is also available. If an application password is set, the administrative tools request such a password. Administration is centralised and only one administrator is allowed at a time.

4.8.1 Usage

A schematic representation of the three levels is presented in Figure 48. The level of security for an application is decided at configuration time, and is set by the administrator by providing different sets of information in the configuration file, depending on the chosen level. The application client, on its side, can register in the Bulletin Board only through the use of the function *tpinit()*, which performs all necessary security checks corresponding to the level set for the application. Depending on the level of security, tpinit() must be provided by the user with a certain amount of information in a special initialisation buffer (the *TPINIT* buffer). All application clients must allocate this buffer before calling tpinit(), and fill it with the amount of information requested by the level of security.

This buffer corresponds to a C structure containing fields for the user name, client type, application password, and other data for authentication. Such a buffer is allocated using tpalloc(), just like any other communication

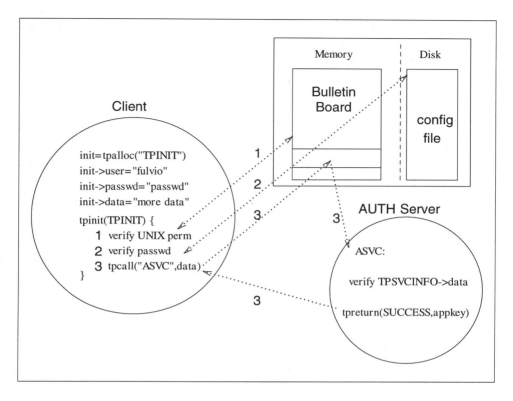

Figure 48. Schematic representation of the three levels of authentication

buffer.[6]

For the first level, the administrator must set the UNIX permissions for the executable program corresponding to the client, and must specify the read-write permissions for the Bulletin Board. For this security level, function tpinit() only verifies the permissions to access to Bulletin Board, and does not require specific information from the user in the TPINIT buffer. This can actually be NULL, unless the client wants to specify its

---

6. This is, by the way, one of the only two cases when an ATMI function can be used before joining the application. The other case is function *tpchkauth()*, which can be used to determine which type of security is configured for the application, and therefore what amount of information must be provided in the TPINIT buffer.

identity with a user name and client type for administration purposes or for being entitled to receive unsolicited notification. This level of security is not suitable for /WS clients, since they are not affected by the UNIX permissions on the machine to which they connect. This is because /WS clients register via a workstation handler, which of course has the necessary permissions.

For the second level, the administrator must set a parameter in the configuration file (see Chapter 6). If this parameter is set, the command used to create the binary version of the configuration file, tmloadcf(1), will prompt the administrator for the definition of an application password and will store it in encrypted form in the configuration file itself. When the client executes tpinit(), it must provide the correct password (the application password, not a UNIX password) in the password field of TPINIT. The tpinit() function matches this value against the value stored in the configuration file. If the values don't match, tpinit() fails and the client cannot register with the application. In the case of WS clients, an encrypted version of the password is passed along with the initial message and is verified by the workstation handler.

For the third level, the administrator must set the name of the application authentication service in the configuration file, and configure an entry for the application server such a service. The authentication server is like any other application server, and the service like any other service. Therefore, the authentication service can receive data and can return the results of its validation. The results are communicated via tpreturn(). They consist of success or failure (i.e. OK or not OK to the user), and of a user application key in one of the parameters (*rval*). This application key is not made available to the user, but is stored by TUXEDO so that it can be silently sent along with every user's requests. Services have this key available in a parameter (*appkey*), and can use it to authorise the execution of the service.

4.8.2 Implementation

I am sure you don't expect me to tell you this, so I won't. Suffice to say that the application password, and the whole of the TPINIT buffer, are never transmitted in plain text. They are encrypted even if the system does not provide encryption mechanisms. For the initialisation phase, TUXEDO provides its own encryption, regardless.

Instead of the internal implementation, it is probably worth spending a few moments to summarise how TUXEDO's security matches the general security features mentioned earlier:

- *Authentication*: This is implemented through the incremental use of UNIX authentication, application password or any alternative method (e.g. Kerberos), and application authentication server. The sufficient amount of information must be provided by an application client, local or remote, in the TPINIT buffer passed to function tpinit(). The use of tpinit() is the only way to get access to the Bulletin Board (and then to the application services). Since this function is provided by TUXEDO, the environment provides the only trusted path for accessing it.

- *Authorisation*: This is implemented through the use of UNIX permissions for the files and memory structures that the client needs to access directly, and through the use of the user's application key for the services requested by the user. Using the user's application key, each service can implement its own version of *access control lists*, although the actual implementation is left to the application. It is expected, however, that in those environments in which DCE's security is available, the server's main provided by TUXEDO will be capable of implementing direct authorisation control using the application key before dispatching the request, reducing the programming requirements for the services.

- *Data encryption*: This is not normally implemented in the TUXEDO functions for sending messages, except for the TPINIT buffer for which encryption functions are provided internally. TUXEDO suppliers, however, would typically add encryption and decryption to the pre- and post-send functions automatically invoked by TUXEDO when sending messages.

- *Auditing*: TUXEDO doesn't provide auditing directly, but provides a function for logging into an application file (ULOG) any messages that the application wishes to log. It is expected that in those environments in which DCE's security is available, the software provided by TUXEDO (tpinit(), the server's main, gateway processes), will make use of those auditing features and will log audit records for users and service requests.

4.9 Summary

In this chapter we have examined those features of the TUXEDO System which allow the implementation of distributed applications over a network of heterogeneous machines. Because these features provide a general framework for various implementations of distributed computing, they have been identified under the name of distributed processing.

First, in order to communicate with one another, the various application components make use of standardised communication paradigms, namely synchronous, asynchronous, and conversational. For these types of communication, suitable programming functions can be used on different types of machines and operating systems. In order to transfer data between each other, all application components make use of predefined communication buffer types, which provide a consistent representation of the application data across machines. Each buffer type is handled internally by TUXEDO, and operations like encoding and decoding are performed automatically.

Apart from the pure task of providing communication facilities, TUXEDO's features in the area of distributed computing allow the implementation of load balancing, prioritisation, and data-dependent routing in a way independent from the programming and in a dynamically tunable way. Through the combination of these features, flexibility and performance can be achieved regardless of the differences between the various components of the application. In addition, features for integrating unsolicited message handling in the application allow for the implementation of a communication protocol outside the standard request/response protocols. This can be used for augmenting the flexibility of the environment and the treatment of asynchronous events.

Finally, for environments which need it, security features are provided for user authentication, authorisation, encryption, and auditing. These features allow the implementation of consistent levels of security for the application across a set of different environments.

5. Transaction Processing

As mentioned in Chapter 2, the subject of transaction processing in a TUXEDO environment is primarily related to the implementation of distributed transaction processing, a specific type of on-line transaction processing characterised by transactions spanning multiple resources and multiple machines. As long as transactions are confined within the boundaries of one single service and one single resource, there is no need for TUXEDO to be directly involved in transactional control. Its role as an open OLTP monitor is best fulfilled by other types of capabilities, both those described in Chapter 4 under the name of distributed processing (consistent communication paradigms, load balancing, data-dependent routing, etc.), and others related to administration and integration of heterogeneous environments, as described in the following chapters.

From industry's perspective, DTP has increasingly become subject to a lot of attention, but this does not necessarily imply that DTP is currently a predominant factor in the decision to move towards Open OLTP. In many environments, such a type of transaction processing is not actually required, and other aspects of interoperability draw more immediate interest. Nevertheless, DTP capabilities are key components of open OLTP monitors, and, even if not used, are considered a prerequisite in a number of cases. This is due to several reasons. As the process of "downsizing" gains momentum, and as the benefits of distributed computing become more appealing to the industry, the requirement to distribute data among different machines is likely to grow, and, along with it, the potential need to perform distributed transaction processing. In an increasingly global economy most types of business rely more and more upon access to different types of data; today's need to access centralised information is quickly becoming the need to manipulate distributed data.

Therefore, when companies begin today to address the issues of distributed computing and start putting together a consistent implementation of heterogeneous distributed environments, sooner rather than later many of them might also have to address the issues of DTP. Planning ahead, the product that companies choose as the basis for distributed computing must also guarantee that it will be possible in the future to address DTP requirements in a consistent fashion.

How quickly DTP will become a common scenario in distributed computing is difficult to say. Because DTP relates to distributed data, the pros and cons of distributing data will be the determining factors. On the one hand, distributing data is appealing; it satisfies the requirements of smaller machines; it allows data to reside near its owners; it helps reduce the impact of failures of individual systems; and it allows the integration at different stages of different types of data. On the other hand, distributing data requires additional administration, adds a degree of complexity to the computing environment, and, perhaps more importantly, it requires a change of attitude and philosophy towards computing as a whole. In general, it is not the availability of DTP capabilities which justifies data distribution, but rather the opposite - the need to distribute data justifies the use of DTP capabilities. So long as there is no business need for it, data distribution and DTP might not be particularly important aspects of distributed computing. There are growing signs, however, that the business need for data distribution is becoming more and more frequent.

So, whether a current or a future need, TUXEDO's support of DTP is one of the strategic features of this product, and it is important to look at how it integrates with the others.

5.1 The DTP model in the TUXEDO framework

To implement DTP in an environment that potentially integrates different software components, it is important to have a model to refer to. The presence of a model helps define the context in which DTP applies, and helps keep the focus on a consistent implementation, independent of the technical details related to the individual components.

An examination of TUXEDO's DTP capabilities must start, therefore, from the description of the model to which they refer. If you are not particularly interested in this conceptual aspect, you might want to skip this section and go to the next, where the actual usage of DTP in TUXEDO's framework is described. Note also that the relationship between TUXEDO's and X/Open's DTP models is discussed in a separate section at the end of the chapter. A diagram of TUXEDO's DTP model is shown in Figure 49. Two different types of logical entities can be identified, *components* and *interfaces*. The components can be briefly described as follows:

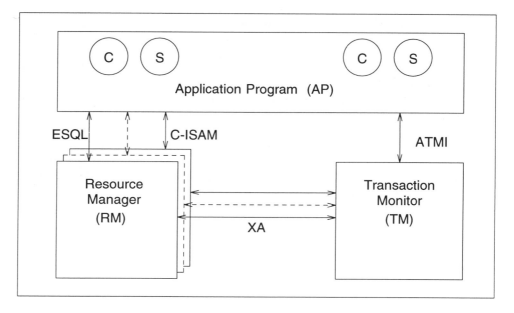

Figure 49. TUXEDO's DTP model

- *Application Program (AP)*: The component that implements the end-user's logic. This includes access to shared resources, definition of the boundaries of transactions, and the decision whether to commit or abort such transactions. In a TUXEDO environment, an application is typically made up of clients and servers, although this separation is not strictly necessary as far as the model is concerned.

- *Resource Managers (RM)*: The various software components that provide the application with access to shared resources. Resources are typically data stores, for example databases or ISAM files, but could be any other type of processing elements, for instance fax machines or disk queues.

- *Transaction Monitor (TM)*: The component that provides the application with control over communication and global transactions. In particular, transaction control is provided by monitoring the progress of transactions and by implementing the commitment and recovery protocols. It is important to note that this component monitors the progress of transactions but does not handle application data. Application data are handled by the application program and by the resource managers. In a TUXEDO environment, TUXEDO itself is the TM.

In order to be able to interact, these components use specified interfaces, to improve portability and interoperability. These are:

- *AP to RM*: This interface allows the application to request work from a resource during a transaction. The TUXEDO System doesn't put restrictions on the type of interface, which is usually the one provided by the RM. Embedded SQL is the most obvious example if the resource is a database, but it could be C-ISAM if the resource is an ISAM file, etc. One characteristic, however, is related to transaction demarcation (begin, commit). In this model, transaction demarcation occurs via the interface between the AP and the TM, and not via the native interface between the AP and RM.

- *AP to TM*: This allows the application to define the boundaries of the transaction, and to communicate with other portions of the application (e.g. make service requests). Via this interface, the application instructs the transaction monitor to propagate all relevant information about the transaction to all involved parties, and to coordinate the commitment or recovery work of all resource managers. In the TUXEDO System, this interface is the ATMI.

- *TM to RM*: This allows the transaction monitor to inform all resource managers about their involvement in a global transaction, to communicate transaction identifiers, and to coordinate the commitment and recovery protocols for the transaction on behalf of the application. In a TUXEDO environment, this interface is called XA (an abbreviation for transaction).

This model is clearly an abstraction of the various types of operation between different entities in a DTP environment, so the first question is usually how the model fits with the reality of an application. In fact, the matching between an application and the model is reasonably straightforward (Figure 50). The application, through the use of the ATMI, defines first where the global transaction begins, then makes service requests (1). Each server, through the use of the native interface with the resource, executes its portion of the transaction (2). At the same time, the TM informs the RM that the work done by the server is part of a global transaction (2'). When all service requests have been completed, the application, again through the use of the ATMI interface, takes the decision to either commit or to rollback the transaction (3). At that point the TM, through the use of the XA interface, coordinates the commitment or rollback of all the resources involved in the transaction (4). Finally, the TM returns to the application the result of the operation (5).

The way in which this sequence of actions can be achieved in a TUXEDO application, i.e. the use of the ATMI for DTP, will be described in the next

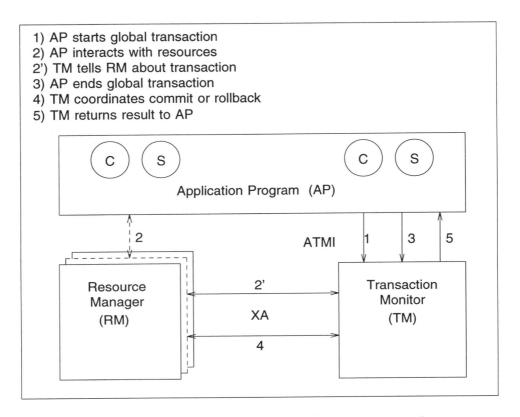

1) AP starts global transaction
2) AP interacts with resources
2') TM tells RM about transaction
3) AP ends global transaction
4) TM coordinates commit or rollback
5) TM returns result to AP

Figure 50. Correspondence between the model and an application

section, so there is no need at this point to examine this subject further. The way in which the application interacts with the resources, i.e. the use of the various native interfaces for the resources, will not be described since this is not particularly relevant for our purposes. On the contrary, the aspects that require more comment and a better examination at this point are the type of capabilities which must be provided by resource managers to fit into this model, and the method with which the commitment and recovery protocols are performed. Let's examine the XA interface and the commit protocol in more detail.

5.1.1 The XA interface

The main purpose of the XA interface is to allow the communication of information about a distributed (global) transaction between the TM and different RMs, with the goal of implementing a transaction coordination protocol capable of satisfying the so-called ACID properties. In a summary, these properties are:

- *Atomicity*: The system will either perform all individual operations on the data, or will ensure that no partially completed operations leave any effects on the data.

- *Consistency*: The execution of a transaction must take all resources involved from one consistent state to another.

- *Isolation*: Operations of current transactions must yield results which are indistinguishable from the results which would be obtained by forcing each transaction to be serially executed to completion, i.e. an end-user application cannot have access to the results of a transaction prior to its completion.

- *Durability*: The system must be able to preserve the effects of committed transactions and ensure the consistency of each resource after recovery from any one of the following failures: permanent irrecoverable failure of durable medium; instantaneous interruption of processing requiring system restart; failure of all or part of memory.

In order to achieve this, it is important that the activity of each resource manager is consistent with the activity of the others, and that each resource manager performs its work according to a protocol. To implement such protocol, the XA interface provides two sets of functions: one provided by the resource managers and used by the transaction monitor, the other provided by the transaction monitor and used by the resource managers.

The functions provided by the resource manager are used by the transaction monitor for:

- initialising the resource in a way that the resource records the fact that it might be used by the application in a global transaction (*xa_open()*). This typically requires the resource manager to allocate a set of structures in which to hold transactional information provided by external entities.

- initiating or resuming the involvement of the resource in a global transaction (*xa_start()*). This requires the resource manager to store information about a transaction identifier provided by the transaction monitor, and to associate the work with this identifier.

- terminating, at least temporarily, the involvement of the resource in a global transaction (*xa_end()*). This requires the resource manager to freeze the content of the structures used during this transaction until used again on behalf of the same transaction.

111

- asking the resource to prepare to commit the work done on behalf of the global transaction (*xa_prepare()*). This requires the resource manager to store permanently all information related to the work done for the transaction in preparation for its commitment.

- asking the resource to rollback the work done on behalf of the global transaction (*xa_rollback()*). This requires the resource manager to release all structures allocated for the transaction and to release the locks on the data structures.

- asking the resource to commit the work done on behalf of the global transaction (*xa_commit()*). This requires the resource manager actually to commit the work and to release the locks held on the data structures.

- recovering incomplete transactions (*xa_recover()*). This requires the resource manager to keep information about all prepared-to-commit work done on behalf of global transactions, and to return a list of the transactions that have been prepared but not yet committed.

- asking the resource to forget about information relating to transactions which had a heuristic completion, i.e. for which the resource manager took decisions outside the agreed protocol (*xa_forget()*). This requires the resource manager to keep information about such transactions until the transaction monitor needs it.

- closing the resource in a way that it records the fact that it will not be used by the application in a global transaction (*xa_close()*). This typically requires the resource manager to terminate its relationship with the transaction manager and not to accept requests under the protocol until a new open operation is again executed.

The functions offered by the transaction monitor are used by resource managers for dynamically registering a non-global transaction into a global one (*ax_reg()*), and for unregistering from it (*ax_unreg()*). These operations constitute an alternative way of initiating and terminating the involvement of a resource manager in a global transaction, in the sense that the resource manager informs the transaction monitor of its involvement only at the time update operations are executed. However, this technique is only rarely implemented by resource managers, and the transaction monitor is usually the entity which controls such involvement.

The resource managers which implement the functions mentioned above are defined as being *XA-compliant*, and can participate in a global transaction coordinated by TUXEDO. Through the use of such functions, the involvement of resources occurs in a consistent way throughout, and when the application decides to commit the transaction, a consistent protocol for commitment, the so-called *two-phase commit*, can be implemented. This is, in the end, the most important reason for the existence of the XA interface, and for the various resource managers to comply with it.

5.1.2 The two-phase commit

When multiple resources are involved in the same transaction, a general theoretical problem is that each resource manager, being in control of its own portion of the transaction (local transaction), could take decisions about the outcome of its own portion regardless of the decisions taken by the others. If, for example, two databases on two different machines are involved in a money transfer, it could happen that the DBMS which performs, say, the deposit, detects an error and correctly decides to rollback the work, while the one which performs the withdrawal doesn't detect any errors and correctly decides to commit the work.

Although acceptable from the point of view of each individual resource because it guarantees the consistency of the local data, this behaviour is clearly disastrous in the context of the global transaction because the ACID properties mentioned above, in particular atomicity, would not be satisfied. Moreover, even if decisions were the same for both resources, but taken at different times, then the isolation and consistency properties would not be satisfied either, since locks would be released at different times. In the absence of these three properties, durability would have no significance.

In order to make sure that all resources take the same decision, one of the possible solutions is to have all resource managers give up their "right" to take decisions, and to leave this task to one single entity. This could either be one of the resource managers themselves, or an external component like the transaction monitor in the model described earlier. In both cases, the entity which assumes the control of the transaction takes the role of *coordinator*, while the individual resource managers take the role of *participants*.

The effect of this solution is that when the time comes to decide the fate of the local transaction, each participant will wait for the coordinator to provide instructions. Also if, prior to the moment when the coordinator takes the decision, circumstances are such that a participant must take a decision, this will always be to rollback the work done until then (i.e. the transaction is presumed aborted).

The coordinator normally uses a two-phase technique for taking the decision and for making sure that all participants perform operations consistently, the so-called two-phase commit protocol or two-phase commit algorithm. The idea behind this algorithm is in itself quite simple (Figure 51): in the first phase the coordinator requests all participants to prepare to commit (1), then waits for all confirmations to come back (2). The

113

preparation consists of the storing in permanent form of all necessary data for actually committing the operation, and not detecting any errors in doing so.

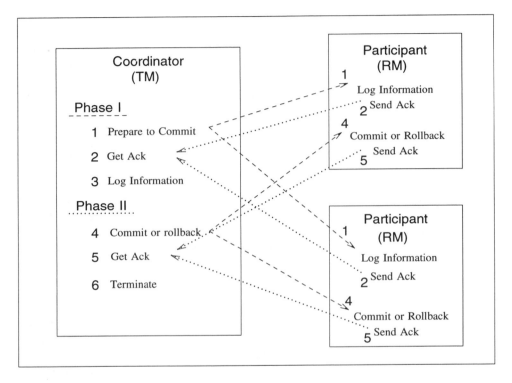

Figure 51. Representation of the two-phase commit

Once all confirmations are back, the coordinator takes the decision to commit or rollback the work depending on whether or not all participants were able to prepare successfully. If the decision is to commit, the coordinator permanently saves information about all participants (3). This action marks the end of the first phase.

In the second phase the coordinator instructs all the participants to actually commit or rollback (4). If the decision is to commit, all participants execute the necessary database updates and release of locks held on the data. If the decision is to rollback, all participants abort the work, even if it was successfully prepared. Once all participants have completed the operation and returned an acknowledgement (5), the coordinator can return the result of the operation to the application (6).

Of course there can be different ways of implementing this algorithm, and that provided by TUXEDO through the use of the XA interface is just one of them. In general, the above operations are the same in all implementations, but, depending on the characteristics of products, certain optimisations are possible. For instance, TUXEDO skips the preparation phase if only one participant is an active party in the transaction (say because the others were involved only in non update operations). Regardless of the implementation, the main purpose of this algorithm is to make sure that data are kept consistent across all the resources. If one of the resources cannot prepare to commit (which is in fact the crucial operation), then all the others are instructed to rollback too. This guarantees that either all operations will have effect, or none will.

An equally important purpose for this protocol is to make sure that data integrity and consistency is achieved in the unlikely but possible event that things go wrong during the execution of this algorithm. In fact, there are several things that could go wrong during the execution of the algorithm, due to failures in processes, machines, peripherals, and networking components. To determine behaviour in such cases, it is probably worth examining some of the most likely scenarios; note that the word "likely" is used assuming that we are in such a situation - as already said, the occurrence of a problem during the execution of the algorithm is in reality a very rare event.

These scenarios can be split into two separate cases: those that can happen before the first phase is complete, and those that can happen after. Relatively speaking, the end of the first phase is the most significant event in the life of the two-phase commit and of the components involved in it. Also, these scenarios assume that timeouts are implemented by both the coordinator and participants, to determine if certain events are not occurring. This assumption is not necessarily valid from a theoretical point of view, but in practice the use of timeouts is a widely used technique, and various implementations of the commit algorithm, for instance TUXEDO's, are based on it.

During the first phase, the end of which is identified by the successful writing in the transaction log of information about all participants, failures to either the processes or machines or the network could occur at different times, and might either prevent certain operations from completing, or, at least, delay their completion. The instants at which failures could occur include:

- *Before the coordinator can communicate the request to prepare-to-commit to the participants*: In this case the participants don't even know that a commit was requested and therefore carry on keeping the information in their stage areas. Depending on the type of failure, the coordinator might or

115

might not be able to restore information about the fact that the application requested a commit operation. If it can within a certain timeframe, then the request to prepare to commit can be communicated and the first phase resumes as if nothing had happened. If it can't, or it takes too long, the application is notified of a failure and all the participants that do not receive a request to commit after a certain time, will abort their local transaction. As said earlier, all resource managers agree to perform an abort if they are forced to take a decision before the coordinator takes one for them. In the implementation of the two-phase commit, this agreement is described by defining the protocol as *presumed aborted*, in the sense that whenever information is no longer available about a transaction, any entity involved, be it the coordinator or the participants, will act as if the available information was that the transaction had to be aborted.

- *After the coordinator has communicated the request to prepare-to-commit to some of the participants but not all of them*: In this case some participants carry out the first phase, while the others don't know they have to. Because of the failure while communicating the request, the coordinator first instructs those participants who have completed the first phase to abort, and returns a failure to the application. Those participants that did not receive the request to prepare will, after some time, presume that the transaction was aborted and will discard all related information. The consistent behaviour for everyone is to abort the transaction.

- *After the coordinator has received some of the replies from prepare-to-commit, but before it has received all of them*: In this case the participants might or might not have completed the first phase successfully. If the communication with all participants is restored within a certain timeframe, and all of them had successfully completed the first phase, then the protocol can continue and the second phase can start. Otherwise, all participants that successfully completed the first phase are instructed to abort at the first occasion, while those that didn't successfully complete the first phase will have already aborted. The consistent behaviour is again an aborted transaction.

- *After the coordinator has received all the replies, but before it could write a log in the transaction log*: This case can only happen because of a failure on the coordinator's side. When the coordinator is available again, because it doesn't have a record of the transaction, it will not instruct the participants to commit. After a certain time, all participants will abort their local transaction. If all participants had replied successfully, this case would have been a little inefficient because it would have aborted a transaction that had satisfied all prerequisites to complete successfully, however, it's still consistent because the application will be notified of the failure, either via timeouts or by the coordinator itself. The consistent behaviour is still an aborted transaction.

Basically, it is possible to draw the conclusion that for any type of failure occurring during the first phase resulting in the protocol being interrupted, the behaviour is a rollback of all the portions of the transaction by all participants. Consistently, the application is always informed of a failure, even before the actual rollback has taken place at all sites.

After the end of the first phase, however, the situation is very different. The coordinator and all participants have by now saved sufficient information to be able to complete the operation as soon as possible, typically when the machine or the network is back and the protocol of the second phase can terminate. Again, we can examine some scenarios, this time related to the failure of either the coordinator or a participant. We also assume that all participants are prepared to wait indefinitely before releasing the locks on a successfully completed local transaction, and that the coordinator is prepared to wait indefinitely for all participants to complete the second phase. Contrary to the assumption made for the first phase, where timeouts were used, the absence of timeouts here is valid from a theoretical point of view, but might have some practical problems, as we will see later:

- *Failure of the coordinator before the second phase is under way*: In this case the participants continue to wait for the second phase to begin, having saved sufficient information for doing so. When the coordinator is back, through the information it had saved, it can contact again all participants and instruct them to perform the second phase.

- *Failure of the coordinator after the second phase is under way*: In this case the participants carry out the actual commit. When the coordinator is back, through the information it had saved, it can recontact all participants and get an acknowledgement about the termination of the second phase.

- *Failure of a participant before the second phase is under way*: In this case the participant had saved sufficient information to continue. When it is back, it is instructed by the coordinator to continue, since it was in the list of participants the coordinator had saved for the transaction.

- *Failure of a participant after the second phase is under way*: In this case the participant had saved sufficient information to roll forward the prepared-to-commit transaction, and therefore it carries out automatically such action and acknowledges the termination to the coordinator.

Unlike failures during the first phase, failures during the second phase lead always to a roll forward. The transaction is always successfully completed, and, when completion is actually achieved, the coordinator returns the outcome to the application. Because the transaction always completes, the coordinator could even return a successful result to the application immediately after the termination of the first phase, since eventually that will be the desired result. This optimisation can bring better performance to the application, since it is free to execute new operations while the second phase is looked after by the coordinator.

In practical terms, though, the assumption that all entities involved in the transaction are prepared to wait indefinitely cannot always be valid. Before the second phase terminates, all participants must keep their locks on the data involved in the transaction, and wait until everyone has completed the job. Unfortunately, if the second phase cannot terminate because of a failure that takes long to be resolved, the locks might have to be held for too long, thus causing inefficiencies to other portions of the application or to other users. In this case the administrator of one of the resources might take the unilateral decision to either rollback or roll forward the local portion of the transaction without taking into consideration the decision of the coordinator (in fact the administrator might not even know in what phase the transaction was). This case goes under the name of *heuristic completion*, and is dangerous for the application because data inconsistencies might be created.

When this is the case, there is very little the coordinator can do to guarantee that a consistent situation is mantained. The XA protocol, however, requires that each RM keeps track of its decision indefinitely, until the coordinator gets to know what had happened. This allows the coordinator to communicate to the application that the transaction terminated in an abnormal way and that some checking is necessary to assess the real situation with the logical database.

In case of heuristic completions, it is the task of the database administrator to find out if inconsistencies were created and if a restart from the backup is necessary to bring back a consistent situation. The use of heuristic decisions is usually discouraged by RM vendors, and is usually also made clear that the procedure for checking the consistency of the data and to restore a clean situation is lengthy and troublesome. However, there are cases when the absolute consistency of data is not so important, and the combination of optimisations and heuristic actions can be beneficial in terms of performance. If, for example, the application is updating the list of items in a food store, it might not be so important to create a situation where there are 1000 tins of peas recorded in the database when there are in fact only 999 on the shelf. If, on the contrary, the application is updating bank accounts, more care might be necessary to the cost of having marginally slower performance.

5.2 DTP in the TUXEDO framework

Having examined the framework provided by TUXEDO's DTP model, the purpose of the XA interface, and the theoretical implementation of the two-phase commit protocol, we can see how things work in practice and how DTP can be set up and used in a TUXEDO application. The development of DTP applications doesn't have to take into consideration most of the aspects discussed in the previous section, since the use of the XA interface and the coordination and recovery of the commit protocol occur transparently. In general, an application must simply define the boundaries of global transactions through the use of ATMI functions, then involve in the transaction all necessary resources through calls to application servers. Each server will access and update the resources through the execution of the services requested.

The involvement of servers and consequently of resources occurs through the use of the capabilities described in Chapter 4. After a global transaction is started, synchronous, asynchronous and conversational requests can be made; message buffers are used to send data backwards and forwards; load balancing, prioritisation, and data-dependent routing can be applied; unsolicited notification can be used to communicate asynchronous events. Some of these features will internally have to take into account the fact that they are being used within a global transaction. For example, messages will have to carry along transactional information, but again this occurs transparently. From the application point of view, the use of these ATMI functions is virtually the same as outside the scope of DTP.

In practice, the use of TUXEDO's DTP is mainly related to the use of a set of different programming facilities, to improve the flexibility and the architecture of the application. For example, clients and servers can explicitly start and commit a global transaction, but under certain circumstances they can request TUXEDO to do it automatically. Service requests can be made within the boundaries of a transaction or outside the transactional protocol. Resources that do not support the XA interface can be accessed while a global transaction is under way. The use of these features is not transparent to the application, in the sense that in order to be able to use them, certain programming techniques must be used consistently and particular administrative actions must be considered.

5.2.1 Usage

Clients or servers can begin a global transaction by using function *tpbegin()*. This takes as its only parameter a timeout for the transaction, e.g. 60

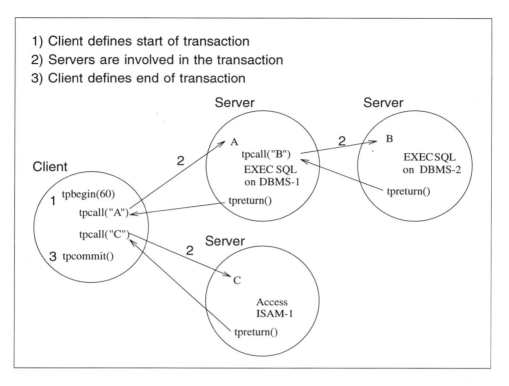

Figure 52. Definition of transaction boundaries - client

seconds. This means that from the moment tpbegin() is invoked, the sequence of calls, the database operations, and the completion of the first phase of the commit protocol must take less than 60 seconds. If this is not the case, TUXEDO will abort the transaction and the application will be notified that a timeout failure occurred. If the application is prepared to wait indefinitely for the transaction to complete, a value of zero for the timeout can be used.

The execution of tpbegin() does not imply any interaction with any resource; it simply notifies TUXEDO that a global transaction has started and that it has a certain number of seconds in which to complete. Because of this, the execution of tpbegin() can occur in any application process, client or server, connected to a resource (Figures 52 and 53) or not. The process that executes tpbegin() is identified as the *initiator* of the transaction.

After tpbegin() has been executed, the process is marked by TUXEDO to be in *transaction mode*. If the process makes multiple service requests, or establishes multiple connections to servers, as will probably be the case since

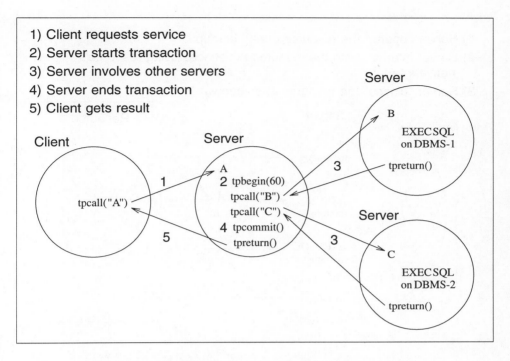

1) Client requests service
2) Server starts transaction
3) Server involves other servers
4) Server ends transaction
5) Client gets result

Figure 53. Definition of transaction boundaries - server

at least two different resources need to be involved to create a true DTP scenario, transactional information is automatically propagated by TUXEDO with the messages. This allows the various servers to dialogue with the resource on behalf of the same transaction. If another process, say one of the invoked servers, executes tpbegin() again, an error is received and no new transaction is started. This is the standard behaviour, although, under certain circumstances (see later on, non participation), a new, separate transaction might be started.

On their side, in order to be able to dialogue with the resource in transactional mode, servers must first of all connect to the resource in a way that makes the resource able to accept work on behalf of a global transaction (figure 54). This is achieved by calling, in the server's initialisation sequence, function *tpopen()*. This function, through information found in the configuration file, opens the database in the correct modality. The TUXEDO-provided server's main executes this function automatically, so there is normally no need to program it. However, if the server has been provided with a personalised init routine, *tpsvrinit()*, then a call to tpopen()

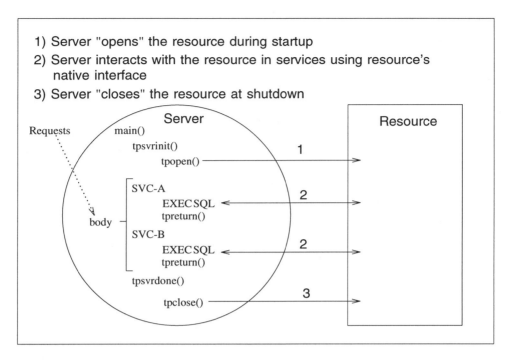

1) Server "opens" the resource during startup
2) Server interacts with the resource in services using resource's
   native interface
3) Server "closes" the resource at shutdown

Figure 54. Server's interaction with the resource

must also be added in this routine (1). If anything goes wrong at this stage, the server will not be started and an error will be logged. If this opening phase is successful, the server will be able to serve requests on behalf of any global transaction. To achieve this, when a request is received in transaction mode, the server's main itself will start a local transaction on behalf of the global one via XA calls to that process's RM. When the service terminates, the code of tpreturn() will terminate the participation in the global transaction again via XA calls.

An implication of this behaviour is that the code of the service doesn't have to provide transaction demarcation through the use of the resource's native interface. In a server which accesses a DBMS, for example, operations like "SET TRANSACTION LEVEL" and "COMMIT WORK" will not be used. If an existing program is converted into a TUXEDO server, these instructions will have to be removed if the server is a participant of the transaction, or will have to be replaced with the pair *tpbegin()/tpcommit()* if the server is the initiator. Apart from this, though, the services will still use the native interface, e.g. embedded SQL, to perform the desired operations at runtime

(2).

At shutdown time, the server will automatically execute function *tpclose()* in order to terminate its connection with the resource. Again, if the server has been provided with a personalised shutdown routine, *tpsvrdone()*, a call to tpclose() will have to be explicitly added (3).

Once the initiator of the transaction is finished with the calls and has received all replies, it can decide either to commit or to abort the transaction. The initiator is the only process allowed to commit its transaction. Any other process attempting to commit or abort the global transaction will receive an error. Although this is not a strong limitation, the most recent version of TUXEDO has been enhanced with two new ATMI functions, *tpsuspend()* and *tpresume()*. These two functions allow a process to give up its right to commit a transaction by suspending its involvement, and another process to resume it and commit it.[7]

The use of *tpcancel()* during a global transaction is forbidden, since this would prevent the initiator from getting all replies and therefore getting the complete list of participants. Also, if tpbegin() is executed in a service, the service cannot invoke tpforward() before committing or aborting the transaction.

The abort of a global transaction is executed using function *tpabort()*, and should be requested every time one of the portions of the transaction returns a failure, i.e. every time the return from a function like tpcall() or tpgetrply() detects an error. If an abort is requested, the transaction will be marked as being aborted, and any work will be automatically rolled back by TUXEDO through an exchange of messages with all resources involved. Service routines can indicate that a transaction must be aborted by using tpreturn() with the TPFAIL flag. This ensures that even if the initiator accidentally calls tpcommit(), the transaction will be aborted.

If all operations are successful, the initiator uses function *tpcommit()* to instruct TUXEDO to perform the two-phase commit and coordinate the global transaction. At the end of this operation the initiator is notified of the outcome, i.e. if the transaction committed successfully or not. If not, TUXEDO and the resource managers will have automatically performed a rollback.

Before calling tpcommit(), the initiator can decide whether it wants to receive the outcome of the transaction after the first or second phase of the

---

7. Because at the time of writing I haven't had the chance to try these functions, I have added this comment only as a pointer. The interested reader should contact Novell or a TUXEDO supplier for additional information.

commit protocol. This can be done by using function *tpscmt()*. As mentioned in the previous section, receiving the outcome after the first phase has been safely logged improves the performance of the application, because the initiator is free to do some new work while the second phase is completed by TUXEDO. The price of this choice, however, is that the application might not become aware of potentially dangerous situations due to heuristic decisions. Of course, the decision as to whether this is acceptable is totally application dependent. By default tpcommit() will return after the second phase, since this is the safest option. The administrator can set a different default behaviour in the configuration file if appropriate.

Finally, any process can obtain information about its involvement in a global transaction through the use of function *tpgetlev()*. The use of this function allows processes, typically servers, to decide if they have to start a transaction. For example, a service for money transfer might verify if it was called in transaction mode or not. If not, it will start a global transaction before calling service "withdrawal" and service "deposit". Otherwise, it will simply make the service calls. This gives the possibility of using a service with different types of clients, for example some that start transactions explicitly and others which simply invoke the service.

From an administration viewpoint, the use of TUXEDO's DTP requires some actions to be performed. Transaction logs must be created on all machines where DTP could occur; opening and closing information for the resources must be specified in the configuration file; relevant service parameters might have to be specified in relation to autotransactions, as explained in the following section; special processes, the transaction nanager servers (TMS) must be added to the configuration. These actions will be described in Chapter 6.

5.2.2 Implementation

Whilst the usage of DTP features in the TUXEDO System is mainly related to the use of a few specific ATMI functions in the application, the implementation is based on work done by both application and internal processes.

DTP fuctionalities are built into the ATMI libraries linked to the application, so that the use of the ATMI guarantees that all necessary actions are transparently performed when used during a global transaction. For example, each server's main performs an xa_start() when it receives a request in transaction mode, while tpreturn() performs an xa_end().

Alongside the work carried out by the ATMI functions, a significant portion of TUXEDO's transactional work is provided by the TMS processes. These are provided by TUXEDO suppliers and are linked with the XA-compliant libraries provided by resource managers. If the application uses different resources, different TMSs will be necessary. Their structure is similar to that of application servers, but they do not contain application code and their function is to serve requests for handling a two-phase commit protocol. Such requests are not issued directly by the application, but rather by the TUXEDO software, for example by the code of tpcommit().

Each TMS is associated to a group of application servers that access the same resource. In this way, TMSs can handle all the commitment work associated to the work done by the servers in the same group (Figure 55).

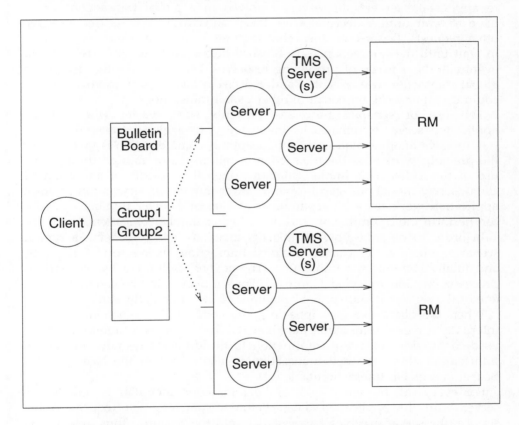

Figure 55. Association between application and TMS servers

For example, one TMS might be associated to three application servers accessing the same DBMS on one machine. The way in which this association is made is a matter of configuration, and will be described in Chapter 6. There is always more than one TMS associated to the same group of servers, both for performance reasons and for avoiding particular cases of deadlocks. Once this association is in place, the TMSs can serve request for transaction coordination on behalf of the work done by the application servers for a certain global transaction. In order to do this, these processes are linked to the same resource as the application servers, and open it at the same way as the application servers do.

The reason why the commitment work is done by separate processes instead of the actual application servers is essentially for performance purposes. If the execution of the two-phase commit was done by code linked to application servers, all servers involved in a global transaction would have to wait until a decision were taken and would not be free to serve other requests. Because of this, other requests from other users would have to wait until the transaction were finished before being served. This would eventually be a waste of processing resources, because while the rest of the global transaction was executed and a decision taken, all individual servers could do other work on behalf of other global transactions.

The use of separate processes prevents such waste; whenever an application server terminates its involvement in a global transaction, it is free to serve another request. In the meantime, some decision is taken about the previous work, and the transaction is committed or aborted through the use of the TMSs. This implementation brings the benefits of an enhanced client/server model one step further; a lower number of servers can perform application work for a higher number of clients; a lower number of TMSs can perform the commitment work for a higher number of servers.

In order to describe how all this fits together, let's consider a a typical scenario, where a client starts a global transaction, makes service requests, and finally commits the transaction. The actions performed by the various processes are illustrated in Figure 56. For simplicity, the behaviour of only one of the servers is shown; the behaviour of the other is the same.

When the client executes tpbegin(), the code of this function generates internally a global transaction identifier (GTRID). This is a unique identifier used to provide consistent information to the different resource managers. Information about the new transaction is also stored in the local Bulletin Board, in a global transaction table (1).

For every call the client makes, the transaction identifier is sent to the server with the application data. Before dispatching the request to the service, the server executes an xa_start() with the resource, thus making the resource aware of the global transaction (2). When the service executed tpreturn(), the function executes an xa_end() in order to end the server's involvement in the global transaction (3). At that point the server is free to serve another request, and does not have to wait until the commitment is done.

When all replies are back, the initiator can commit the transaction. This is

1) Client starts global transaction - entry allocated in BB
2) Client makes a call (e.g. B) - server starts local transaction
3) Service returns - tpreturn() ends local transaction
4) Client commits the transaction - TMS invoked
5) TMS coordinates two-phase commit
6) TMS returns result to the application

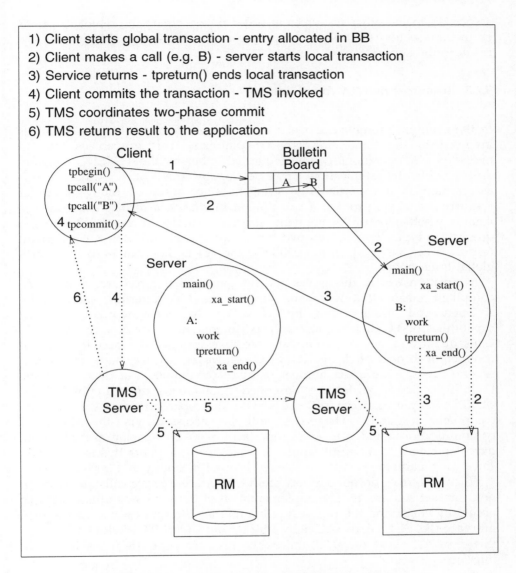

Figure 56. Implementation of DTP - example

the point when the TMS gets into the picture. tpcommit() requests one of the TMSs to coordinate the two-phase commit, typically one associated to the first group of servers involved in the transaction(4). This TMS interacts directly with the local resource, and exchanges messages with one TMS associated to the other resources in order to coordinate the remote portions of the transaction (5). When the protocol terminates, the TMS returns the result to the application (6).

5.2.3 Resources non XA-compliant

In the example presented above, the main assumption is that the resources involved in the transaction are XA-compliant. This guarantees that all necessary XA operations can be requested either by the TUXEDO software linked with the application processes or by the TMSs. Although this assumption is not particularly stringent since most of today's popular resource managers provide XA-compliant interfaces, a recurrent question is usually whether non XA-compliant resources can also be used. Actually, the question is typically split into two further questions: (a) if non XA-compliant resources can be used with TUXEDO; and (b) if they can participate in a global transaction.

A quick answer to this is yes and no. Saying that a resource is non XA-compliant means that it cannot support the DTP interface specified by X/Open and implemented by TUXEDO. In other words, the DTP capabilities of TUXEDO cannot be used in conjunction with such resources. Consequently, a non XA-compliant resource cannot take part in a global transaction coordinated by TUXEDO. However, as we have mentioned several times, there are a number of other capabilities that do not involve DTP. In particular, all features described in Chapter 4 are still applicable. A TUXEDO application can still use servers that open and access a non XA-compliant resource. They can still be accessed via the described communication paradigms, and properties like load balancing, prioritisation, data-dependent routing still apply. In many environments this is sufficient, since such features provide the desired level of flexibility and performance.

When resources do not support the XA interface, service calls are made in non transactional mode. The implementation of transactions in these services occurs by specifying the transaction boundaries through the native resource interface (i.e. SET TRANSACTION LEVEL and COMMIT WORK). Of course this does not allow for DTP, unless the resource supports it via its native interface.

5.3 Autotransactions

In many applications the idea of calling a service corresponds to that of calling a transaction. This is mainly inherited by mainframe OLTP applications where programs on the mainframe would typically be transactions, regardless of the actual operation or the type of transaction, be it local or global. When this way of seeing the operations needs to be maintained, either for historical reasons or for preserving the philosophy adopted by a certain development environment, the programmers of both clients and servers will not want to define the boundaries of the transaction explicitly. They will simply want to invoke a transaction, i.e. in TUXEDO terms, a service.

If the service/transaction operates on one single resource, there is one-to-one mapping between the service and the transaction, and therefore the execution of the service will also correspond to the execution of the transaction. Because of this, TUXEDO will not have to be involved in the coordination of the transaction and the use of TUXEDO's DTP will not have to be taken into account. On the contrary, if the service requested makes other service calls, this might result in a global transaction. This requires the boundaries to be defined somewhere, using TUXEDO's semantics.

An easy way to set such boundaries is to configure the service in autotransactional mode. For an autotransactional service, TUXEDO begins a global transaction when the server is invoked, and commits the transaction when the server returns the reply to the requester. In this way, a global transaction is automatically executed every time someone invokes the service. For example, a service for money transfer might be configured as autotransactional, so that if the service is not called in transactional mode, a global transaction will be started. However, if the service is already in transactional mode, a new one will not be started. This implementation of the transfer service is an alternative to the one presented earlier, in which the same service would first invoke tpgetlev(), then explicitly start a transaction if not in transaction mode already.

5.3.1 Usage

The use of autotransactional services is usually straightforward, since no programming is required. All that needs to be done is to set a parameter in the configuration file for the service, and to specify the timeout value which TUXEDO will use at the execution of tpbegin(). Of course, this applies only to services that either directly or indirectly access XA-compliant resources. When that is not the case, the use of TUXEDO's DTP is impossible and consequently the use of autotransactional services is impossible too. The transactional work for the resource will have to be defined through the resource's native interface (e.g. SET TRANSACTION LEVEL and COMMIT WORK).

5.3.2 Implementation

The implementation of autotransaction is presented in Figure 57. Information about the autotransactional characteristics of a service is stored in the Bulletin Board. The call made by the client is no different from any other service call, and no tpbegin()/tpcommit() are used (1). When the server reads the request, it verifies whether the service is autotransactional. If it is, before dispatching the request to the corresponding routine it starts a global transaction through the use of tpbegin() and puts the process in transaction mode (2). This is done transparently in the server's main, i.e. no programming is necessary. If the request arrives as part of a client's transaction, the server skips the call to tpbegin() and simply joins the client's transaction (i.e. it becomes a participant).

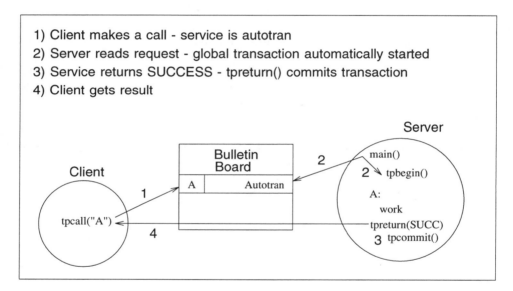

1) Client makes a call - service is autotran
2) Server reads request - global transaction automatically started
3) Service returns SUCCESS - tpreturn() commits transaction
4) Client gets result

Figure 57. Autotransactions - implementation

When the service terminates, i.e. it executes tpreturn(), the server performs tpcommit() or a tpabort() depending on whether the value returned was SUCCESS or FAIL (3). Again, this is done transparently in the code of tpreturn(). Finally, the reply is sent to the caller (4). If the value was SUCCESS but the commit fails, the caller is returned a failure.

Unlike the case where the application code explicitly calls tpbegin(), in which calls to tpforward() are forbidden before committing the transaction, autotransactional services can terminate using tpforward(). In this case, TUXEDO itself commits or aborts the transaction at the end of the forwarding chain, before returning the final reply to the originator of the request.

5.4 Non participation

Once a TUXEDO environment is set up for distributed transaction processing, all calls made in transaction mode will by default propagate transactional information. This instructs the server to use XA calls to involve the resource in the transaction. There are cases, however, when this behaviour might be undesirable or impossible.

If, for example, one of the calls made within the transaction boundaries is irrelevant to the transaction, it might be acceptable that the result of such a call does not affect the result of the transaction. If, for instance, during the execution of a money transfer a call is made to an audit server, it might be preferable to implement the transaction in a way that a failure in writing the audit log should not prevent the transaction from successfully completing. Similarly, if one of the calls involves a resource which does not support the XA interface, for example a printer, it might be acceptable to consider this call outside any transactional semantic.

In both cases, TUXEDO allows the use of a special flag during the service call, to signify that the execution of the request will occur outside the boundaries of the global transaction currently under way. This gives the application better control of what constitutes a transaction, and restricts the implementation of transactional control to only the essential elements of the transaction, rather than on all operations regardless.

5.4.1 Usage

Non participation in a global transaction is simply a matter of setting a flag, TPNOTRAN, in tpcall(), tpacall(), or tpconnect(). The setting of this flag is compulsory if during a global transaction calls are made to servers interacting with a non XA-compliant resource. If this flag were not used, the call would fail because the server wouldn't be able to initiate the involvement of the resource in the transaction, and the whole transaction would have to be aborted.

5.4.2 Implementation

If the TPNOTRAN flag is set, no transactional information is passed along with the call, and therefore the server will not attempt to execute an xa_start() with the resource. Failures in the execution of the service, and a subsequent call to tpreturn() with flag TPFAIL, will not mark the transaction for abort. It is also true, however, that a success of this service and a subsequent abort of the transaction will not rollback the work done by the server, so the use of this flag must be carefully considered.

If the called service is autotransactional, or if the service uses tpbegin(), a new independent transaction is started. The commitment or abort of this does not affect the commitment of abort of the other. Therefore, the use of TPNOTRAN in combination with the start of a separate transaction must therefore be used with caution too, since in many cases it might be unsuitable.

5.5 The DTP model from X/Open

The model for DTP presented at the beginning of this chapter was developed for TUXEDO, and as such is only directly applicable to it. The same model has however been adopted by X/Open as their standard reference model for DTP. X/Open's model encompasses most of TUXEDO's technology, but includes also technology contributed by other suppliers like OSF™, Transarc®, NCR™, and DEC™. Its main purpose is the definition of the reference entities in a generic DTP environment, in which not just different resources, but also different applications and different TP monitors, can be integrated within global transactions.

Depending on the emphasis we want to put on the various components, X/Open's model can be represented in different ways. One of these, the closest to TUXEDO's representation, is presented in Figure 58. This is not an official representation, i.e. one which would be found in the published X/Open documentation. It is rather one which I have chosen to put together in a single picture all elements currently defined.[8]

With respect to TUXEDO's model, the main difference is related to the definition of the TM. While in TUXEDO's model the TM (transaction monitor) provides transaction and communication control, in X/Open's

---

8. There are several documents published by X/Open which refer to the DTP model. These are listed in the bibliography.

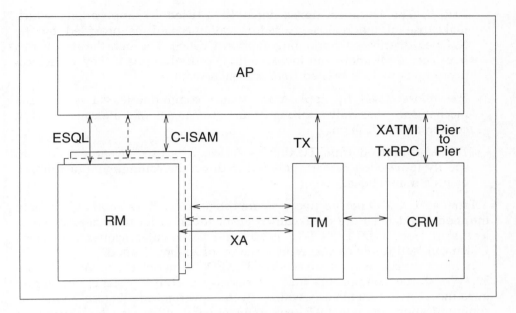

Figure 58. X/Open's DTP model (complete)

model the TM (transaction manager) provides only transaction control. Communication control is provided by an additional component, the *communication resource manager* (CRM). This component is theoretically separate from the transaction manager, although a TP monitor would probably integrate both of them. The communication provided by the CRM occurs according to different paradigms, for example request/response or conversational, and may encompass the propagation of information about global transactions.

Since the communication resource manager is a separate component, not necessarily bundled with the transaction manager, there are different interfaces that an AP might use to request communication services. The model provides for three different interfaces, and, in addition, it also defines a specific interface between the application and the transaction manager. In a summary, these four interfaces are:

- *XATMI*: Derived directly from TUXEDO's ATMI, it can be used by applications which use a communication paradigm based on service requests, and as such is particularly suitable for client/server applications.

- *TxRPC*: The so-called transactional RPC, used by applications which make use of the remote procedure call mechanisms provided by the X/Open distributed computing support (XCDS). Through the use of this interface, applications can invoke remote procedures as if they were local procedures with associated transactional semantics.

- *Pier-to-Pier*: Used by applications which communicate via a dialogue mechanism, basically through an exchange of messages in a conversational fashion.

- *TX*: Also derived from TUXEDO's ATMI, it is used by applications to specify transaction demarcation and to direct the commitment or rollback of such transactions.

From a TUXEDO perspective, it is important to see how TUXEDO fits into the model and what are the common elements. In order to understand this, let's start from TUXEDO's DTP model and work out a sequence of steps which can lead to the chosen representation of X/Open's model.

A more precise way of presenting TUXEDO's model is shown in Figure 59. Whilst the components and interfaces are still the same, the figure introduces two elements which were overlooked before. One is communication in the DTP environment, the other is the degree of separation within an AP, as the AP might in general be seen as the collection of individual applications (e.g. client and server programs).

In TUXEDO's model, we assumed that when a call is made via the ATMI, the request was sent to another portion of the application by the entity called the TM, as if it was an omnipresent entity. Equally, when a global transaction is started, we assumed that transactional information was propagated where necessary by the same entity, and that when the two-phase commit was performed, the TM coordinated the protocol as if it were an entity on all machines.

In fact, from a logical point of view, the functions that the TM performs are related on the one hand to the definition and coordination of transactional information, and on the other to the propagation of such information to all the individual components of the environment, typically the clients and servers in the application. If we consider these two functions, the entity called the TM can in fact be split into two subentities, one specifically dedicated to the transaction management, the other dedicated to the auxiliary function of communicating information, possibly transactional information, across the DTP environment (Figure 60).

Because of this separation, the entity which in the TUXEDO environment is called the TM (transaction monitor) tends to disappear, and is replaced by two others. One we can call a transaction manager (TM)[9], and the other we

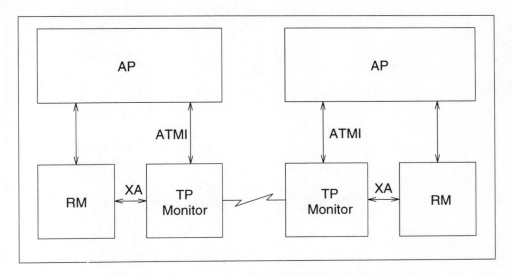

Figure 59. Representation of TUXEDO's DTP model

can call a communication resource manager (CRM). This separation resembles very much the separation between the distributed processing and transaction processing capabilities of TUXEDO. Accordingly, we can split the ATMI interface into two parts, one performing pure transactional operations (tpbegin(), tpcommit, etc.), and one performing generic communication operations (tpcall(), tpconnect(), etc.). This approach matches X/Open's, and leads to the creation of two separate interfaces, one between the AP and the TM, and the other between the AP and the CRM. Because the ATMI includes both, the subset that relates to the TM can be associated to X/Open's TX, and the subset that relates to the CRM can be associated to X/Open's XATMI (Figure 61).

In addition, support for the TxRPC interface has been added. Although support of one of the three defined AP-to-CRM interfaces is sufficient for claiming compliance to the model, as of mid-1994 TUXEDO was the only product to support at least two of the interfaces. This can be seen as a competitive advantage, because it allows consistent administration of applications coded in two different styles, as well as integration of DCE-

---

9. Note the use of the same acronym with a different meaning.

135

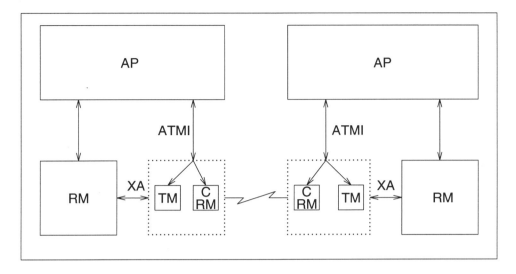

Figure 60. Subentities in the TP monitor

based environments.

The differences between TUXEDO's native ATMI functions and the X/Open's standard ones are minimal, but must be taken into consideration. Before we move to the comparison of the two interfaces, though, for the sake of completeness it is also worth examining another interface, the one between the TM and the CRM.

This interface is not explicitly shown in Figure 61 and is only marginally considered in X/Open's current model, but it has been the subject of interest in the industry and has generated some debate about its meaning and importance.

The purpose of a standard interface between the TM and the CRM is to allow the use of different CRMs by the same TM under the same global transaction. Since this resembles the use of the XA interface for integrating different RMs under the same global transaction, this interface has sometimes been referred to as the *XA+*.

There is a fundamental difference, though, between the XA+ and the XA; whilst the latter provides the framework for integrating different existing products in the model and for resolving from a theoretical and practical point of view the difficulties related to the interoperability of such products, the former is mainly theoretical. Whilst there exist different RMs on the market, and therefore their interoperability is a practical issue, at the moment no equivalent CRM products are available. In certain OLTP

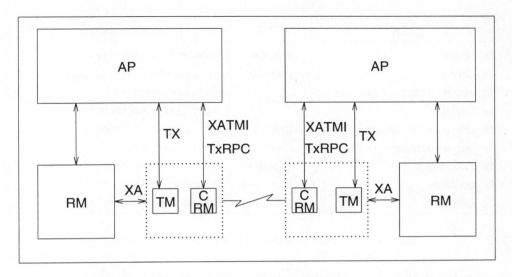

Figure 61. Correspondence between TUXEDO's and X/Open's DTP models

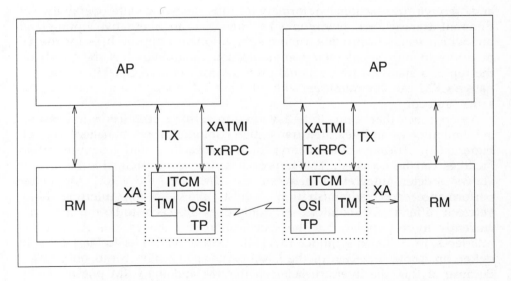

Figure 62. Integrated transaction communication manager

monitors the CRM capabilities are actually provided by entities separate from the TM, but there is no evidence that such entities will ever become

TX	ATMI	Description
tx_open	tpopen	Open the AP's resource managers
tx_close	tpclose	Close the AP's resource managers
tx_set_transaction_timeout	tpbegin	Set transaction timeout
tx_begin		Begin a global transaction
tx_set_commit_return	tpscmt	Set return point of commit
tx_set_transaction_control	-	Select chaining mode
tx_info	tpgetlev	Obtain current transaction information
tx_commit	tpcommit	Commit a global transaction
tx_rollback	tpabort	Rollback a global transaction

Figure 63. Correspondence between ATMI and TX

products, to be purchased separately from OLTP monitors.

The reason usually given why CRMs may exist as separate products is that in this way a transaction manager could use different CRMs to transmit and receive transactional information, thus allowing interoperability of different transactional environments. However, an alternative option and one which seems to provide a more straightforward approach, is for the TP monitors to implement their communication capabilities (i.e. the CRM) on the top of a standard transactional protocol, for example OSI-TP, so that the native CRM can communicate with all other TP monitors implementing the same protocol.

An approach that seems to be favoured in existing products is to consider a TP monitor as an integrated transaction communication manager[10] (ITCM, Figure 62). Through this entity, both transaction and communication facilities can be accessed. This approach seems to be preferable because it allows stricter integration between the TM and the CRM for better performance and administration, whilst allowing for interoperability between different TP monitors. Not only does this seem to be the approach currently more popular, but the specifications for the various AP-to-CRM interfaces in X/Open's model (XATMI, TxRPC, and Pier-to-Pier) already define an implementation of the CRM protocol machine based on OSI-TP. Because of this, the interface between the TM and the CRM doesn't really

---

10. I have seen this approach and this terminology first used by Bull Machines.

XATMI	ATMI	Description
Typed buffer functions		
tpalloc	tpalloc	Allocate a typed buffer
tprealloc	tprealloc	Increase the size of a typed buffer
tpfree	tpfree	Free a typed buffer
tptypes	tptypes	Get information about a typed buffer
Functions for request/response services		
tpcall	tpcall	Send a synchronous request
tpacall	tpacall	Send an asynchronous request
tpgetrply	tpgetrply	Receive an asynchronous reply
tpcancel	tpcancel	Cancel a call descriptor
Functions for conversational services		
tpconnect	tpconnect	Establish a connection to a service
tpdiscon	tpdiscon	Terminate a connection abortively
tpsend	tpsend	Send a message in conversation
tprecv	tprecv	Receive a message in conversation
Functions for dynamically advertising service names		
tpadvertise	tpadvertise	Advertise a service name
tpunadvertise	tpunadvertise	Unadvertise a service name
Functions for writing service routines		
tpservice	service	Template for service routines
tpreturn	tpreturn	Return from a service routine
-	tpforward	Forward service to another service

Figure 64. Correspondence between ATMI and XATMI functions

need to comply to any standards, since the native interface is as effective and the whole ICTM allows for better internal optimisation and more consistent administration.

5.5.1 ATMI versus TX and XATMI

As said, the ATMI interface has been adopted by X/Open in the reference DTP model, but in doing so it has been split into two separate interfaces, the

XATMI	ATMI	Description
C language buffer types		
X_OCTET	CARRAY	Array of characters which may contain the NULL character
X_COMMON	VIEW	C structure
X_C_TYPE	VIEW	C structure
-	FML	Fielded buffers
X_C_TYPE	STRING	Array of characters terminated by the NULL character
COBOL language record types		
X_OCTET	CARRAY	Array of characters which may contain LOW-VALUE characters
X_COMMON	VIEW	COBOL record
-	STRING	Array of characters which may not contain LOW-VALUE characters

Figure 65. Correspondence between ATMI and XATMI buffer types

TX and the XATMI.

The TX interface roughly correspond to the functions for defining the transactional properties of the application, and include functions like *tx_begin()*, *tx_commit()*, and *tx_rollback()* in correspondence to tpbegin(), tpcommit() and tpabort(), as presented in Figure 63.

The meaning of these functions is virtually the same, but a few differences can be noted: the transaction timeout is not set directly in tx_begin(), but rather through the use of a separate function, *tx_set_transaction_timeout()*; tx_commit() behaves like tpcommit(), but can also implement a chained transaction mechanism, by which a new transaction is started immediately after the current one has been completed. This behaviour is much like that of a synchronisation point and is determined by the use of function *tx_set_transaction_control()*. With the native ATMI, the application would have to use tpcommit() and tpbegin() in strict sequence to achieve the same result. The commit return is set with *tx_set_commit_return()* instead of tpscmt(). Function tpgetlev() is replaced by a more general function, *tx_info()*, that provides information not just as to whether a global transaction is under way at a particular moment, but also about the timeout, the state of the transaction, and the current transaction branch identifier. Because TUXEDO is TX-compliant, these functions can be used in place or alongside the corresponding ATMI.

ATMI	Description
Functions for unsolicited notification	
tpsetunsol	Set the unsolicited message handler
tpchkunsol	Check for unsolicited messages
tpbroadcast	Broadcast a message
tpnotify	Send an unsolicited message
Functions for connecting to the transaction manager	
tpinit	Join the application
tpterm	Leave the application
tpchkauth	Check the security level
Functions for initialising an application server	
tpsvrinit	User written initialisation routine
tpsvrdone	User written termination routine
Functions for service priorities	
tpsprio	Set priority of next request
tpgprio	Get priority of last request
Functions for stored requests	
tpenqueue	Enqueue a message in a disk queue
tpdequeue	Dequeue a message from a disk queue

Figure 66. ATMI which do not have correspondence in XATMI

The XATMI interface corresponds more closely to a subset of the remaining ATMI functions, both in names and syntax (tpcall(), tpconnect(), tpalloc(), etc., as shown in Figure 64), and therefore TUXEDO is inherently compliant to such an interface.

The main difference between the ATMI and the XATMI is about message buffers (Figure 65). The use of FML buffers and string buffers is based on the availability of specific software, so these buffer types are not allowed in XATMI functions. Views and carrays are allowed, but under different names (*X_OCTET*, *X_COMMON*, and *X_C_TYPE*) and with a slightly different meaning in relation to the allowed types of data. The different names are mainly cosmetic changes, but also indicate the fact that certain capabilities provided by TUXEDO with its native buffers, for example data-dependent routing, are not required for compliance to the model. Because TUXEDO is XATMI-compliant, XATMI buffer types can be used instead or alongside the

ATMI buffers.

To complete the comparison, it must also be noted that the union of the TX and XATMI interfaces does not correspond to the entire ATMI. Those ATMI functions which correspond to TUXEDO's specific features live outside this model, although they can be used alongside it. These functions are listed in Figure 66. As a product, the TUXEDO System provides a richer set of features than those defined by the X/Open model. Features like unsolicited notification, prioritisation, and forwarding of service requests are specifically provided by TUXEDO, and so are customisable routines for the initialisation and termination of application servers. Enqueuing of service requests into disk queues is provided by a subsystem of TUXEDO (System/Q), so all of these can be seen as TUXEDO extensions to enhance the standard environment.

5.6 Summary

In this chapter we have examined the features related to DTP. The importance of these features is directly related to the importance of data distribution in current and future computing environments, and is expected to play an increasingly strategic role as the establishment of distributed computing gains momentum.

TUXEDO's features in this area are implemented according to a model which defines the components of a DTP environment and the programming interfaces between them. In particular, the interface between the transaction monitor and the resource managers, the XA, provides a consistent method for the implementation of a two-phase commit protocol for transaction coordination. In such a protocol, resource managers are instructed by the transaction monitor whether to commit or abort a global transactions.

TUXEDO's DTP model has become the basis for the standard DTP model defined by X/Open, and many of TUXEDO's elements can be now identified in it, for instance the XA, TX, and XATMI interfaces. The model encompasses interfaces derived from other products, and adopts the TX interface as the sole mechanism for communicating transactional information between the application and transaction managers.

From an application's perspective, the definition and execution of global transactions is done through the use of the ATMI interface or its X/Open counterpart. These allow for the definition of transaction boundaries and for the involvement in the same transaction of any number of application servers. Internally, the coordination of global transactions is provided by specialised processes, the transaction manager servers. This method frees the application servers from the task of participating in the two-phase commit protocol, thus providing for better performance. To allow additional flexibility, autotransactions can be defined as well as non transactional properties for certain service requests.

6. Administration

To build a complete application environment, programming is not the only aspect that needs to be considered. In fact, and in many senses more importantly, setup and administration are crucial activities as well, since the effectiveness of all application components largely depends on them. In a distributed environment, where the components could be different software packages, databases, printers, and various other types of peripherals, the setup and administration of the application requires a number of different administrative actions, probably independent of one another. If the environment includes TUXEDO, a set of TUXEDO-related operations will also have to be carried out.

The administration of a TUXEDO-based application involves essentially two different types of activities, typically identified as *system programming* (configuration) and *day-to-day administration*. These activities have a significant impact on the effectiveness of the application, and require a clear understanding of both the application's and TUXEDO's architecture. The role of a TUXEDO system programmer and/or administrator can therefore be a delicate one, and it must be realised that someone with sufficient expertise should be involved early in the the design of the application's architecture, even before the actual programming begins.

Having said that, the actual process of configuring and administering a TUXEDO application is quite straightforward, and with the help of the administrative tools provided by the standard TUXEDO software or by other vendors, it can be made reasonably simple and automatic. Especially for the day-to-day administration, it is usually possible to prepare a set of administrative procedures which can be invoked automatically at the occurrence of certain events so that, even in complex and high-availability applications, the human intervention can be significantly reduced.

In this chapter we will examine both activities. Configuration, though, is specific and you might want to skip it if you are not particularly interested in the actual contents of a TUXEDO configuration file.

6.1 Configuration

In all TUXEDO environments, an application is described in a configuration file traditionally called the user bulletin board configuration (UBBCONFIG). The system programmer, who is in fact the owner of the application, will typically prepare this file once before the application is started for the first time, and then will add or tune some parameters at a later stage. The UBBCONFIG is an ASCII file divided into a number of sections, each defining the characteristics of certain components of the application. Apart from one, which must be the first in the UBBCONFIG, all sections can appear in any order, and some of them can be omitted if the corresponding information is not relevant for a given application.

Although separate, these sections have a logical correspondence, as presented in Figure 67. The figure should be read as follows: each application has general characteristics and specific resource requirements, valid for the whole environment (RESOURCES); within the limits imposed by these characteristics, each application is typically made up of a number of machines (MACHINES), each of them having network characteristics (NETWORK) and hosting groups of servers (GROUPS); each group is made up of servers (SERVERS), which in turn are made up of services, possibly the same for all servers (SERVICES); finally, services can be associated to specific routing criteria, which determine to which group or machine a request for a certain service will be sent (ROUTING).

Note that no information is specified about clients. Clients are not associated with any specific machine or server, and don't have to be configured. Each client will dynamically register itself in the Bulletin Board when it joins the application (i.e. when it executes tpinit()).

Without examining the actual syntax of this file (an example is provided in Appendix A; system programmers will find all necessary information in the relevant product's handbooks), let's have a look at the content of the various sections.

6.1.1 RESOURCES

This is the section which must appear first in the UBBCONFIG, and which is used to provide general information for the whole application. An example is provided in Figure 68. In this section, you must specify identification

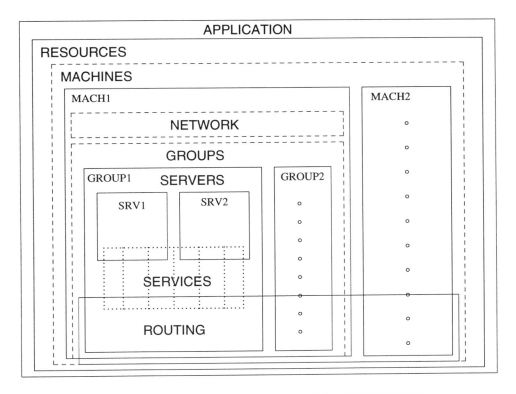

Figure 67. Logical representation of the UBBCONFIG

information for the application, the access permissions for the internal TUXEDO resources, the machine which will perform the master functionalities (master and backup master are discussed later in this chapter), and a number of other general parameters. These include the level of security, the handling method for unsolicited notification, the application timeouts for message send or receive, and the frequency of sanity checks. Quite importantly, the definition of the maximum numbers of processes allowed in the application, the maximum number of services, and the maximum number of global transactions active at the same time are also specified here. These last parameters determine the size of the internal structures of TUXEDO's name server (the Bulletin Board), and the number of resources needed at the operating system's kernel level (hence the name of the section).

This example includes a master and a backup master, server migration, and load balancing. If parameters are omitted, default values are provided.

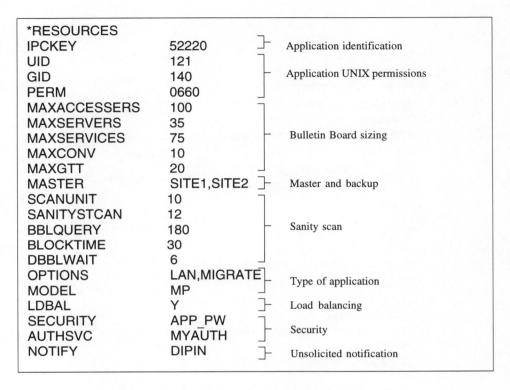

Figure 68. Example of a RESOURCES section

Although defined here for the whole application, some of these parameters can be redefined on a per-machine basis, in order to tune the usage of resources on different systems more effectively.

6.1.2 MACHINES

This section describes all the System/T machines involved in the application (also called *nodes*). Workstations and PCs, which only perform client functionalities and do not have System/T on board, are not described in this section or elsewhere in the configuration file. Similarly to the native clients, they register themselves dynamically once they establish a connection with a System/T machine.

An example of the MACHINES section is provided in Figure 69. The information for each machine includes a logical machine identifier. This

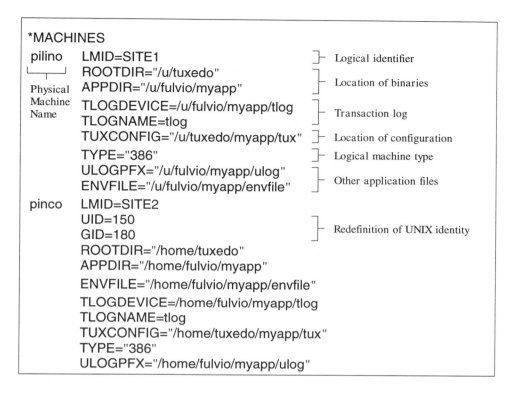

Figure 69. Example of a MACHINES section

allows us to identify the machine unequivocally, regardless of its physical name, since this might change if the machine were replaced or if there is not a consistent representation across different systems. Other parameters provide information about the location of the TUXEDO executables on that particular machine, the location of the application, and the location of various other files, including the transaction log and the configuration file. For the latter, the value of this parameter specifies where the file will be propagated by TUXEDO once the application is started. While TUXEDO and the application must be installed on every machine in advance, the configuration file and the Bulletin Board are propagated to all machines at startup time, so that all machines receive the latest information.

In addition, the maximum number of processes and transactions can be redefined if the values specified in the RESOURCE section are not suitable for one particular machine. As a result, less or more kernel resources might be required, and the size of the Bulletin Board will vary accordingly. This is the typical case when the network of System/T machines comprises both small and large systems, where the resource occupation has different impact on the performance and efficiency of each individual system.

Finally, a particular parameter is used to identify the type of the machine (TYPE). This is an arbitrary definition, for example "386" can be used to represent all Intel 386™ and 486™ machines, and is used by TUXEDO to determine whether message encoding and decoding is necessary between two machines (because of different data representation). In practice, if two machines have different TYPE, TUXEDO will perform encoding and decoding. This is done using the external data representation from Sun Microsystems, the so-called XDR™ interface.

6.1.3 NETWORK

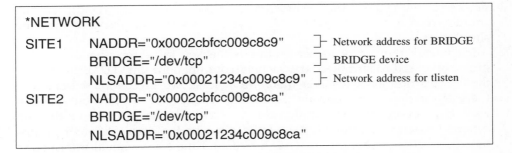

Figure 70. Example of a NETWORK section

This section describes the network characteristics of all System/T nodes involved in the application, and therefore there will usually be as many entries in this section as in the MACHINES section. An example is provided in Figure 70. The parameters specified here are the network addresses of two specific TUXEDO processes needed on the machine, the BRIDGE and the Network Listener. If the networking implementation on the machine requires the network device to be specified (e.g. TLI), this is also provided here (e.g. /dev/tcp). The specification of network addresses allows the TUXEDO application to be booted on all machines from a central machine (the master), and also allows non master machines to connect and exchange messages with other non master machines.

Because, in a network with more than a few systems, it would be extremely inefficient and expensive to establish connections among all machines at boot time, TUXEDO implements a *lazy connection* scheme. In this scheme machines initially connect only to the master node. Each machine establishes connections with the other machines when the first message needs to be sent. This reduces the boot time, and typically also the overall number of network connections open at any time, since usually not all the machines have to exchange messages with all the others.

6.1.4 GROUP

In a TUXEDO application, servers do not exist as individual entities, but rather belong to a group. The existence of groups gives the possibility to define a set of common characteristics for the servers, such as the machine on which they run, which type of resource they access, and which transactional information is related to the resource they access. In addition, it gives the possibility to perform easier runtime administration on the servers, for example the migration from one machine to another (where all processes with the same characteristics have to be migrated), or the shutdown of a resource (where all servers accessing the resource must be shutdown).

In general, the use of server groups is the key to performing distributed processing and distributed transaction coordination. In TUXEDO terms, there is distribution whenever there are at least two groups of servers, and there is distributed transaction processing whenever a transaction spans at least two server groups. Groups don't necassarily have to be located on different machines, although this would often be the case. Different groups in a transaction access different resources, and the transactional information associated to each group gives TUXEDO the possibility of coordinating different resources within the same transaction.

Although it is possible to have only one server in a group, if it really has unique characteristics, each TUXEDO application will be normally made up of several groups, each of them having several servers (possibly multiple instances of the same program). The GROUP section is used to provide information about the common characteristics of the application servers belonging to a certain group. As shown in Figure 71, these characteristics include the location (i.e. on which machine the group is located), the alternate location (in case of migration), the transaction manager server which will be used to handle transactions involving the group, and, finally, the information each server must use in order to open or close the resource accessed by the group (if this is XA-compliant).

Perhaps a little surprisingly, an entry for a group does not provide information about which servers belong to it. This is because different instances of the same server might belong to different groups, and therefore it is left to each instance of a server to indicate to which group it belongs.

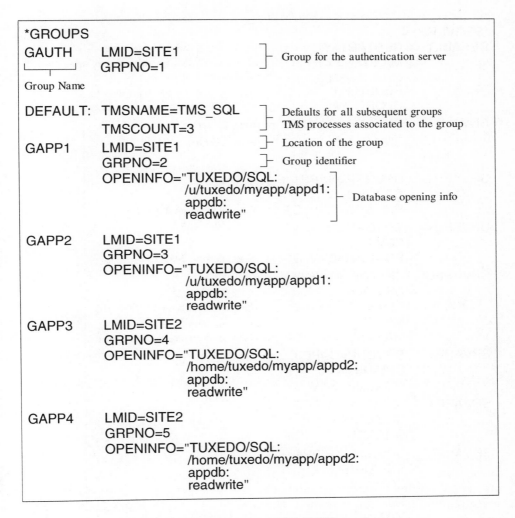

Figure 71. Example of GROUPS section

6.1.5 SERVERS

In this section are listed all application servers. An example is shown in Figure 72. Each server entry defines the server name (the name of the corresponding executable program), the group to which the server belongs, and whether it supports conversations or not. Multiple instances of the same servers must be repeated, unless they all belong to the same group, in which

151

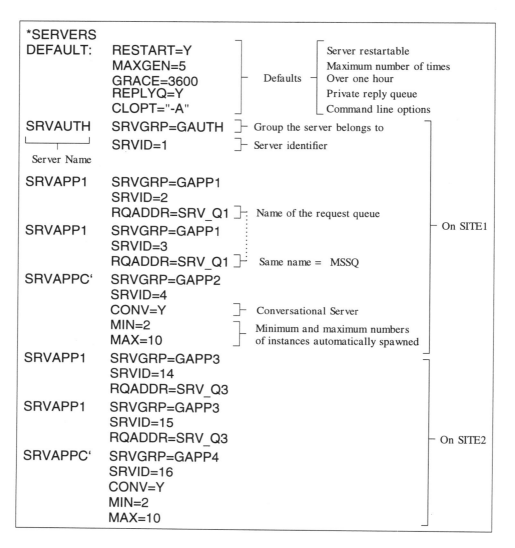

Figure 72. Example of SERVERS section

case it is possible to specify a single entry and a multiplication factor. Each server must be assigned, explicitly or implicitly, a unique numeric ID to identify it among a set of the same servers in the same group. Startup options instruct the server about what services it must advertise and what files it must use as standard output and standard error. Other options are available, including application options which are passed to the server to personalise its startup and services execution.

Other parameters are used to assign a logical name to the server's request queue, and to create a private reply queue. The logical name for the request queue allows the definition of multiple server single queues by defining the same logical queue name for more than one server (see Chapter 4 for a discussion about MSSQ).

As with groups, server entries do not specify which services are advertised by the server. Again, this is because the same service could be advertised by more than one server in more than one group, and therefore it is left to each individual service to specify which group it is associated with. The association of a server to a group means that the servers in the same group will use the same properties for such service.

6.1.6 SERVICES

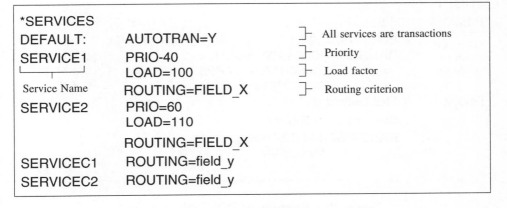

Figure 73. Example of SERVICES section

This section describes all possible services in the application. An example is shown in Figure 73. The parameters corresponding to a service entry include the service name, the server's routine name corresponding to the service (the same service could be excuted by different routines in different servers), and the group in which the service is advertised. If a service must be advertised in more than one group (for example, when there are multiple databases and the same services must be available for all databases, say service DEPOSIT), then multiple entries for the same service may be specified with a different group association, so that different parameters can be provided.

On the contrary, if a service must be advertised with the same properties by all servers, one single entry for the service is sufficient.

Other parameters for the service include its priority, its load factor (see Chapter 4 for a discussion about these), and specification of autotransactional properties (see Chapter 5). As discussed earlier, load factors and priorities can be different for the same service in different groups. This applies for instance to the case where the same service is offered on two different machines, one slower than the other, in which case the load factor should be different.

Finally, a special parameter is the routing criterion used to route requests to the service. In order to guarantee consistent routing among groups, all entries for the same service must specify the same routing criterion.

6.1.7 ROUTING

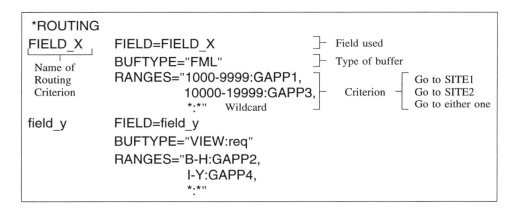

Figure 74. Example of ROUTING section

This section describes the routing criteria for data-dependent routing (see Chapter 4). An example is provided in Figure 74. Entries describe individual routing criteria, which usually define which field in the request buffer must be used, and which are the associations between data values and groups. Fields can be FML fields or view elements, and restrictions can be set on the types of buffers for which a certain criterion applies.

When defining the ranges, numeric or alphanumeric values can be specified, as well a "wild cards" (the asterisk). The use of a wild card in the ranges means that any field value not matching one of the defined ranges will fall in a general category, and that requests with such values will be routed to a specified group. In turn, if the specified group is a wild card, the request will be routed to the first available group, if there is one available. If no wild cards are specified, and a value falls outside the specified ranges, an error will be communicated to the requester.

6.1.8 Configuration tools

The UBBCONFIG is an editable ASCII file. For efficiency reasons, the TUXEDO software reads configuration information from a more compact binary file, traditionally called the tuxconfig. In order to create a binary tuxconfig from the UBBCONFIG, the system programmer will use tmloadcf(1). This command provides a few options, including one which gives the chance to calculate how many kernel resources are needed for booting the application described in the particular configuration. This helps with the tuning of the operating system's kernel before the application is started.

From an existing tuxconfig, the system programmer can create an editable UBBCONFIG through the use of tmunloadcf(1). This can be done if the initial UBBCONFIG is lost (every administrator knows that these things can happen), but also for re-creating a UBBCONFIG that includes those parameters which were not esplicitl specified in the initial one; for these tmunloadcf(1) extracts the default values.

6.2 Day-to-day administration

The day-to-day administration of a TUXEDO application typically starts after the application clients and servers have been developed (at least an initial subset of them), the configuration file has been prepared, and a binary copy of the configuration has been produced through the use of tmloadcf(1). At this point the application is ready to be booted, and the booting can be considered the first act of application administration.

In fact there is also a small number of preliminary actions to be carried out, but because these occur only once before the application is started for the first time, they can be considered separately. Apart from such preliminary actions, the administration of a TUXEDO application can be divided in the following set of operations:

- Boot and shutdown

- Information display

- Dynamic modifications

- Dynamic reconfiguration.

The combination of these operations allows the administrator to make sure that either the application is working as expected, or that it can be repristined or enhanced to the desired level of effectiveness. These operations are normally carried out from a unique point of administration (which, at least initially, is the application master machine), and are performed through the use of a set of administrative tools. Without examining the actual use of these tools (TUXEDO administrators will find all necessary information in the relevant product's handbooks), let us have a look at the functionality of these tools and at the types of operations that can be performed.

In addition to the actions performed by the administrator, certain portions of the applications can be set up or configured in a way that some degree of automatic administration is possible. These are also presented at the end of this section.

6.2.1 Preliminary actions

Before an application can be started for the first time, there are a few TUXEDO-related preliminary actions to be carried out. Of course TUXEDO-related actions might not be the only ones, for instance a database might have to be installed, activated, tuned, and populated, but for our purposes all actions outside the scope of TUXEDO's administration will not be considered here.

First of all, a copy of the TUXEDO binaries must be installed on each machine, in the directory specified in the MACHINES section of the UBBCONFIG. Equally, a copy of the application, or at least the necessary portion of it (typically the application servers which must be booted on that machine, the relevant field tables and view tables, and the various types of native application clients, if there are any) has to be installed in the directory specified in the UBBCONFIG. If the network comprises different types of machines, the administrator will have to make sure that a suitable version of the TUXEDO binaries and of the application are installed. In the case of different resources, the application servers and the TMSs will have to be those linked with the correct libraries. The way TUXEDO and the application can be installed is not really a matter for discussion here, as it very much depends on how packaging and distribution are handled.

Second, if the application is expected to use TUXEDO's transactional capabilities, the administrator must reserve on all the machines a portion of disk necessary to host the transaction log (this portion of disk has a

TUXEDO-defined structure and is called, in TUXEDO terms, the *device list*). On the master machine the administrator must not only reserve such space, but also explicitly create the transaction log. On the other machines, the latter operation is automatically performed by the boot sequence when the machine is first connected to the TUXEDO application. The creation of the device list, and, on the master, of the transaction log, is performed through the use of *tmadmin(1)*, the main TUXEDO administrative tool. This can be used for these initial operations and for other operations which will be examined later.

Finally, the administrator must start on all the machines a TUXEDO listener process (the tlisten(1)), which is used by the master machine to connect to all other machines during the application startup. The network address used by the tlisten on a certain machine must be the same as the one specified in the corresponding entry in the NETWORK section of the UBBCONFIG. The activation of the tlisten is usually included in the init procedures of the machine startup, so that every time the machine is physically booted, the tlisten becomes immediately available. Once these operations are completed, the true day-to-day administration can effectively begin.

6.2.2 Boot/shutdown

Unlike other software environments, for example RDBMSs, the startup of a TUXEDO environment can be slightly more complex than just starting the proper TUXEDO software on all the machines. If the startup of a DBMS consists of initialising shared memory structures and putting the database on line, i.e. actions related only to the system, the startup of TUXEDO includes also the startup of those application components under the direct control of TUXEDO, i.e. the application servers.

Whilst the application clients start when the user executes them, the servers must be made available beforehand, since they are resources provided by the TUXEDO environment, regardless of the individual users. Therefore, starting a TUXEDO application requires booting the proper TUXEDO processes as well as the application servers, perhaps not all of them at the same time. In a simple case where all servers must be started, the action of booting the application can be particularly straightforward, but in other cases the administrator might have to decide which servers or which machines will have to be booted and in what order.

The administrator, working on the TUXEDO master machine, can start the application using command *tmboot(1)*. This command can only be run on the MASTER machine, which is the only one at that point which has all necessary information, i.e. the binary version of the configuration file. It

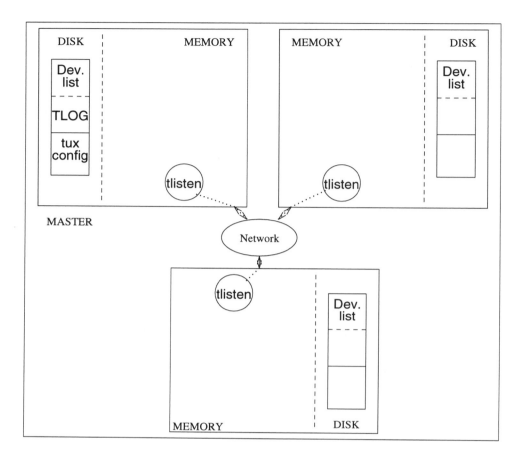

Figure 75. Before boot

accepts a number of options to perform a complete or partial boot of the application. These options give the possibility to indicate which machines, groups, and servers must be initially started. From the information provided in the command line, and the information contained in the tuxconfig, tmboot first starts TUXEDO's administrative processes on all indicated machines, and then all necessary application servers on such machines. This command is typically used in command line form, although there exist graphical tools, based on tmboot, capable to provide a more intuitive handling of the startup procedures.

The execution of tmboot results in the configuration file and the Bulletin Board to be propagated to all indicated machines, and in the activation of all necessary administrative and applicative processes. Errors in the booting of certain components are communicated as error messages as well as recorded in the user log file.

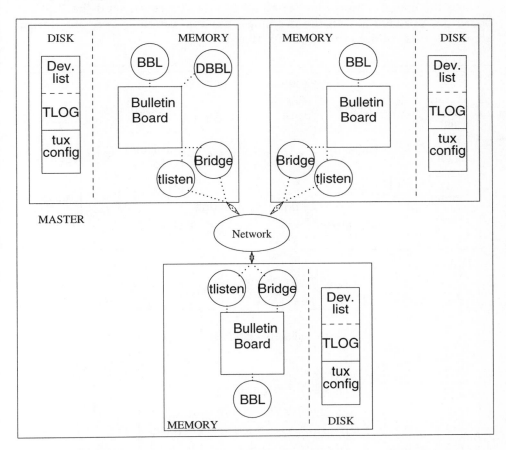

Figure 76. Step 1: Start the TUXEDO software and propagate information

The complete boot sequence is presented in Figures 75, 76, and 77. From a situation where all preliminary actions have been performed on all machines (Figure 75), tmboot first starts the administrative processes on the master machine (DBBL, BBL, and BRIDGE), then propagates the configuration file to the other machines, creates the transaction logs (if necessary), and starts the administrative processes on the remote machines (Figure 76). These operations are carried out by remote commands executed through the use of the tlisten, which in turn uses a remote TUXEDO agent provided with the TUXEDO software (the *TAGENT*). When the remote BBLs start, they synchronise with the DBBL and receive a copy of the Bulletin Board.

Once the configuration file, the administrative processes, and the Bulletin Board are available on all the machines, the application servers are started according to a configurable sequence (Figure 77).

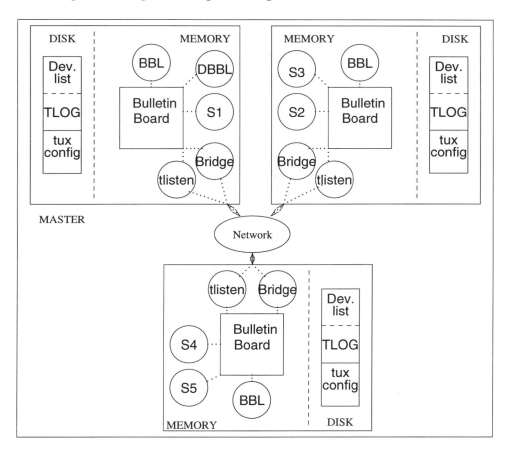

Figure 77. Step 2: Start the application servers

Apart from the initial startup of the application, tmboot can be used at any other moment for booting components of the application that had not been booted yet. This can be done without having to stop the active components. Once a steady situation is achieved, boot scripts can be prepared for easier administration.

Command *tmshutdown(1)* is used with the opposite effect, to stop the entire application or portions of it. The administrative processes on one machine cannot be stopped if there are application servers running on such a machine. A complete shutdown automatically stops all servers and all administrative processes on all machines. As with booting, stopping one machine or one server can be done while the others are still available and executing their work.

6.2.3 Information display

Once the startup operations have been completed and the application is running, the administrator must be able to get information about the application components, to be able to decide whether some action is needed.

The display of information about a TUXEDO application is provided by tmadmin(1). Invoked in "browsing" mode, this tool gives the possibility of gathering information about all the components on all machines. Although it is usually used on the machine where the administrator is working, tmadmin can be executed on any machine of the network, and, for browsing purposes, there can be multiple instances running on different machines. The possibility to run it anywhere gives the possibility to prepare automatic scripts which can be executed as a result of certain events, so that, for example, recovery actions can be initiated automatically by any machine detecting a fault.

This tool works like a shell and puts the administrator in a command mode, with a set of commands available. Typically such commands allow the administrator to get information about clients (name, location), servers (location, group, availability, work done), services (location, status, work done), net (connected machines, partitioned machines, network traffic), and about the active transactions, general application parameters, statistics, etc. Some examples are presented in Figure 78. Various options are also available to restrict the scope to a particular machine, server, service, and to set verbose or non verbose output.

Given the fact that the standard tmadmin is available with a command-line interface, its use might prove in certain cases a little unfriendly. However, there are alternative implementations in the market which provide better interfaces in order to make the extraction of information easier and more straightforward.

6.2.4 Dynamic administration

In response to certain events, for instance the failure of one of the machines

161

Print information about all clients on machine SITE1

> pclt -m SITE1

LMID	User Name	Client Name	Time	Status	Bgn/Cmmt/Abrt
SITE1	fulvio	teller	3:10:22	IDLE	35/34/1
SITE1	kathryn	teller	1:22:38	IDLE	12/12/0

Print information about servers in group BANK2

> psr -g BANK2

a.out Name	Queue Name	Grp Name	ID	RqDone	Load Done	Current Service
TRANSFER	Q-TRAN	BANK2	1	30	2700	TRAN
ACCOUNT	Q-ACC-1	BANK2	5	16	940	DEP
ACCOUNT	Q-ACC-2	BANK2	6	19	970	(IDLE)
INQUIRY	Q-INQ	BANK2	11	155	1550	(IDLE)
INQUIRY	Q-INQ	BANK2	12	155	1550	BAL

Print information about services in group BANK2

> psc -g BANK2

Service Name	Routine Name	a.out Name	Grp Name	ID	Machine	# Done	Status
TRAN	TRAN	TRANSFER	BANK2	1	SITE2	30	AVAIL
DEP	DEP	ACCOUNT	BANK2	5	SITE2	10	AVAIL
DEP	DEP	ACCOUNT	BANK2	6	SITE2	7	AVAIL
WITHD	WITHD	ACCOUNT	BANK2	13	SITE2	6	AVAIL
WITHD	WITHD	ACCOUNT	BANK2	14	SITE2	12	AVAIL
BAL	BAL	INQUIRY	BANK2	21	SITE2	94	AVAIL
BAL	BAL	INQUIRY	BANK2	22	SITE2	95	AVAIL
ACCNO	ACCNO	INQUIRY	BANK2	29	SITE2	61	AVAIL
ACCNO	ACCNO	INQUIRY	BANK2	30	SITE2	60	AVAIL

Figure 78. Examples of use of tmadmin in browsing mode

in the network, the administrator might need to intervene and either execute recovery actions, or change the characteristics of certain components of the application. In other cases, such as peak hours, the administrator might have to tune the number of available servers in order to respond more effectively to a higher number of service requests. In general, the administrator, or an automatic script executing administrative procedures, will, at times, have to modify something in the applicative environment.

Modifications can be applied through the use of tmadmin(1) in its more extended capabilities. Again, this can be done on any of the machines in the network. Contrary to what is possible for the display of information, however, the possibility of modifying the application environment is restricted to one invocation of tmadmin at a time, i.e. tmadmin in browsing mode can be invoked from multiple locations at the same time, whilst in active mode it can only be invoked fron one location at a time. This is a safe approach, as it prevents people from executing conflicting operations at the same time. The existence of an active instance of tmadmin does not prevent the invocation of one or more instances of tmadmin in browsing mode.

Change load factor for service WITHD in server ACCOUNT

> chl -g BANK2 -i 5 -s WITHD 80
> chl -g BANK2 -i 6 -s WITHD 80

Clean processes on machine SITE1

> bbclean SITE1

Boot one more instance of server ACCOUNT

> boot -g BANK2 -i 7

Suspend service ACCNO in all servers reading from queue Q-INQ

> susp -q Q-INQ -s ACCNO

Figure 79. Examples of use of tmadmin for dynamic administration

Examples of dynamic administrative actions are shown in Figure 79. The actions that can be performed include: pure administrative functions such as the change of the application password; tuning operations such as the modification of timeouts, priorities and load factors; clean-up operations such as the removal of dead processes or restart of dead servers; boot or shutdown operations on administrative and application processes; and, finally, suspension/resumption and advertisement/unadvertisement of services. Operations related to specific cases of recovery are the activation of the backup master and the migration of application servers. These are discussed later in Sections 6.2.6 and 6.2.7.

During the execution of dynamic administration procedures, the components of the application not affected can keep on executing without alteration and without having to be stopped. For example, if the master machine has become unavailable, the other machines in the network and all the services can carry on with their work while the backup master is being activated. Similarly, if a service offered by a server is unadvertised, the server itself can continue executing other services without having to be stopped first.

All the types of modifications mentioned above are registered and propagated to all Bulletin Boards on all machines, so that they take immediate effect. However they are valid only until the application is active. If the application is shut down completely (i.e. all Bulletin Boards are removed), a successive boot will reinstate the situation described in the configuration file. The only way to make the changes permanent is to invoke a dynamic reconfiguration procedure along with, or as an alternative to, the dynamic changes.

6.2.5 Dynamic reconfiguration

During the lifetime of the application, it is likely that at various points modifications will have to be made to the configuration, either for recording changes performed in the Bulletin Board (for example, a new priority for a service), or for adding components which were not initially present (for example, a new machine or a new server). In order to be permanent, these changes have to be recorded in the binary configuration file, the tuxconfig.

The simplest way to modify the tuxconfig is to stop the application, change the UBBCONFIG (the order of these two actions is not important), rebuild the tuxconfig (after the application was stopped), then restart the application.

Although this can be done during scheduled maintenance intervals, the need to stop the application might not sometimes be the best option, for example in those environments where continuous availability must be provided, or in large configurations where the restart of the whole application on all machines would be too long a process.

In these cases, it is possible to reconfigure the application dynamically without having to stop the entire application. If the changes are additions of servers or machines, the current application doesn't have to be stopped at all, since the old components are not directly affected. If the changes are modifications to existing entries, the components corresponding to such entries will typically have to be temporarily stopped. A certain number of parameters, those which have an impact on the size of the Bulletin Board (maximum number of accessers and routing criteria) cannot be dynamically reconfigured and a full shutdown of the application is required.

To perform dynamic reconfiguration, TUXEDO makes available a tool called *tmconfig(1)*, also accessible from within tmadmin via the config command. This tool, through a simple (and not particularly nice) interface, allows the administrator to retrieve entries in the tuxconfig, change parameters, and record the changes back in the tuxconfig. In a network configuration, the changes are propagated automatically to all tuxconfig files on all machines, and in the unlikely event that the propagation fails on one machine, a warning will be printed (this usually implies more serious problems, probably requiring a stop and reboot of the machine involved; in this case an updated tuxconfig will be re-sent anyway). If necessary, the administrator can create a UBBCONFIG from the new tuxconfig through the use of tmunloadcf, to keep track of the changes.

The modifications made to the tuxconfig do not immediately affect the Bulletin Board. However, after the modifications are made and the modified components are activated or reactivated, the modifications become available in the Bulletin Board as well. For example, after a new machine is added, the machine can be started immediately and at that point the relevant entries in the Bulletin Board will be updated. The same applies to servers, services, etc. Once a server is started, or a service is advertised, the newly modified/added parameters will be picked up in the Bulletin Board.

6.2.6 Backup master

Among the various administrative actions that can be performed through the use of tmadmin(1), there are some that can usually be of special interest and particular importance for the good functioning of the application. One of these is the possibility of activating a backup master machine, should the master fail.

In TUXEDO terms, the master machine is the machine from which the application is started and on which, at runtime, a particular administrative process, the DBBL (see Chapter 3), performs a sequence of actions. These are mainly aimed at verifying that all other machines are still running, and guaranteeing that they are still receiving all necessary information.

Contrary to what might seem immediately intuitive, the TUXEDO master machine doesn't necessarily have to be a machine where application functionality is provided, for example the database and related application servers. It might be so if this makes the overall administration easier, but, as far as TUXEDO is concerned, it might just as well be a small machine sitting on the desk of the administrator, within easy reach. The purpose of this machine, in TUXEDO terms, is simply to boot/shutdown the application and to host the DBBL.

Whichever the machine, during the lifetime of the application there might be cases when it becomes unavailable, either because it must undergo scheduled maintenance, or because the machine itself or the network fail thus disconnecting it from the rest of the application. When such conditions occur, the rest of the application is still running, but the possibility of detecting failures and performing administrative actions is severely limited. In the end, the application would run with some degradation and might eventually fail completely.

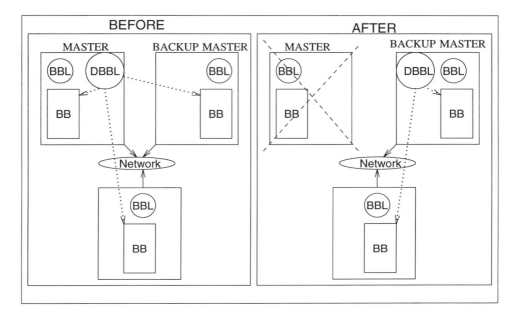

Figure 80. Migration in case of failure of the master machine

To avoid this, it is possible to configure a backup master machine in the UBBCONFIG. Like the master, this machine could either be a dedicated machine, possibly idle for most of the time, or one of the other machines, probably in the vicinity of the administrator. The reason why it should be in the vicinity of the administrator is a pure practical one (easy access), and it could be any other machine with System/T on board. A PC or workstations running only System/WS cannot be a backup master.

When it becomes necessary, the administrator or an automatic script on his/her behalf can run tmadmin on the backup master and execute a particular command to migrate the master functionality. This migration (Figure 80) consists of stopping the DBBL on the old master (assuming this is still available), and starting a new DBBL on the backup master. The latter

166

becomes the acting master. The new DBBL synchronises with the other machines and carries on working as usual. Apart from some rare circumstances, the switch from master to backup master and viceversa, if this is deemed preferable after the initial master is again available, will pass unnoticed to the users and to the application processes.

6.2.7 Server migration

Another administrative action which can add a degree of flexibility to the good functioning of the application is the migration of application servers.

As we have seen in the section dedicated to configuration, a group of servers is normally associated to one particular machine, meaning that all servers belonging to it run on the specified machine. In the event that the machine becomes unavailable, either because of a failure of the machine itself or a failure of the network, the servers belonging to all the groups resident on that machine become unreachable. At that point it is not possible to route service requests to any of them until the machine is back on the network.

Although safe from the application perspective (requests will either fail because services are unavailable, or will be routed to other machines, if possible), the loss of application servers will almost certainly have an impact on the effectiveness of the application and possibly on its performance.

In order to reduce the impact of the loss of a machine, it is possible to configure the groups of servers in such a way that they can be hosted on an alternate machine. Of course this might not be possible in all cases, but if another machine can offer the same functionality, then server migration can become an easy way to restore both functionality and performance in a very short time. For example, if a group of servers handles print requests, these can be migrated to another machine where another printer is available, thus maintaining the print services available to the application.

Cases which involve databases are usually a bit more difficult to handle, because server migration might not be of any use if the database is not migrated too. However, in environments which require high application availability and various degrees of fault tolerance, the same data are usually made available to different machines through the use of shared disks or disk mirroring, and therefore server migration can provide significant benefits in such environments. An example of this is presented in Figure 81, where two machines share the same disk. Before the problem with one of the machines occurs, the two server groups, possibly providing different services, are located on different machines. After one of the machines becomes unavailable, the server group resident on it is migrated to the other machine. This change is registered in the Bulletin Board, and therefore

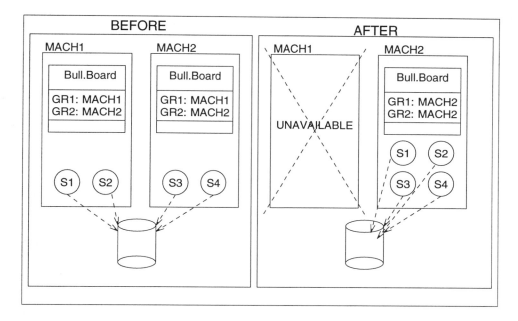

Figure 81. Server migration: data still available

requests for those servers are subsequently routed to the new machine.

In fact, even in cases where data are no longer available, server migration can still be useful. An example of this is presented in Figure 82. After the migration, instead of executing the request, migrated servers could simply store the requests in permanent queues, for later execution when the original machine is restored. This cannot be taken as a granted alternative, since simply enqueuing requests might not always be possible, but in various circumstances it could offer a viable alternative. It must be noted, however, that the switch between executing the service and storing the requests requires some additional programming in the application servers. TUXEDO does not provide this feature automatically, since, of course, it is strictly application dependent. Servers will explicitly have to take the decision to either execute the service or enqueue the request depending on whether they are running on the primary or the alternate machine.

Servers migration can be performed centrally by the administrator through the use of tmadmin(1) or by a script on his/her behalf, regardless of the actual location of the two machines involved. By executing a specific sequence of commands, the groups on the unavailable machine can be started on the alternate one. If all groups can be migrated to the same alternate machine, as would often be the case, the administrator can migrate

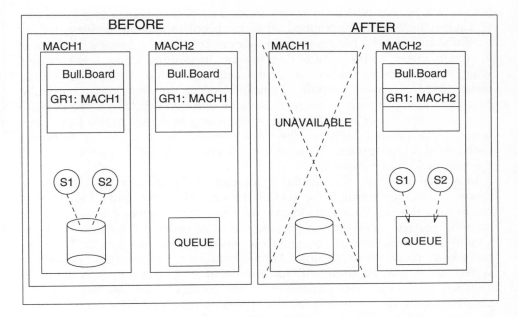

Figure 82. Server migration: data not available

all of them in one single command.

When server migration is executed, servers are started on the alternate machine but the content of the memory queues on the unavailable machine are not accessible any longer. The requester will be informed, via timeouts, that the request cannot be executed, but it will be its task to retry the request if the application logic requires so (i.e. TUXEDO cannot re-create the contents of memory queues on the alternate machine). The important thing to note, though, is that the migration occurs while the rest of the application is running, and in many cases could even pass unnoticed. Moreover, because it is TUXEDO's task to handle the routing of service requests, an application client which retries a request (or an internal process on its behalf, see System/Q in Chapter 7) will not notice that the request is now being routed to another machine.

6.2.8 Automatic server restart

During the lifetime of an application, it might sometime happen that certain servers terminate abnormally. This is typically due to hidden errors in the application. Under certain conditions these errors cause the process to die (e.g. a bad pointer which causes a core dump), and in these cases the server will normally have to be stopped while the problem is being investigated.

Whilst this is not a big problem in a development environment, the loss of a server might cause severe degradation in a production environment, where services might need to be continuously available. Moreover, because these hidden errors would typically occur under very particular circumstances, probably in unpredictable or untested conditions, the services offered by the server would execute without any problems most of the other times. The unavailability of the server might be a waste of resources because, although potentially faulty, the server could still execute correctly the vast majority of requests.

In a case like this, the administrator can explicitly take the decision to restart the server through the use of the administrative tools. However, it might take time to the administrator to notice that a server has died, so the manual restart could prove impractical. In order to help with these situations, it is possible to configure the servers in such a way that TUXEDO can restart them automatically if certain conditions are verified. Automatic server restart can be used without additional programming; it is simply a question of setting a few parameters in the configuration file. Basically, it is possible to specify, for each server, if it is restartable and how many times it can be restarted within a specified interval of time.

This gives the possibility to decide in advance what is the acceptable level of stability for a server. If, for example, one knows that a certain server receives on average 20,000 requests a day (statistics can be obtained through the use of the administrative tools), then it could be acceptable to have it die twice a day, but perhaps not ten times. Therefore, the parameters for the server restart could be set to, say, five times per day. This means that TUXEDO will automatically restart the server up to five times in the same day and will ignore the restart from the sixth time onwards. The administrator will not be involved in this, and from the sixth time the server will be effectively off-line. In many cases this makes it possible for the server to be available for as long as possible while the problem is being investigated.

Automatic server restart is a feature mainly provided by the BBL. When a server dies, its entry in the Bulletin Board is still available because the server did not have the chance to perform the proper exit sequence. The BBL checks at regular intervals the availability of local servers by reading the entries in the Bulletin Board and sending a signal to the process. If the process is not alive, the BBL reads in the corresponding entry whether the process is restartable, how many times, and what is the executable program corresponding to it. If all conditions are satisfied, it starts a new process. This new server, through the information still available in the Bulletin Board, impersonates the old one and inherits information about the queue from which the dead process was reading (this too is still available, because, being an object separate from the processes, it doesn't get destroyed if the process attached to it dies). It then starts serving the requests which were still in the queue, if any. The one request which was being executed at the time of the failure is not resumed, and the requester is (or it has already been) informed about the failure through the expiry of timeouts. If the server cannot be restarted, the BBL tries to re-route the outstanding requests to another equivalent server, if one exists, or sends a failure message to the requesters.

In relation to automatic restart, each server can be associated with a personalised restart procedure. This is typically a shell script or a program executed by the BBL every time the server is restarted. A simple use for this is the display of a message on the console and the writing of a record on a printer, to warn the administrator that the server had to be restarted because of some errors. Personalised restart procedures are invoked but not provided by the BBL, which by default simply logs a message in the application log file.

6.2.9 Dynamic service advertisement

In a TUXEDO application, servers are typically made up of a number of services, automatically advertised by the server itself when it starts up. The advertisement is done by reserving an entry in the Bulletin Board for each one of the services. At that point all processes become aware of these services and requests can be sent to the server.

A server would usually advertise all its services, but, at certain times, it might be necessary to make some of them unavailable. This could happen, for example, if the business requires certain services to be offered only during working hours. Control over the services offered by a server can be obtained in different ways, and this makes the overall administration more flexible and efficient.

Firstly, in the configuration file it is possible to specify for each server which services must be advertised at startup time. By default it would be all of them, but a list can be specified instead. This allows control over the services which have to be advertised whenever the server starts, and those which are optional.

Secondly, the administrator is allowed at any time to advertise/unadvertise services dynamically during the execution of the application. This can be done through the administrative tools, which allow to advertise/unadvertise a service across the whole application or within an individual server. If a service is unadvertised, its entry in the Bulletin Board is removed so that new requests are not be routed to the server. The function itself is still available in the server, which means that the requests already in the queue can still be served.

Thirdly, the server itself can be programmed in such a way that it can advertise/unadvertise services dynamically at the occurrence of certain events. This is possible through the use of two ATMI functions, *tpadvertise()* and *tpunadvertise()*. These functions can be used from within any of the services, and have an effect on all the services offered by the server in which they reside or on all the servers in the same MSSQ.

A typical use for these functions is to automatically advertise/unadvertise services at certain times during the day. For example, if the service for loan authorisation has to be enabled only during working hours when a supervisor is available, the service can be programmed in a way that it checks for the time at every request, and if the time is past 5.30 pm, it automatically unadvertises itself. This is an alternative to the administrator running a procedure at 5.30 pm to unadvertise all such services.

Another possible use is when a service detects error conditions that would prevent other services from working. For example, if a service for bank deposits detects a write error on the database, it might notify the administrator through unsolicited messages, unadvertise itself, and unadvertise also the service for withdrawals, which might suffer the same problem. It might on the contrary leave service for enquiries available, as it might still be able to perform read operations. This behaviour allows for a more timely handling of error conditions. In the example, this could help prevent further corruption of the database, as unadvertisement could occur even if the administrator was not immediately available for a manual unadvertisement. Moreover, the unadvertisement would affect only one particular server and not, for instance, the same server on another machine where the database has no problems and deposits and withdrawals can still be executed.

The programming of these functions is usually straightforward, since they require only the service name as a parameter. If a server attempts to advertise a service already advertised, or to unadvertise a service already unadvertised, the request is simply ignored by TUXEDO.

6.3 Summary

In this chapter we examined the concept of administration of a TUXEDO application. Administrative tasks can be split into two separate categories: configuration (system programming) and day-to-day administration. Configuration consists of the preparation and maintenance of the configuration file for the application. This activity has a significant influence on the good functioning of the entire environment. The configuration file describes all the components of the application, but not the application clients, which register themselves dynamically.

Apart from the setup of the configuration, some preliminary actions must usually be carried out before starting the application, but once these have been executed, the day-to-day administration is mainly made up of the use of an administrative tool that provides centralised administration over the entire application. Such a tool can be used on any machine in the network, either in browsing mode or in active mode. In the latter case, however, only one instance can be active at any one time to avoid the execution of conflicting operations. Through the use of such a tool, the application administrator can gather information about the various components of the application, and perform corrective or tuning actions while the application is running.

Some corrective actions relate to the migration of specific functionalities, typically that of the master machine, or of application servers. Dynamic additions are also possible, and, through the use of another tool, dynamic reconfiguration can be performed while the application is running. The system can be configured so that it performs a certain number of administrative actions automatically, for example the restart of application servers. Programming functions are also provided to the application services in order to advertise or unadvertise services automatically in response to specific events.

7. Extensions

The features presented in the previous chapters are provided by the core component of TUXEDO, System/T, which is mainly available on UNIX and UNIX-like systems as the basis for different types of distributed applications, transactional or not. This might be sufficient in some environments, but the role of an open OLTP monitor is not completely fulfilled if it does not allow the integration of systems as well.

If we look at the general characteristics of enterprise computing, there are three tiers of computer systems to take into consideration. These are shown in Figure 83. Personal computers and/or workstations are available for the individual user and provide the vast majority of desktop facilities. Minicomputers are available at departmental level and provide a set of locally shared facilities like printing services, disk space, different applications, and local data. Mainframes are available at enterprise level and provide access to corporate data. The integration of these three levels in a single distributed application is more complicated than that of different UNIX systems, especially because of the lack of standards. At the same time, is a very strict requirement for many companies, which find this tiered approach effective and either do not wish to abandon it for a number of specific reasons, or cannot afford to to do it because of the investments already made in all three tiers.

In order to provide a viable UNIX solution to enterprise computing, an open OLTP monitor must provide the possibility to integrate the other components into the same application environment. In a TUXEDO environment, this is mainly achieved through the use of two extensions, which can be used in addition to System/T to make TUXEDO's features available to non UNIX systems. These extensions normally go under the name of System/WS and System/HOST, although certain TUXEDO suppliers, depending upon the requirements of a particular environment, or

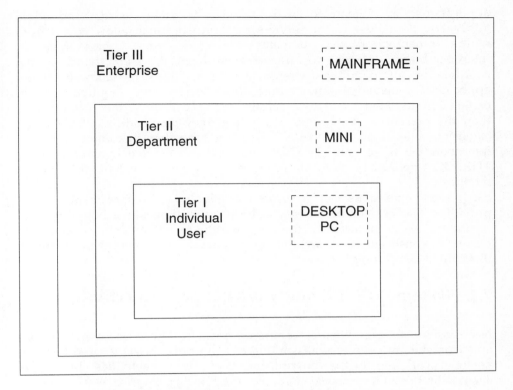

Figure 83. The three tiers of enterprise computing

upon their proprietary OLTP product offering, will sometimes package these components with System/T under a single name. In general, all TUXEDO suppliers make information available about the actual composition of their product.

Besides the features offered for broadening the scope of System/T towards enterprise computing, OLTP environments may require additional features with respect to those offered by System/T, in particular batch processing facilities and alternative queuing mechanisms for services or transactions. Because these features are useful only in the context of specific environments, they are provided outside the scope of System/T as an extension called *System/Q*. This is a subsystem that allows the implementation and administration of recoverable disk queues.

Finally, beyond the scope of today's enterprise computing, a new approach to Open OLTP requires that not only different systems and resources are integrated within a single application, but that entire applications are integrated with others. In other words, individual applicative domains and the services they provide must allow access from within other applicative domains and vice versa. Such type of interoperability extends to transactional control, and therefore the coordination of distributed transactions must also be allowed across applicative domains. Again, because these features are required only in certain environments, and to a certain degree constitute the future rather than the present of distributed computing, they are made available as an extension called *System/DOMAINS*. This is a subsystem that allows both the interoperation of separate TUXEDO applications, and the interoperation of TUXEDO applications with applications under the control of different TP monitors.

All these extensions can be used individually or in combination, thus providing TUXEDO environments with several options and a high degree of flexibility. More importantly, they provide the set of capabilities needed to create a consistent software platform suitable for present and future distributed computing.

7.1 System /WS: PC and workstation connectivity

Needless to say, the types of computers most widely used today are PCs and workstations. In a typical working environment, these are used both for personal work and for the accomplishment of business activities. In a travel agent's branch, for example, PCs are used for back-office work such as preparing travel arrangements for customers, and for front-office operations such as flight bookings or timetable enquiries. Whichever the case, the commodity of a desktop PC is something desirable and more and more companies are improving productivity by providing their employees with them.

Apart from the fact that PCs are already there, there are multiple reasons why PC connectivity might be desirable or necessary, both economical and practical; companies who deploy new applications or migrate old applications want to use the most convenient options in terms of hardware and software; companies who use UNIX applications separate from PC applications increasingly need to give PC users access to the UNIX services; PCs have better graphical interfaces and therefore allow the development of more appealing front-ends; PCs make use of their own CPU for the processing associated to screen handling, so the presence of a high number of users does not affect the performance of the server system in this respect; the full power of the system can be used for the execution of the application services.

In general, wherever PCs are available to employees, there is a strong requirement that the employees are given the chance to execute all necessary operations from them. This is valid for most types of environments, including OLTP ones. Although the use of PCs is not the typical scenario in traditional OLTP, where ASCII terminals are still the most widely used type of input/output devices, the presence of PCs in such environments is becoming at least part of most evolution plans, and is certainly a factor to be taken into consideration.

When PCs are used in conjunction with UNIX environments there are usually two possibilities in terms of connectivity; PCs are used either as emulators of native UNIX terminals, or as individual machines in a network, probably a local area network (LAN), or, more rarely, a wide area network (WAN). In the case of emulation of a native UNIX terminal, a PC behaves exactly like a native terminal, in the sense that it corresponds to a UNIX process running on the CPU and in the memory of the UNIX server. In a TUXEDO environment, this means that the process can directly access the structures provided by System/T on the UNIX machine, i.e. it can directly become an application client. Because of this, no special connectivity features are needed from the TUXEDO point of view.

In the case of distributed computing, on the contrary, the PC does not correspond to a UNIX process and does not share resources with the UNIX server, in particular it doesn't share the memory. A program or process running on the PC cannot access the structures provided by System/T and as such cannot directly become an application client. This is the functionality provided by System/WS (or, in short, /WS). This extension provides application connectivity for PCs and workstations which do not or cannot have direct access to System/T[11] (Figure 84).

Because the function of a PC user corresponds, in TUXEDO's philosophy, to that of a client, System/WS allows a user to execute on the PC an application program equivalent to a native System/T application client. In this framework, PCs are not used to provide services to the rest of the environment, so it must be noted that System/WS does not allow the execution of application servers on PCs. Except for a small number of cases, this is not a limitation since the functionality of a PC is, in the vast majority of environments, that of a client machine.

Being the equivalent of native System/T application clients, PC clients can use the same programming interface as the native ones (ATMI functions and

---

11. In practical terms, this includes the case of UNIX systems that only require client connectivity for users. In this case, each UNIX user is considered as a separate WS client. To keep the language easy, though, we will assume that a /WS client is a PC user, since this is the most intuitive approach.

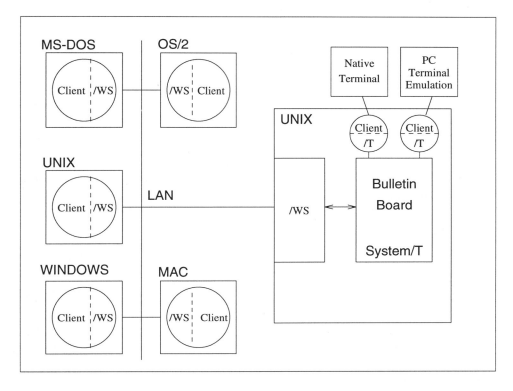

Figure 84. Native and PC clients in a TUXEDO environment

buffers, or their X/Open counterpart), thus guaranteeing maximum portability between environments. System/WS is made up of ATMI libraries for PCs or workstations (MS-DOS, MS-WINDOWS, OS/2, Apple Macintosh, and, of course, UNIX), and of specific processes activated on System/T machines. These processes provide, on behalf of the PCs, the appropriate links with System/T's internal structures and with the rest of the application components.

7.1.1 Usage

Because the purpose of System/WS is to re-create on a PC the same functionality as for native System/T users, its use doesn't have to be more complicated than that of System/T for native clients. In fact, TUXEDO's API is exactly the same for System/T and System/WS and so is the functionality. PC clients join the application via tpinit(), make service requests via tpcall(), establish connections via tpconnect(), start and terminate transactions via tpbegin()/tpcommit(), send and receive unsolicited messages, and so on.

The differences in implementation are completely transparent to the application. This also means that the TUXEDO code for a native client doesn't have to be modified in order for it to run as a PC client, and viceversa. This doesn't imply that any native clients will run unmodified as a PC client, but that the modifications are not related to TUXEDO. The extent to which a native client would have to be modified depends very much on the PC environment, the type of user interface, and possibly on the development tools used. If, for example, a 4GL tool is used to create screens, these probably won't need modifications on a PC supporting the same 4GL, and a simple recompilation/relink should be sufficient. If specific UNIX interfaces are used, such as curses(3), then the migration to a non UNIX PC could involve the change of the interface in its entirety. Other differences might be due to the use of 16 bit operating systems, typically in the representation of numeric variables. While TUXEDO makes up for the differences as far as TUXEDO calls are concerned, other portions of the client might have to be adapted as well.

In any cases, these considerations do not directly affect the functionality of /WS. Equally, the same tools for building native clients are available for building PC clients, so not only is the TUXEDO programming the same, but so is the environment for creating clients. These tools use the recommended type of C or COBOL compiler for the specific environment, and typically require only specific command-line options. Finally, tools are also available for creating and using FML or VIEW buffers in the same fashion as the native environment.

The only real difference in the usage of a native client relates to a couple of administrative actions, since special processes must be configured and started on the UNIX server for supporting the PCs. The configuration involves the addition of one or more entries for the workstation listener (WSL) in the SERVERS section of the UBBCONFIG. This server program handles connection requests from PCs and sets up the environment for handling the messages generated by the PCs. The workstation listener needs some parameters, in particular the network address for receiving connection requests from the PCs, and the number of internal processes which will have to be started for multiplexing the PCs (the workstation handlers). On the PC side, an environmental variable must be set before the client is started to provide the network address of one of the available workstation listeners. Such a variable can contain a list of network addresses, so that the connection procedure will have alternative possibilities should the connection with the first address be impossible. Finally, again in the configuration file, the maximum allowable number of workstation clients must be specified. This can either be the same for all machines, or a different one for each machine that may have PC clients attached.

In terms of networking, the /WS libraries are linked on the top of the TUXEDO network library. This is usually based on sockets implementations of TCP/IP, and therefore any such type of networking can be used. Typical networking packages include Novell's LAN Workplace® and FTP's PC/TCP®. Through the use of products like SLIP®, RS232 connectivity can also be used. One thing to note is that network packages on PCs, especially on MS-DOS, do not usually follow any specific standards, so not all TCP/IP packages will work. We must make sure that the /WS libraries are linked with the same TCP/IP package installed on the PC. This situation is unusual on UNIX PCs, for which standard TLI or sockets TCP implementations are available, and is getting better on MS-WINDOWS and OS/2, where the existance of pseudo-standards like WINSOCK, and the use of dynamically linked libraries (DLLs), make the use of different networking packages more straightforward.

7.1.2 Implementation

While the usage is virtually the same as the native environment, the implementation of /WS clients is very different, since, basically, it has to cope with a network in between the client and the Bulletin Board. The concept behind the implementation of /WS is quite straightforward; because the PC isn't able to attach directly to the Bulletin Board, it must make use of some entity that has got such ability and that can perform operations on its behalf. This entity is the workstation handler (WSH), which runs on System/T machine. The WSH receives messages from the PC, performs the operation requested via information found in the message or in the Bulletin Board, and forwards to the PC any messages generated in response to the operation requested. An example of how this is implemented is presented in Figure 85. When the PC invokes a service, the code of tpcall() on the PC forwards the request to the WSH (1). The WSH accesses the Bulletin Board, performs all necessary operations like load balancing and data-dependent routing, and then sends the request on behalf of the PC (2). When the service is finished, the server sends the reply to the WSH (3), which then forwards it to the PC client (4).

The workstation handlers are special types of clients which impersonate PC clients on System/T machines. Such processes are created automatically by the workstation listener, depending on some configuration parameters. Typically, each WSL creates at boot time a configurable number of WSHs, where each one is allowed to handle up to a configurable number of PCs

1) tpcall() on PC forwards request to WSH

2) WSH makes the call on behalf of the client

3) Server replies to the WSH

4) WSH forwards reply to the PC client

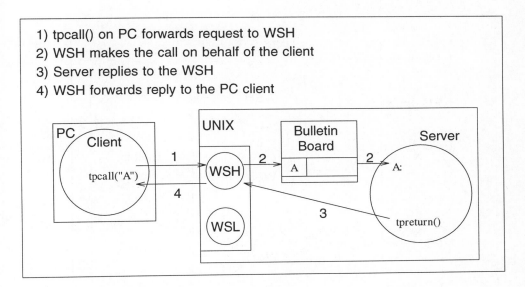

Figure 85. Implementation of tpcall() through /WS

(Figure 86).

Because each WSH usually handles tens of PCs, PC connectivity is beneficial for the UNIX server in terms of occupied IPC resources. Unlike the instance of native clients, where each client uses its own IPC resources, PC clients share the IPC resources of the WSH to which they are connected, thus reducing the overall amount of IPC resources on the server.

Each PC is assigned to a WSH by the WSL at the time when it joins the application. The procedure under which a PC is put in communication with a WSH is presented in Figure 87; when executing tpinit(), the PC reads the address of the WSL and establishes a connection with it (1); the WSL chooses one of the available WSHs, the one which has the fewest connections at that moment, then acknowledges the request and provides the PC with the address of such WSH (2); from that moment on, the PC communicates directly with the WSH, using a new private address (3).

While there usually are some workstation handlers on each System/T machine, the number of workstation listeners per machine is typically one. This is because a connection request is a rare action in comparison to the requests for services, etc., for which multiple simultaneous requests are likely to arrive at any time. If it is expected that many PCs might request the connection at the same time, multiple instances of the WSL can be configured, so that connection requests can be handled better. Equally, if there are multiple networks connected to the same machine, one or more

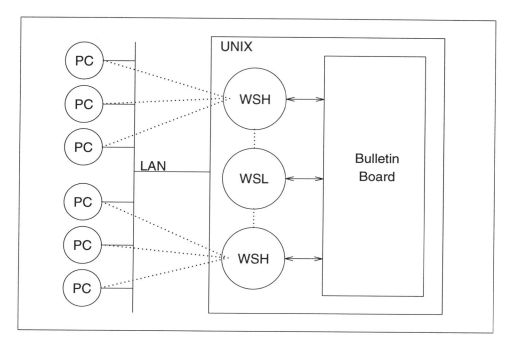

Figure 86. Workstation listener and workstation handlers

WSL can be configured per each LAN.

Once the connection has been established and a PC is assigned to a WSH, all operations go via the WSH. The WSH, handling multiple PCs, keeps a context for each of them, and, depending on the PC involved in a certain message, it impersonates it and updates information regarding it. This involves requests, expected replies, conversations, timeouts, transactions, etc. It must be noted, though, that if the connection drops and cannot be recovered by the underlying network software, the PC client must explicitly reconnect to the application, i.e. dropped connections are not automatically re-established. After a reconnection, the PC client is assigned a new context.

7.1.3 Relationship with System/T

Since System/WS is used in connection with System/T, the operations performed by PC clients make use of System/T features. Following is a summary of how the features presented for System/T are implemented in relation to the use of PC clients.

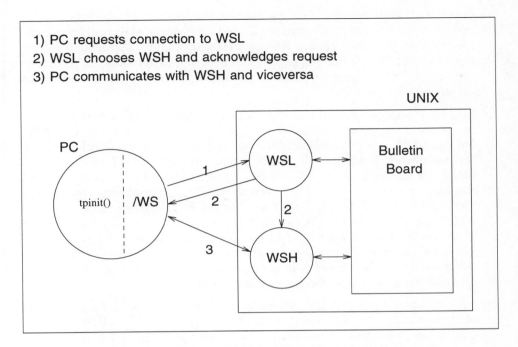

1) PC requests connection to WSL
2) WSL chooses WSH and acknowledges request
3) PC communicates with WSH and viceversa

Figure 87. Connection procedure for /WS clients

- *Joining the application*: When the PC client executes tpinit(), a connection with a WSH is established in the way described in the previous section. During this process, an entry for the client is allocated in the Bulletin Board, which makes the client appear as if it was effectively attached to it. Because of this, the client's identity becomes known to the application servers and to the administrative functions. Allocating one entry, though, means that there must be sufficient room in the Bulletin Board for it. Should all entries be used, the WSH will attempt to use an entry from those configured for native clients before reporting a failure.

- *Buffer allocation*: PC clients allocate buffers directly on the PC, and use them for requests and responses. The WSH is not involved in the allocation, since this is an action local to the client. However, when messages are sent and received, it will internally allocate/reallocate buffers in order to be able to store the messages to and from the PC. Field-ids and VIEW descriptions can be made available to the PC client through the use of tools equivalent to those for the UNIX side, so buffer allocation can include FMLs and VIEWs. The WSH must have on the UNIX machine the same field-ids and/or the same VIEWS, if data-dependent routing must be performed on behalf of the client. All necessary environmental variables used to access the files must be specified in the environment file for the WSL. If new application buffer types are added to the buffer type switch, the WSH must be relinked with such buffer types in order to be able to handle them on behalf of the client.

- *RPC-like paradigm*: As already mentioned, when the PC client makes a service call, the code of tpacall() will simply pass the request to the WSH on the UNIX machine. The WSH acts a surrogate client, and, through the use of the native tpacall(), looks into the Bulletin Board and performs the various necessary operations (load balancing, data-dependent routing, message send, etc.). When the PC client reads the reply, tpgetrply() reads the reply buffer local to the PC, a sort of reply queue in which the WSH will have forwarded any messages it received as a result of the request made on behalf of the client. On the server's side, when tpreturn() is called, a message is sent to the WSH, which was the actual client as far as the server was concerned. It is then the WSH's task to forward the message to the appropriate client.

- *Conversational paradigm*: Like in the case of RPC-like calls, the execution of tpconnect() on the PC passes the request to the WSH, which establishes a connection with the server and passes back the connection descriptor to the client. During a conversation, the code of tpsend() passes the message to the WSH, which sends the message to the server. When the client attempts to receive a message, the code of tprecv() reads a message from the local message queue, or waits if there isn't one. If the client executes a tpdiscon(), the code of tpdiscon() sends a message to the WSH so that this operation is performed on its behalf.

- *Load balancing*: This is performed automatically by the WSH when it executes the call on behalf of the PC, so the implementation is not different from that of native clients. Another type of load balancing is performed by the WSL, which assigns a connection to the WSH which has the fewest, thus balancing the number of connections among WSHs.

- *Prioritisation*: The assignment of the priority for the request is done by the WSH when it executes the call on behalf of the PC, so, again, the implementation is the same as that of native clients. If the client uses tpsprio() to change the priority of a request, the code of tpacall() on the PC passes this information to the WSH, which makes the request using the specified priority.

- *Data-dependent routing*: This is performed automatically by the WSH when it executes the call on behalf of the PC, so in this case the implementation is the same as that of native clients. However, as mentioned before, the same field-ids and/or VIEWS as those used by the PC must be available on the machine where the WSH resides for the routing to be possible.

- *Unsolicited notification*: A PC client can set its own message-handling function, and, via the direct or indirect use of tpchkunsol(), can receive and handle unsolicited messages like native clients. When an unsolicited message is directed to a PC client, this is forwarded to the WSH, which, in turn, sends the message to the PC. Unlike native clients, PC clients cannot receive signals and therefore the only method for receiving unsolicited messages is through the use of the ATMI.

- *Server migration*: WSLs and WHSs cannot be easily migrated as a result of a machine crash or similar. This is because they are associated to a certain machine address, and unless the alternate machine can take over the network address of the one which became unavailable, the migration is impossible. In order to handle these cases of machine failure, an alternative approach usually consists of keeping standby WSLs and WSHs on another machine, and to specify multiple addresses for the PCs to connect to. If the connection with one machine drops, a new tpinit() will try to connect to the alternate addresses.

- *Security*: Apart from the establishment of a connection with a WSH, the operations performed by tpinit() for a PC client are the same as those for native clients. These include the verification of the password and of other authentication information provided in the TPINIT buffer. When a password and other authentication information are required, the TPINIT buffer is encrypted by the /WS software before sending it over the network, so that its content cannot be intercepted. If the client is assigned an application key for authorisation purposes, this is stored in the client's code and is passed along with all requests the PC client makes, thus allowing the use of authorisation functions in the services. If encryption routines are added to the buffer handling procedures, these must be made available to the PC and to the WSHs.

- *Transactions*: PC clients can initiate and terminate transactions like native clients. When tpbegin() is executed, the code of tpbegin() on the PC sends a message to the WSH. This initiates a global transaction on behalf of the client by allocating a corresponding entry in the Bulletin Board. All subsequent operations requested are in transaction mode, and, as such, are handled by the various processes as if they originated from a System/T process. When the PC client commits or aborts a transaction, the code of tpcommit() or tpabort() passes the request to the WSH, which executes the operation on their behalf. Any action which provokes the transaction to be aborted is communicated to the PC client in the same fashion, so that all interested ATMI function returns the proper error status codes to the application. If the communication between the PC and the WSH drops before a commit or abort is requested, the transaction will be aborted because of timeouts, and, when the PC client reconnects, it will have to reissue the request (unless stored requests were used - see System/Q). If the communication between the PC and the WSH drops after the commit or abort request was submitted but before the result is sent to the PC, when the PC client reconnects it must to enquiry the resources to find out the result of the transaction. The same applies if the connection drops after the PC requested an autotransactional service, but before the reply arrives.

7.2 System/HOST: mainframe connectivity

The advent of powerful minicomputers and workstations has generated in recent years a new approach to computing, and a large number of companies, software vendors, computer manufacturers, etc., have gradually modelled their product offerings more and more around distributed architectures and distributed environments. Many companies have adopted such architectures as the basis of their business and use products like TUXEDO to enhance the environment and to prepare the ground for future evolutions in a consistent environment. Among these companies, some may have been users of mainframe systems at one point in the past, but, with the advent of minicomputers, they have switched to more flexible environments, perhaps to proprietary systems first, and then more towards UNIX-based systems. In such companies the use of mainframes has lasted only for as long as the technology did not provide viable alternatives, and the investments made in these systems have been gradually superseded by investments in more open systems until the complete removal of mainframes from their computer base occurred.

Continuing this trend, which seems at this point irreversible, a significant number of businesses are now looking at TUXEDO as one of the possibilities for undertaking the change. Among these, a certain percentage is looking at a complete replacement of the mainframe environment with a set of different systems, probably existing ones plus new ones. In this case they are prepared to make investments into re-engineering applications, and into having a fresh new start with an eye on openness, interoperability, vendor independence, etc. TUXEDO is an appealing product in these cases, since it specifically addresses these requirements.

However, this approach is quite drastic; once the decision to change is made, the replacement of the mainframe environment is carried out in a single step, as this is less troublesome than trying to mix the old and the new. Unfortunately, an even higher percentage of companies cannot afford this drastic approach, either because it would be too expensive in one go, or because the timeframes would not be suitable. Such companies have the choice to stick to the present environment until times are more suitable, but, if pushed by the business conditions, they try to undertake a gradual migration. In order to help with this type of migration, TUXEDO makes available System/HOST, a component that gives the possibility to access, from within a TUXEDO-based application, services, and programs resident on mainframe systems (hosts).

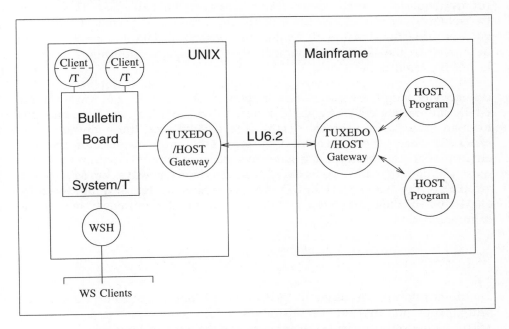

Figure 88. Schematic representation of System/HOST

As shown in Figure 88, mainframe connectivity is provided by gateway processes resident both on the UNIX and on the mainframe side. The gateways on the UNIX side perform essentially two actions: they advertise the services offered by the host, so that the application can request such services as if they were offered by native System/T application servers, and convert the data passed into the format suitable for the programs on the host. On the mainframe side, TUXEDO's gateways adapt TUXEDO's request/reponse protocol to the mainframe's own mechanism.

Through the use of System/HOST, a staggered migration can be achieved.

Initially, for example, only the front-end programs can be moved to UNIX or PC systems in the form of application clients, while all back-end programs are still resident on the mainframe. When this is in place, the TUXEDO software routes client's requests to the /HOST gateways, and through them it delivers the reply to the clients. As a second step, when time and resources allow, part of the data and part of the back-end programs can be moved away from the mainframe onto a UNIX server system, and application servers can be developed instead of the old programs. At that point the migrated services are no longer advertised by the gateways, but by the new application servers. Accordingly, TUXEDO routes requests to such servers rather than to the gateways. This occurs transparently, so that the initial investment in the development of the front-ends is protected. Finally, all remaining portions of data and programs can be moved to the UNIX environment, thus freeing the application from the use of the mainframe.

Of course mainframes are not all the same, and different types of connectivity might be necessary. In general TUXEDO's gateways on the UNIX side are based on the CPIC interface for accessing host environments over an SNA LU6.2 protocol. TUXEDO's gateways on the mainframe side cannot be very general, because they must take into consideration the host environment. In practice, such gateways exist for certain environments, the most popular of which being MVS/CICS. While gateways for MVS/CICS are part of the "vanilla" TUXEDO product, others are typically produced by OEMs when they integrate TUXEDO with their proprietary mainframe solutions.

7.2.1 Usage

The description of the usage of System/HOST can be split into three areas: setup, programming, and administration.

The setup of the /HOST extension can be straightforward, as it only encompasses a small set of administrative actions on the UNIX and mainframe side; however, it requires familiarity with both types of environments. On the UNIX side, gateways must be added to the UBBCONFIG, one instance or more depending on the expected traffic. Each gateway must be provided with the list of the services it must advertise, and with an environment file which defines the information necessary to connect to the host environment. In the case of CICS, for example, information include a CICS application identifier, LU6.2 configuration parameters, maximum size of the exchanged data, and a correspondance table between the advertised service names and the CICS programs, if these are not the same.

On the mainframe side, the TUXEDO gateways must be installed and configured as part of the environment. In the case of MVS/CICS, for example, VSAM datasets must be allocated, VSAM files must be created, and, finally, CICS resources must be defined and initialised. This is typically carried out once and for all by the system programmer.

The programming of a TUXEDO application that integrates mainframe programs is also quite straightforward, but, depending on the applicative environment on the mainframe, it must take care of certain possible differences between such environments and UNIX. On the UNIX side, the application can request host services using tpcall() or tpacall() just as if they were on the UNIX system, which means, that not only can the ATMI functions be used with the same syntax, but also that TUXEDO buffer types can be used. The TUXEDO gateways translate such buffers from ASCII to EBCDIC and viceversa, but, inevitably, certain rules apply. In particular, an FML buffer must contain a field stating the name of a VIEW into which it can be converted, since the concept of FML will probably not exist on the mainframe. The UNIX gateway must be provided with VIEW files which describe this correspondence, so that they can convert requests that use FML buffers backwards and forward. Also, for types of data like packed decimals, which do not typically exist on UNIX systems, a special data type is made available by TUXEDO so that the application clients can make use of it if the mainframe programs do.

On the mainframe side, the TUXEDO gateway provides the communication of service requests and data to the appropriate program. The way in which the program gets data in input and returns data to the gateway depends largely on the environment, and modifications to existing programs may be necessary in order to be able to integrate with TUXEDO. In the case of CICS programs, for example, all programs which can directly be invoked must link to a TUXEDO-provided program for getting the input (TGETBUF), and, at the end of the execution, must return data and control to the TUXEDO gateway via an XCTL to another TUXEDO-provided program (TRETURN). This specific behaviour is shown in Figure 89; when the request is made, a message is sent to the mainframe via the gateways (1); the host gateway passes the message to a TUXEDO-provided CICS program, which executes a LINK to the requested program (2); the CICS program executes a LINK to program TGETBUF for reading the data (3), and, when it terminates, returns data and control to TRETURN (4); on return, the mainline program passes the data to the host gateway (5), which forwards them to the client via the UNIX gateway (6).

The administration of the gateways and the programs on the mainframe can be done via tmadmin(1). The control over the UNIX gateways occurs via normal commands, as for any other application server. The control over mainframe programs occurs via specific commands, which allow inspecting

189

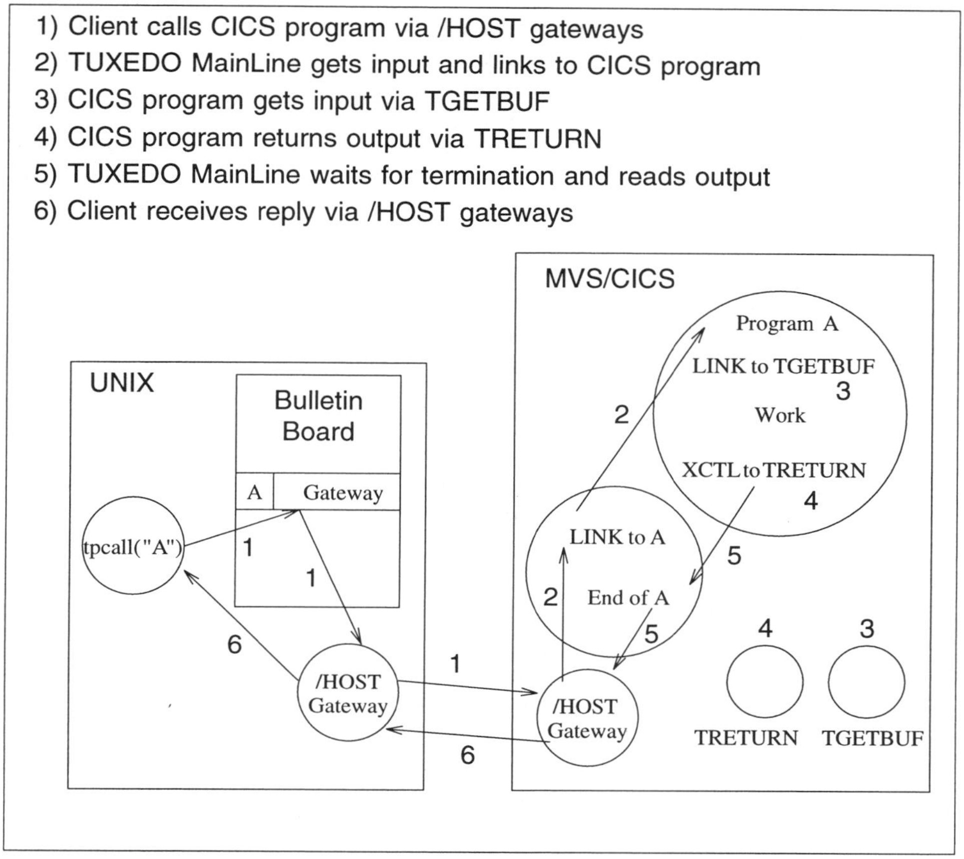
1) Client calls CICS program via /HOST gateways
2) TUXEDO MainLine gets input and links to CICS program
3) CICS program gets input via TGETBUF
4) CICS program returns output via TRETURN
5) TUXEDO MainLine waits for termination and reads output
6) Client receives reply via /HOST gateways
MVS/CICS
Program A
LINK to TGETBUF
3
Work
XCTL to TRETURN
4
2
UNIX
Bulletin Board
A
Gateway
tpcall("A")
1
1
LINK to A
End of A
2
5
5
6
1
/HOST Gateway
/HOST Gateway
6
4
3
TRETURN
TGETBUF

Figure 89. Programming with System/HOST in a CICS environment

the activity of such programs, gathering statistics, and performing reconnections should the connection drop. These specific administrative requests are forwarded to the TUXEDO gateway on the mainframe side. In addition to the administration via tmadmin(1), /HOST usually provides a set of batch utilities for the host environment. In the case of MVS/CICS, for example, these utilities are used to print history records about the calls made from the /T application, to delete history records, and to flush records from temporary storage queues to a history file.

7.2.2 Implementation

As said, the implementation of /HOST is based on the use of gateway processes, both on the UNIX and mainframe sides. On the UNIX side, gateways advertise services as if they were application servers, but on receipt of a request forward it to a gateway counterpart on the mainframe according to a correspondence table provided by the administrator. During the boot phase, gateways establish a connection over the LU6.2, then advertise the necessary services. Multiple instances of the same gateway can exist. These can be put in a MSSQ set, if this helps with the traffic handling. Also, gateways towards different host environments can coexist in the same application. In general, a gateway performs the necessary data conversion, typically from ASCII to EBCDIC, then forwards the message over the LU6.2 connection. In TUXEDO's implementation, access to the LU6.2 is performed through standard CPIC functions. When receiving a reply from the mainframe, the gateways forward the reply to the requester, either directly or via the BRIDGES and workstation handlers.

On the mainframe side, gateways are programs that receive a message and then communicate with another program. Different implementations require different gateway programs. In the case of MVS/CICS, for example, a TUXEDO mainline program, that receives control from the gateway and interprets the request, is also provided. There can be multiple gateway programs on each mainframe, and multiple instances of the mainline program. Such programs also accept administrative requests, for example requests from tmadmin(1) to report statistics on the number of requests. Depending on the implementations, there can be various other auxiliary programs. In the case of MVS/CICS, for example, a couple of programs for creating and deleting a history file are provided, and also an abend handler.

7.2.3 Relationship with System/T

In reference to the features of System/T presented in Chapter 4 and 5, their use in an application involving System/HOST can be summarised as follows:

- *Communication paradigms*: Given the nature and the purpose of the /HOST extension, clients can request the execution of programs in RPC-like form, both synchronous and asynchronous, but cannot establish conversations with a program on the mainframe. The conversational protocol provided by TUXEDO does not match the implementation of message exchange in host programs. Also, the use of conversations would probably require extensive modifications to the existing

191

mainframe program; this would defy the purpose of the integration.

- *Communication buffers*: As already said, TUXEDO's typed buffers can be used by a System/T application which requires services off a mainframe. A packed decimal data type exists as part of VIEWs, so that packed decimal data can be specified and used even if such type of data would not normally be used between System/T processes. The UNIX gateways translate ASCII data into EBCDIC and viceversa, and, if FML buffers are used, convert them into VIEWs. This requires that FML-VIEW correspondence tables are made available to the gateways.

- *Load balancing*: Load balancing applies when requests are sent to the UNIX gateways, if there is more than one. Once the gateway reads the request, it sends a message to the mainframe gateway, but in doing so no specific load balancing applies.

- *Prioritisation*: Again, prioritisation applies to requests sent in the queue of the UNIX gateway. Each gateway reads requests (i.e. propagates requests to the mainframe gateway) in priority order.

- *Data-dependent routing*: This mainly applies when there are multiple groups of gateways communicating with different mainframes. For example, assuming that part of the data is on one mainframe and part on another, data-dependent routing can be transparently used by the TUXEDO software to route a service request to the group of gateways which communicate to the mainframe hosting the associated data to the current request buffer. The same concept applies also in the case where application data is split between UNIX machines and the mainframe, in which case requests can be transparently routed either to a System/T application server or to a gateway.

- *Unsolicited notification*: This feature is not applicable. /HOST programs, like any other application servers, do not receive unsolicited messages, so the gateways do not have to provide any functionality for propagating such messages. Also, existing /HOST programs do not include notification to TUXEDO clients, so support for this functionality is not needed.

- *Dynamic advertisement*: This is not applicable. The UNIX gateway cannot be programmed to advertise/unadvertise mainframe services directly, and mainframes program do not use such a technique. It is possible, though, to advertise/unadvertise mainframe services dynamically through the use of the administrative tools.

- *Server migration*: UNIX gateways can be migrated to other machines, provided that the appropriate environment files are available on the alternate machines. If the migration occurs as a result of the crash of a machine, the requests and replies present in the gateways' queues at the time of the crash are lost (unless System/Q is used). The TUXEDO processes involved in the request will simply be informed of the failure.

* *Security*: For the /HOST extension, security may apply in relation to the opening of the connection between the UNIX and the mainframe gateways, to the propagation of information for service access control, and to the encryption of data between UNIX and the mainframe. Since these depend on the security features implemented in the mainframe environment, none of these areas can be directly addressed by a generic /HOST implementation. Typically, customisations are provided by the various OEMs in relation to the security features provided in each environment.

* *Transactions*: The request of execution of programs on the mainframe under a global transaction demarcation is not possible with the current generic implementation of /HOST. Transactions can be requested as long as they are all carried out on the host, but transactions spanning the UNIX environment and the mainframe environment at the same time are not supported. This is mainly due to the fact that different host environments provide different transaction coordination methods for which there is no standard implementation. Given the nature of migration paths, where data and functionality are usually migrated together, the need for such a feature is not a particularly severe limitation. However, when this is a requirement, implementations of /HOST by individual manufacturers can be customised to allow this type of transaction processing in conjunction with certain mainframe environments. In addition, it is expected that the generic /HOST extension provided by Novell will be enhanced to support global transactions involving MVS/CICS environments.

7.3 System/Q: stored requests

The synchronous and asynchronous request/response paradigms described in Chapter 4 are effective when the operation have to be performed at the time the request is originated, and when the only expected delay, typically short, is determined by the number of other requests already present in the memory queues of the servers. If the execution time of a service is expected to be long, the asynchronous paradigm permits better handling of the waiting time, as it provides for the execution of other operations while the service is being executed. In general, the combination of both mechanisms allows for a fast turnaround of requests and responses. However, these request/response protocols make basically three assumptions: (1) a server can be reached with the request; (2) the server will read and execute the request as soon as possible; (3) failures during this timeframe will cause the request and any associated transaction to fail.

For several OLTP applications, these assumptions might not always be valid or necessary. If, for example, a request is made when the machine where the server resides is unavailable, using the standard request/response mechanisms such request will fail and the client will have to retry later. Also, if the server serves the request but the reply doesn't make it to the client because of some failure, the client will have to decide whether it must submit the request again. In both cases, these problems might prevent the application from satisfying the so-called "exactly once" criteria, for which the request for a transaction must be submitted only once.

Other cases might not always be adequately handled through the submission and execution of a request as soon as it is generated. If, for example, a client submits a very low priority request, or one not particularly urgent, this will still be executed as soon as possible, perhaps delaying the execution of higher priority requests and causing inefficiences, for example, during peak hours. On the contrary, it might be preferable to delay the execution of such a request until night, when there is less traffic. Equally, if an application was used in two different locations, each of them accessing one copy of a database, the synchronisation of both databases would need the use of distributed transaction processing, probably making the performance of the system slower. In fact, it might be preferable to make the cross updates only at the end of the day as a batch procedure, allowing for better efficiency at runtime. Finally, if a transaction included, for example, the transmission of a fax, a simple problem of busy line would make the transaction fail. On the contrary, it might be preferable to complete the transaction by saving the text of the fax and resubmitting it later.

In all these cases, and obviously in several others, the standard request/response mechanism requires additional programming to work around these drawbacks, and in some cases it might prove inadequate altogether. A straightforward handling of such cases is on the contrary provided by *System/Q*. This subsystem gives an application the possibility of storing service requests into permanent queues on disk, by providing a set of processes that read the requests at a later stage,[12] submit them to the appropriate server, and store the results of the operations in a permanent

---

12. The later stage can be any time after the enqueuing stage, be it 2 seconds or 2 days. It can only be qualified in a specific environment or application.

reply queue. The application process which stored the request is then allowed to read the reply at an even later stage, or perhaps simply to forget about the request knowing that this will be executed later.

The emphasis of this implementation is on allowing service requests to be stored in permanent queues instead of being sent immediately to an application server. In doing so, an important aspect is also to make sure that when these are finally submitted, the application servers won't have to do anything special to handle them. They can simply serve them as if they had been requested in that precise moment. In this way the application servers don't have to be modified when used in conjunction with System/Q.

This approach is useful in all the scenarios presented in the previous page. In the case of machine failure, for example, the request can be stored just once into a disk queue; TUXEDO can be left with the task of repeating the submission should the first attempt fail for any reason. In the case of peak usage, requests for low priority services can be stored in the queue and TUXEDO can submit them during the night. In the case of cross-updates, the updates to the local database can be done at runtime, whilst those for the remote database can be enqueued and executed during the night, or at the first suitable chance, should any failure occur in the meantime. Finally, in the case of the transaction involving the transmission of a fax, the request and the text could be saved in a queue and the transmission could be tried and retried by TUXEDO later, as many times as necessary.

System/Q is based on the idea of queue spaces. Queue spaces are resources made available to an application, just like databases (Figure 90). The interface to access such a type of resource is provided by TUXEDO as an extension to the ATMI, and allows for enqueuing and dequeuing messages in such queues. In addition, administrative tools and processes are made available to create and administer the queue space and its queues, and to perform at runtime specific operations such as the submission of one of the requests to an application server.

Because enqueuing and dequeuing must be reliable, queue spaces support the transactional semantic, and transactional control is provided implicitly and explicitly through the use of an XA-compliant implementation. Enqueuing and dequeuing is performed through the use of TUXEDO-provided processes, which initiate global transactions when requests are enqueued, dequeued, or submitted to application servers, and when replies are enqueued back. In its role as a resource manager, System/Q handles queue updates within global transactions, and guarantees commitment or rollback of such operations within the transactional context defined by the application.

The use of queue spaces in an application can also benefit from the set of features generally made available by System/T. Enqueuing can be done in a local or remote queue; priorities or other ordering criteria can be used; in

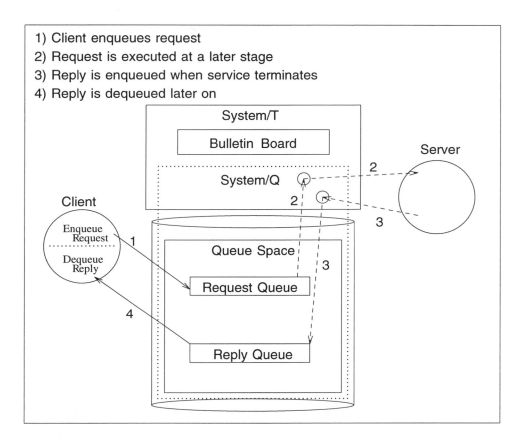

1) Client enqueues request
2) Request is executed at a later stage
3) Reply is enqueued when service terminates
4) Reply is dequeued later on

Figure 90. Schematic representation of the System/Q subsystem

the presence of multiple queue spaces, data-dependent routing is applied; in the presence of multiple enqueuing servers, load balancing is applied. Equally, dequeuing can be done by a combination of different criteria, for example by priority after a certain time; when requests are finally submitted to a server, data-dependent routing and load balancing are applied. Overall, System/Q is a consistent extension of the request/response mechanism, which can be used to make it more suitable to delayed processing, and to increase the availability and the efficiency of an application.

7.3.1 Usage

The use of stored requests (or stored messages, as they would be best described), consists of a mix of administrative actions for setting up and configuring the environment, and the use of a couple of programming functions in conjunction with some TUXEDO-provided server processes.

The main administrative task is related to the definition and creation of queue spaces and queues. *Queue spaces* are portions of disk dedicated to contain message queues; each application can use as many as necessary, although one on each machine is usually sufficient. *Queues* are collections of messages in a queue space, for example all request messages for a certain service, or all error messages generated as a result of requests dequeued from such queue space. Roughly speaking, a queue space could be seen as a database, a queue could be seen as one of the database's tables, and each message could be seen as one of the table's records. Unlike a database, though, this type of resource imposes certain constraints in terms of creation of tables and record layout, since these have to match certain defined structures.

The setup of queue spaces is possible through the use of an administrative tool, *qmadmin(1)*. Like the database tools for creating/administering databases, it allows the application administrator to allocate a certain amount of space on the disk, then to create within it specific queues. The creator of queue spaces and queues must work in close relationship with the application programmers to decide the actual content of the queue space, since the programming will have to take this into account. In general, the main action is to decide what queues belong to a queue space, and what criteria can be used to enqueue messages. Valid criteria are FIFO, LIFO, by priority, by time, at the top of the queue, and also by message identifier, in the sense that the message can be placed ahead of a message with a particular message identifier.

The administrator creates one queue per service, and assigns each queue the same name as the corresponding service (Figure 91). In addition, the administrator can create reply queues to store replies (if necessary), failure queues to store failure messages (if necessary), and, for his/her own benefit, an error queue to store error messages. It must be noted that failures and errors are different concepts in this context. A failure is an unsuccessful return from the requested service (e.g. the service used tpreturn() with flag TPFAIL), and the client will probably be interested in it. An error is the result of a problem with the execution of the service that prevented System/Q from receiving the result (e.g. a timeout due to a network failure). This is not interesting for the client, but is interesting for the administrator who might have to decide whether some actions need to be carried out.

Other aspects that can be taken into consideration include the queue capacity limits, in the sense that it is possibile to establish automatic administration procedures when limits are reached, for example when the queue is 75% full. Another aspect is the number of retries that can be allowed if the submission of the request fails. In this case, it is possible to define the delay after which the next attempt should be made.

Another administrative task consists in the definition, in the application's configuration file (the UBBCONFIG), of the System/Q processes involved in the application (Figure 91).

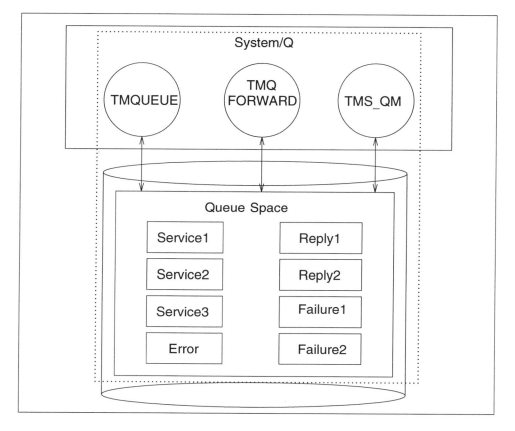

Figure 91. System/Q processes

These include: an enqueuing server (TMQUEUE(5)), transparently used to enqueue requests in the proper queue once the appropriate enqueing function has been invoked by the application; a specific transaction manager server (TMS_QM), used to coordinate global transactions involving the queue space; a request-forwarding server (TMQFORWARD(5)). When this server is added to the configuration, it is transparently used to dequeue requests when they reach the top of the queue, submit such requests to the appropriate application server, wait for the reply, and store the reply and/or possible failure messages in the queues. The use of the forwarding server is by far the most commonly used approach for dequeuing and executing stored requests, although, in certain cases, application servers can be built specifically for this task.

If System/Q is added to an existing application, both the creation of queues and the addition of the above processes can be done dynamically through the use of tmconfig(1). That is, the application doesn't have to be stopped to have System/Q added. New clients will probably have to be used, though, in order to be able to use the functions for enqueuing/dequeuing.

The programming of stored requests is related to the use of two specific ATMI functions, *tpenqueue()* and *tpdequeue()*. Function tpenqueue(), as the name suggests, can be used by an application process to enter a request in the queue associated to the service which will eventually have to be executed. As such, this function is similar to tpacall(), in the sense that it specifies a name where the request must be sent and the data buffer corresponding to the request. Because the data buffer will be sent to an application server, the same buffer types as the ones for tpacall() can be used, i.e. either one of the four default types (ATMI), or one of the three standard ones (XATMI), or any other defined by the application and added to the TUXEDO buffer switch.

A difference with respect to service calls is that a control structure is used to determine exactly the behaviour for the enqueuing of the request and the reply. This structure, shown in Figure 92, is passed as a parameter to the function and is used to define the enqueuing technique, the priority (if necessary), the time at which the request must be entered (if necessary), the name of the reply queue in which the reply will be stored, and the name of the failure queue in which the possible failure message will be stored. The structure also contains a set of return parameters, the most significant of which is a message identifier used to read the reply. A special parameter is an application-defined correlation identifier. This is kept consistent across queues and allows the retrieval of information about a specific request, regardless of the queue in which such information resides (for example, the reply or the failure queue). Upon successful return, the request is guaranteed to be in the appropriate queue, and the message ID corresponding to the enqueued message is made available in the control structure passed as a parameter. If the operation fails, the reason for failure is also available in the control structure.

tpqctl structure		
flags	⊢	Indication of which values are set
deq_time	⊢	Absolute/relative time for dequeuing
priority	⊢	Enqueue priority
diagnostic	⊢	Reason for failure
msgid	⊢	ID of the message before which to queue
corrid	⊢	Correlation ID to identify the message across queues
replyqueue	⊢	Queue name for the reply message
failurequeue	⊢	Queue name for the failure message
clientid	⊢	Client identifier (returned by TUXEDO)
urcode	⊢	Application user-return code
appkey	⊢	Application authentication key for the client

Figure 92. Control structure for enqueuing/dequeuing

An exception occurs when the enqueuing is invoked within a global transaction, in which case the successful return of tpenqueue() does not automatically guarantee that the message is in the queue; the actual presence of the request in the queue is subject to the outcome of the transaction, and the request will actually be removed if the transaction fails. If, for example, a global transaction is made up of runtime updates to a local database and the enqueuing of a request for batch updates to a remote database, failure in the local updates causes the storing of the request to be rolled back.

Function tpdequeue() is used to dequeue messages from one of the available queues, and is typically invoked in two cases: either by the application process which previously enqueued a request, in order to read the corresponding reply message, or by an application server (service, in fact), in order to dequeue a stored request explicitly and perform the desired function. This latter usage is an alternative to the use of the TUXEDO-provided TMQFORWARD server, and requires specific programming of the application servers, for dequeuing the request and enqueuing the reply. Unless really necessary, i.e. unless the simple dequeue-forward-enqueue mechanism provided by TMQFORWARD is not sufficient, this is not the preferred way of implementing application servers because this will make such servers unusable with the other request/response paradigms. On the contrary, the TMQFORWARD server is specifically designed to make it possible to use normal application servers together with the System/Q.

Furthermore, the explicit use of tpdequeue() in a server also requires that transaction control be explicitly provided. For example, a transaction will have to be started before dequeuing the message and committed after the reply has been enqueued, so that a failure in the execution of the service will restore the request in the queue for a later retry. LIke tpenqueue(), tpdequeue() too is passed a control structure. Through this structure, information about the reply queue, failure queue, client identification, client authorisation key (if applicable), and message ID is made available to the process which dequeues the message.

The day-to-day administration is performed through the use of qmadmin(1). Like database administrative tools, qmadmin allows the administrator to browse within the queue spaces or the individual queues, and if necessary to perform changes to the existing configuration, for example enlarging the queue space. In addition, the administrator is also allowed to remove messages from the queues if these are known to be no longer useful, to change parameters for the requests, to inspect the error queue, and to perform active control over pending transactions. In this last case, the administrator can heuristically commit or abort pending transactions to free the involved data structures and administrative processes, with all the troubles that this might imply (see Chapter 5).

7.3.2 Implementation

Enqueuing and dequeuing is not performed directly by the application processes. This would not be a general approach, since the queue space involved might not reside on the same system as the process which wants to execute these actions, for instance a remote PC client. Instead, tpenqueue() and tpdequeue() generate a request for a dedicated System/Q server, TMQUEUE, which executes the operation on their behalf. TMQUEUE servers are similar to normal application servers, except that they only serve requests for entering and extracting messages into System/Q queues, and that they only accept requests generated by those two particular ATMI functions or by the administrative tools. These processes are local to the resource (the queue space), and there can be as many as necessary. The administrator can add new instances if the current ones cannot cope with the amount of enqueuing/dequeuing requests.

Because queue spaces are resources used to store application data (messages), updates to such type of resource need to be performed under transactional control. Being XA-compliant resources, transactional control can be specified either implicitly or explicitly through the use of the ATMI functions for transactions, tpbegin(), tpcommit(), and tpabort(). This also implies that dedicated transaction manager servers, the TMS_QMs, are made available for coordinating or taking part in a global transaction. Again, these TMSs are local to the resource and there can be as many as necessary (at least two, as for any TMS).

On the server's side, the application can either explicitly dequeue requests and enqueue replies, or, more probably, make use of another System/Q process, TMQFORWARD. This dequeues requests, calls the corresponding application server, and enqueue the result of the service's execution. As said, this approach is preferable because it allows the use of the same application servers as those used in the normal request/response mechanism, whilst the other requires servers to be specifically coded. Again, the TMQFORWARD process is local to the queue space and there can be multiple instances per each queue space. Each instance of TMQFORWARD monitors the queues in a queue space and executes the request that gets to the top of the queue.

The typical implementation of the enqueuing/dequeuing mechanism is shown in Figure 93. The first operation is enqueuing a request at time I. The client starts a transaction and then executes tpenqueue(). This function calls TMQUEUE, which executes the update in the desired queue, then returns the result of the operation. The client then commits the transaction so that the request is actually stored in the queue. During this operation the TMS_QM is involved to coordinate the commitment of the transaction.

It must be noted that if the client's purpose is just to enqueue the request, the execution of tpbegin() and tpcommit() is somewhat redundant and an alternative way would be simply to call tpenqueue(). In this case, TMQUEUE will detect that there is no active transaction and will implicitly start and commit one around the update operation of the queue. In many other cases, however, the enqueuing will occur among a set of other operations, for example direct calls to other application servers, so the client will have to explicitly start a global transaction in order to guarantee that the enqueuing is consistent with the execution of the other operations.

At time II, when the request has reached the top of the queue, TMQFORWARD executes the request on behalf of the client. In order to do so, and to guarantee that either all operations are executed or none, it starts a global transaction, dequeues the request (it does it directly, doesn't need to use TMQUEUE), and calls the service. Because the call is in transaction mode, the operations performed by the server belong to the same transaction that dequeued the request. If the call fails for some reason, i.e. the service returns failure, TMQFORWARD aborts the transaction so that the request is rolled back in the queue for a later retry. At this point there is no need to enqueue a failure message; it's just like not having executed the request yet. If the service returns success, TMQFORWARD enqueues the reply in the reply queue, if there is one, then commits the transaction. The request is actually removed from the request queue, the data are updated, and the reply is stored in the reply queue. If any one of these operations

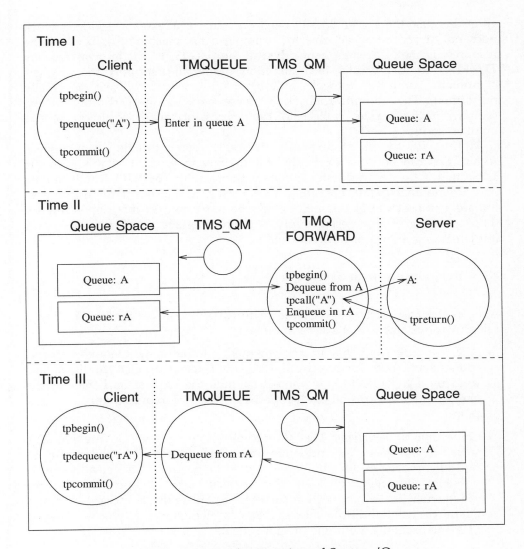

Figure 93. Implementation of System/Q

fails, the whole sequence is rolled back so that the situation restarts from the beginning.

Because all these operations are executed in transaction mode, all entities involved must be able to support the XA protocol. System/Q operations are supported by the TMS_QM, while the application servers must have associated a specific TMS for the resource they deal with. If there isn't one, either because the server doesn't need one (i.e. it accesses a resource which does not support transactions, for example a fax machine), or because the resource is not XA-compliant, then a null TMS is made available by TUXEDO to allow calls in transaction mode and support the an XA-compliant commit protocol, although no commit/rollback is really performed. The commit/rollback in these cases is applied only to the request in the queue, subject to the successful/failed execution of the invoked service.

At time III, the client dequeues the reply, using function tpdequeue(). Again, this can be done explicitly or implicitly in transaction mode, in the sense that if the client doesn't initiate a transaction, TMQUEUE will initiate one around the update operation. One reason why a client might want to initiate a transaction at this point could be, for example, that depending on the dequeuing of a successful reply, it might enqueue another request, thus implementing a kind of flow control.

7.3.3 Relationship with System/T

Also in the case of System/Q, the features provided by System/T play a role at various stages. Let's see a summary:

- *RPC-like paradigm*: This is implemented internally by tpenqueue() and tpdequeue(). Both functions call TMQUEUE using tpcall(). tpcall() is also used by TMQFORWARD, when it submits the request on behalf of the client, and therefore all the properties of service requests apply at that point.

- *Conversational paradigm*: This is not related to System/Q. The requests stored in the queue are individual ones, and do not allow the storing of multiple messages for the same server in a single conversation. It is possible, however, through the explicit use of tpenqueue() and tpdequeue() in the application servers, to read multiple messages from a queue or from multiple queues, thus implementing a type of delayed message exchange with one or more clients.

- *Communication buffers*: All ATMI and XATMI buffers can be enqueued into disk queues. If the application defines other buffer types, TMQUEUE and TMQFORWARD must be regenerated in order to be able to handle them.

- *Load balancing*: This applies at the time tpenqueue() and tpdequeue() are executed by the client, in the sense that the least loaded TMQUEUE server is chosen. Requests to TMQUEUE have all the same load, since they are all for the same type of request (enqueue). Load balancing also applies when TMQFORWARD submits the request on behalf of the client. The load factors stored in the Bulletin Board are used as with any other service requests.

- *Prioritisation*: This applies when TMQFORWARD submits the request on behalf of the client. The priority associated to the service is used. Another form of prioritisation is provided by the control structure associated to tpenqueue(). This allows you to specify the enqueuing by priority, in the sense that the message is stored ahead of the messages with a lower priority. This type of prioritisation is not related to the priority handling of System/T.

- *Data-depending routing*: This applies when tpenqueue() and tpdequeue() are used, in the sense that if there exist multiple queue spaces, then routing criteria can be defined for determining which space should be used. This allows, for example, requests for a certain service to be enqueued in different queues, depending on whether the queue is local to the service. Data-dependent routing is also used when TMQFORWARD calls the actual service, if multiple groups of servers can offer the same service.

- *Unsolicited notification*: This feature does not normally apply in the context of System/Q. However, unsolicited messages in relation to stored requests could be used once the application server has finally received the request; in this case the server could send a notification to the client immediately before executing tpreturn(), to communicate that the request has eventually been executed and that it is worth trying to dequeue the reply.

- *Security*: In the context of System/Q, security is implemented by propagating the client's identity and its application key along with the stored request, so that authorisation can still be performed by the application servers when they receive the request. Security is also implemented at administrative level in the sense that an administrative password might have to be provided to use qmadmin().

- *Transactions*: This topic has been mentioned in the previous sections. Queue spaces are XA-compliant resources and specific TMS processes are provided. Enqueuing and dequeuing always occurs in transaction mode, whether or not the application process has started a transaction. If a transaction is active, TPNOTRAN can be used during the call to tpenqueue() or tpdequeue(), so that such operation is not included in the current global transaction. In such a case, however, the consistency of the operation is not guaranteed with respect to the current transaction. For the rest, the transactional behaviour is similar to that of any other resource involved in a global transaction.

7.4 System/DOMAINS: multiple domain connectivity

All features provided by System/T and the extensions seen so far can be used to design and develop distributed applications. These, at least in theory, can integrate any number of System/T machines and any number of workstations and mainframes. The glue that holds together this potentially high number of entities is TUXEDO's name server, the Bulletin Board, as it provides information about all the components of the application. The Bulletin Board is created from information stored in a single configuration file, and is administered from a single location through the use of dedicated administrative tools and processes.

Because there is no theoretical limit to the number of components that can be configured in the same application, and because the systems involved can be geographically remote, large organisations can design a single application integrating all locations and all components at the same time. A bank, for example, could have all branches connected within the same application, thus allowing on-line operations between branches during normal front-office hours. The time needed for money transfers between branches might be in the range of a few minutes instead of a couple of days; customers might have immediate access to up-to-date account details from any branch, etc. This approach satisfies the desire to have the entire organisation share the same procedures and data, but removes the need to refer to a central machine.

However, the implementation of such an environment as a single application might prove somewhat inefficient, both from the business point of view and from a more specific TUXEDO one. On the business side, intralocation operations might not be very frequent and might not require a constant connection to all other locations; confidentiality of operations might require that certain services are not made available to all locations; unavailability of certain machines might not always have to result in additional work for others; potential growth in specific locations might have to be taken into consideration. On the TUXEDO side, the configuration of a large number of machines and application servers would certainly increase the size of the Bulletin Board and would require a large number of update operations between nodes to keep all information consistent; administration from a central location might become too complicated; recovery procedures might take longer than expected; restart operations might become very lengthy altogether.

Instead of a single application, it might be preferable to have a set of independent applications (*domains*), each one configured and administered separately. This is the purpose of *System/DOMAINS*. This subsystem allows an application domain to make available services to other applications, and to access services offered by other applications. Access to services occurs through the use of the same request/response mechanism as for the intra-application requests, i.e. without having to distinguish between calls directed to components of the same application and others directed to external ones (Figure 94).

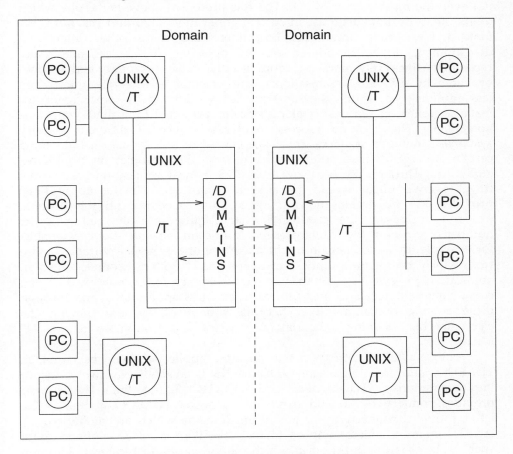

Figure 94. Representation of System/DOMAINS

Moreover, if transactions span multiple domains, the system makes sure that transactional information is propagated and that a two-phase commit algorithm is implemented across domains.

In the case of the banking system mentioned earlier, for example, each

207

branch, or perhaps a local group of branches, could constitute an applicative domain and have direct interaction with all the components within such domain. At the same time, through the use of /DOMAINS, they could occasionally execute services, say transfers, towards other domains and vice versa.

The provision of a more flexible environment for large organisations is just one of the possiblities of System/DOMAINS and to a certain extent is not even the most important one. The role presented above is the one which offers the most immediate use in current application environments, but if we look a few years down the line, there are some other interesting developments to be considered. For example, we already see that many types of business rely more and more heavily on access to data and services provided by different organisations, which cannot be integrated, and even less administered, within the same applicative domain. A travel agent, for instance, relies on separate booking systems provided by airlines, railways, hotels, etc. The booking process involves the use of different enquiry systems, a number of phone calls, keeping seats and rooms on hold for a certain amount of time, double checking with the customer on the phone, and so on. Through the use of /DOMAINS, a local application used at the travel agent's office would be able to coordinate all the applications provided by the organisations involved, thus speeding up the process, probably increasing the productivity, and, quite possibly, reducing the number of errors in the whole process. A little further still, it is conceivable, for example, that each person might make use of a personal portable device from which to execute a number of operations. Through a connection to an application provided by a local company, perhaps for a monthly fee, you could then gain access to many different business applications, and through these execute operations like checking your bank account, paying the electricity bill, booking a holiday, purchasing a season ticket to see AC Milan,[13] etc.

Of course you cannot expect that all these applications will be based on TUXEDO, and for this reason /DOMAINS is available in two different implementations, /TDOMAINS and /OSITP (Figure 95). The former provides connectivity to and from homogeneous TUXEDO domains. The latter provides connectivity to and from domains which are monitored by any TP monitor which complies to the OSI-TP protocol. Compliance with such protocol is the direction in which the industry and the technology are

---

13. For American readers: AC Milan is a soccer team. Many people, especially in Milan, believe they are the best. I only do when they win - which, luckily, happens quite often.

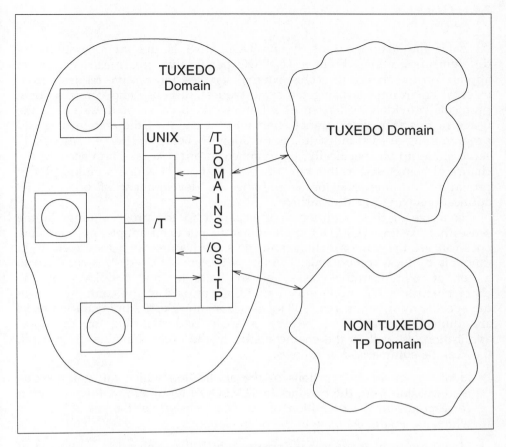

Figure 95. /TDOMAINS and /OSITP

moving, so it is reasonable at this point to think that all major products will comply to such implementation in a reasonably near future.

Given the above, System/DOMAINS can be seen both as the basis for today's distributed computing in large environments, since it allows to structure the business in a set of separate segments with autonomy of administration, yet sharing data and services, and also as TUXEDO's link with the future of distributed computing, since it allows businesses to expand through cooperation with other organisations and not necessarily through acquisition of functionalities.

7.4.1 Usage

As said, the main goal of System/DOMAINS is the interoperability of different applications. From a TUXEDO perspective, this means giving an application the chance to access external services and receive requests from external environments using the same request/response and conversational protocols provided by System/T's framework. Because of these goals, the usage of this subsystem cannot enter into the merit of the architecture and programming of each individual application. If clients and servers, especially servers, had to be specifically programmed in order to take into account the chance of being used in this type of configuration, TUXEDO's philosophy of providing a framework for simplifying the development of open OLTP applications would be diminished.

The usage of this extension is transparent to the programming, in the sense that existing TUXEDO applications do not need adaptation, and new ones can use the same functions and the same features as if they were used uniquely by local components. The use of System/DOMAINS is confined to a set of administrative tasks related both to the definition of the characteristics of the multidomain environment, and to the configuration of the specific information relevant to each domain. Such administrative tasks are quite important and require a clear understanding of the local application, as well as the characteristics of the other domains. In general, they can be summarised as follows:

- identification of the portions of the application which are going to be made visible from the outside. In TUXEDO's terminology, this operation corresponds to the definition of the *local domain*, i.e. the set of services which are made available to the other domains.

- identification of the external domains which the application is allowed to access (*remote domains*).

- addition in the application's configuration file (UBBCONFIG) of a group of gateway servers (*domain gateways*). These are made available with the /DOMAINS software to handle the communication to and from the remote domains and to perform bidirectional transaction control. They must belong to a dedicated server's group and must be configured in a MSSQ, i.e. they all read from the same queue. The addition of the dedicated group and its corresponding servers can be done dynamically through the use of tmconfig(1).

- addition of a gateway administration server, GWADM(5), a process provided by the /DOMAINS software for executing administrative functions for the gateway servers group. These functions include the gathering of configuration information on behalf of the administrator and the logging of transactions originating from a foreign environment.

- definition of a configuration file specific for domains interoperability (DMCONFIG). This is separate from the UBBCONFIG, since it contains information related to the interoperability of the local application with others, which is independent of the application itself. Information contained in this file include the name of the various domains, the type of domain (TUXEDO or OSI-TP), logical identifiers, and the network addresses through which the domains can be accessed. Other information include the list of the services which constitute the local domain, the list of the remote services, information about data-dependent routing, and the definition of access control lists for the implementation of security over multiple domains. This file is compiled into a binary version (BDMCONFIG) through the use of command *dmloadcf(1)*, and is used at boot time by the gateway servers to find the addresses of the domains they need to connect to, to set the services they must advertise, and to set all parameters for the handling of incoming and outgoing requests.

- addition in the UBBCONFIG of a domain administrative server (DMADM(5)), supplied with the /DOMAIN software for providing run-time administration of the BDMCONFIG file. Administrative functions include the gathering of information on behalf of the administrative tools, and the execution of operations requested by the gateway admin server, GWADM.

Once this work is done, the /DOMAIN software can be started using standard System/T tools like tmadmin(1) and tmboot(1). At this point, the situation on the System/T node where the gateway servers are resident looks like the one presented in Figure 96; on disk, System/T and System/DOMAINS configuration files are present; in memory, System/DOMAINS processes are active. The two administrative processes receive requests from the administrative tools, while the gateway servers receive requests from the application clients and deliver requests to the application servers.

At runtime, administration of the /DOMAINS components is performed via a dedicated administrative tool, *dmadmin(1)*. Like tmadmin(1), this tool is an interactive command interpreter which can be used to browse into the activity of the domain gateways, to change the execution of certain components dynamically, and to reconfigure the domain dynamically. Information which can be displayed includes the list of the remote domains connected, the list of the remote services, the list of the local advertised services, and the list of active transactions. Operations that can be performed include the advertisement or unadvertisement of local services, the

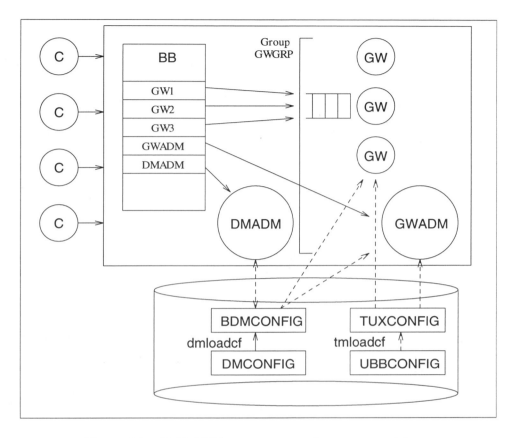

Figure 96. /DOMAIN components after setup and boot

activation or deactivation of an audit trace, and the administration of the transaction log. Configuration parameters that can be changed, added, or removed include local and remote services, routing criteria, access control lists, and the local domain password.

7.4.2 Implementation

As already mentioned, the implementation of /DOMAINS is based on a set of gateway processes which handle outgoing and incoming messages (Figure 97). Outgoing messages are typically requests or replies to an external domain, but could also be protocol messages generated by the local application during the commitment of a global transaction involving other domains. Similarly, incoming messages are typically requests or replies from an external domain, but could also be protocol messages generated by an external domain during the commitment of a global transaction involving the local domain.

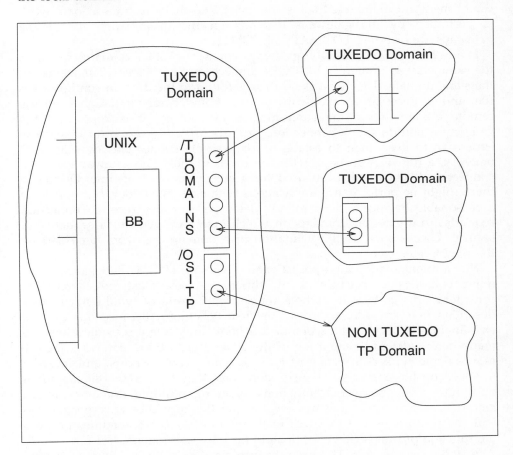

Figure 97. Connection to multiple domains

To be used for routing requests to external domains, gateways read at boot time information about the remote services, and advertise them as if they were local. Consequently, when any process in the local application executes a tpcall() or tpconnect(), the message is sent to the gateway as if it were a normal application server. The gateway will then read the service request and send it over to the domain it deals with. When a reply or message arrives, the gateway forwards it to the process that originated the request. In this behaviour, the gateway is very similar to a workstation handler, except it handles a set of processes (the remote application) instead of a set of workstations.

While this behaviour is common to all gateways, the way connections are established and maintained across domains, and the way transactional work is perfomed by the gateways depends on the instantiation, i.e. if the gateways are of type /TDOMAIN or /OSITP.

In the case of /TDOMAIN, gateways connect to other domains much in the same way as System/T BRIDGEs connect to other System/T machines in the same domain. The network address is found in the domain configuration file, and, if necessary, a password is also provided for validation from the remote domain. Once the connection is established, it is kept until the gateway is shutdown. If connections are expensive to keep, or at least more expensive to keep than to establish, for example connections over an X.25 network, a timeout can be specified in order to make the gateway drop the connection if it has not been used for a certain amount of time. Of course there might be performance implications with such behaviour, but hopefully a reasonable balance can be found. Gateways can also receive connection requests from external domains, in which case they perform a sequence of security checks such as the validation of a domain password provided by the remote gateway.

The implementation of transactional work in /TDOMAINS gateways is quite complicated because many different cases must be taken into consideration. In fact, the whole transactional protocol would have to be described here in order to clarify the real behaviour. Because this type of examination is beyond the scope of this book, only a few considerations are made here; gateways keep a log of the active transactions; gateways receive requests and replies on behalf of local or remote TMS servers, and in order to speed up the execution of such operations, they have TMS functionalities built into them; because transactions spanning multiple domains have a hierarchical structure, gateways ensure that this structure is respected and that the protocol is not violated; in doing so, they can sometimes perform the function of transaction coordinators for the local domain.

In the case of /OSITP, each communication with a remote domain constitutes a *dialogue*, and a dialogue is used for all operations related to a transaction: data transfer, transaction control, error notification, etc. Therefore, the establishment of a connection and the execution of transactional work are more strictly integrated. Moreover, because OSI-TP does not define a specific application context, one is defined for interoperability with TUXEDO environments, and a specific protocol is used. This protocol is defined in the X/Open XATMI specifications and constitutes TUXEDO's implementation of the functionality of a communication resource manager. /OSITP gateways can be seen as CRMs in the X/Open DTP model (see Chapter 5). In order to clarify the behaviour of these gateways, we would have to describe the entire OSI-TP protocol, but because this goes outside the scope of this presentation of /DOMAINS, only a few comments are made; once a gateway receives a service request for a remote service, or a connection request, or a commit request, it establishes a dialogue with an entity in the remote domain and performs the operation according to the predefined protocol; encoding/decoding functions for the data can be provided to the gateways to handle the different formats across heterogeneous domains.

7.4.3 Relationship with System/T

With reference to the features provided by System/T, the relationship between these and the /DOMAINS environment can be summarised as follows:

- *RPC-like paradigm*: Local application processes can use tpcall(), tpacall(), and tpgetrply() for requests to remote services; no difference at programing level. Servers can serve remote requests and return replies to remote processes. Also, services can forward a request to a remote service.

- *Conversational paradigm*: Local application processes can connect and exchange messages with remote services; if necessary, they can drop connections, in which case all transactional implications are looked after by the gateways.

- *Communication buffers*: Application messages can be of any one of the types allowed. For TUXEDO-to-TUXEDO communication, the whole range can be used; for TUXEDO-to-non TUXEDO communication FML buffers are not allowed, but if corresponding VIEWS are available, these can be used for conversion.

- *Load balancing*: This is applied to incoming requests, when the gateways forward requests from a remote domain to the local servers. For outgoing messages, because gateways are in MSSQ, load balancing is not applied, as all messages end up in the same queue; however, MSSQ still allows for requests to be load balanced among gateways. Another form of load balancing is performed when an incoming connection request arrives; this is assigned to the gateway which has got fewer connections open at that time.

- *Prioritisation*: Remote services can have an associated priority, and the priority for the request can be dynamically modified. Gateways read service requests by priority and propagate it to the remote domain, if this is a TUXEDO one. Equally, if a request has an assiciated priority, this is sent along with the call to the local application server. Priorities are not implemented in TUXEDO-to-non TUXEDO interoperation, since there is no provision for this features in the standard protocol.

- *Data-dependent routing*: This applies when a local application process makes a call; the group to which gateways belong to can have routing criteria associated, so that a call to a service can either be routed to a local group or to the gateways for sending to a remote domain. In addition, the gateway can apply another level of data-dependent routing to decide which one of the remote domains should be chosen. For this second level, routing information is available in the domains configuration file (BDMCONFIG).

- *Unsolicited notification*: This is not supported in the /DOMAINS framework. Unsolicited messages are not sent to the gateways for propagation to remote domains. Apart from not being particularly useful, this would require a change in the way clients are identified across different domains, and, in the case of /OSITP, also a standardisation of this type of communication.

- *Server migration*: Gateways can be migrated to other machines, but, because incoming connections cannot be automatically reassigned to the migrated gateways, this operation is not as straightforward as the migration of application servers within a single application.

- *Dynamic advertisement*: Advertisement/unadvertisement across domains is not supported. Like in the case of unsolicited notification, this feature is useful within the context of a single application and does not have implications in terms of interoperability.

- *Stored requests*: tpenqueue() can be used to store a request for a remote service. The TMQFORWARD process can then forward the request to a gateway for remote execution, and store the reply back when the gateway returns it. tpenqueue() can also be used to store a request in a queue which belongs to a remote domain, in which case the local gateway forwards the request to the remote TMQUEUE for enqueuing. This feature is only supported for TUXEDO-to-TUXEDO interoperability since there is no provision in the OSI-TP protocol for such a type of operation.

- *Security*: In the /DOMAIN framework, the first level of security is provided by the definition of the local domain; basically, only a subset of the domain's services is made visible to remote domains, and only requests for those services are accepted. A second level is provided by access control lists; for each service, a list of remote domains can be specified, so that requests for a certain service are accepted only if originating from one of the specified domains. A third level is provided by domain passwords; when remote gateways request a connection with the local one, they are authenticated against a password specific to the domain. In addition, audit facilities are provided to track the operations performed by the gateways.

7.5 Summary

In this chapter we have presented a set of extensions to the TUXEDO environment that help enhance the framework provided by System/T, and make its features more adaptable to specific requirements of distributed computing. The first two extensions, System/WS and System/HOST, allow a TUXEDO environment based on UNIX systems to encompass systems like PCs and mainframes, thus creating a more suitable environment for enterprise computing.

System/WS provides an application with the possibility to run TUXEDO clients on PCs and workstations which do not have System/T. This extension provides the same API and the same functionality as for native clients, which guarantees code portability as well as integration of desktop computing facilities within an OLTP application. This extension is implemented through the use of workstation handlers on the System/T system, where each workstation handler handles a configurable number of workstations.

System/HOST provides an application with the chance to access mainframe programs from within a UNIX-based TUXEDO application, through the use of the same request mechanism as used for native TUXEDO application servers. This helps integrate mainframe facilities within an open systems application, and helps design migration paths based on interoperability. This extension is based on the use of gateways both on the UNIX and on the mainframe side. Gateways handle requests, responses, and data conversion to and from the TUXEDO application. Although several instantiations are available for different mainframe environments, the most popular is that for MVS/CICS environments. In such an instantiation, existing mainframe programs link to a TUXEDO-provided gateway for transmitting data to the UNIX side. Programs in the CICS environment can perform any type of transactional work, but this is not coordinated with any distributed transaction processing carried out by TUXEDO.

The other two extensions enhance TUXEDO's framework for enterprise computing in the areas of request/response processing and interoperations with other applications. System/Q provides an application with the chance to store service requests in permanent queues on disk for delayed processing. This technique can be used for implementing the "exactly once" criterion, for augmenting the recoverability/availability of applications, and for increasing the runtime performance of an application by delaying unnecessary processing. Batch processing can also be implemented through this extension. The implementation of System/Q is provided by set of administrative processes that help define and use queues under a transactional semantic.

System/DOMAINS provides an application with the chance to request services from remote applications, and to offer services to remote environments. The use of this extension allows on the one hand to split a large application environment into multiple independent applications; on the other hand, it allows business environments to grow through interoperation with other environments. Each domain can make use of TUXEDO's features, including the coordination of global transactions across domains. System/DOMAINS is available in two instantiations, one for interoperation of homogeneous TUXEDO application, the other for interoperation with other heterogeneous OLTP environments monitored by other OLTP products. In both cases, the implementation is based on gateway servers which connect to remote domains and forward requests and replies back and forth. The internal implementation of communication and transactional work is based on an internally defined protocol in the case of TUXEDO-to-TUXEDO interoperation, and on the OSI/TP protocol in the case of TUXEDO-to-non TUXEDO interoperation.

8. Selected Topics

When examining the TUXEDO System, an important aspect is no doubt to understand what features the product makes available; the previous chapters hopefully helped in this direction. However, when software products offer features for building capabilities into applications rather than features *perse*, that is, when products provide technology rather than end-user functionality, an equally important aspect is to examine how the individual features can be used together, to see their effectiveness in relation to the characteristics of specific business environments. Due to the wide scope of distributed computing and Open OLTP, the links between TUXEDO's individual features and the eventual capabilities of TUXEDO-based applications may not always be evident, so certain questions have become recurrent in relation to the product and certain topics have become the subject of widespread attention.

The purpose of this final chapter is therefore to present some of the areas in which people more often focus their attention when looking at the TUXEDO System. Admittedly, this is not an extensive examination of all areas that are subjects of attention in relation to TUXEDO, but only some of the more general. The topics discussed here include: (a) two subjects that reflect the desires and concerns of many business environments, namely business modelling and high application availability; (b) two topics that result from recurrent questions, i.e. how can we decide if TUXEDO is suitable for a certain environment, and what does it mean migrating an application environment towards TUXEDO; and (c) very briefly, a topic that has already been treated in Chapter 5, but that is repeated here for those who were not interested in the technicalities of TUXEDO DTP, namely the use of non XA-compliant DBMSs in a TUXEDO application.

I have chosen these subjects because they have a degree of general

219

validity and can be discussed at a level that does not require too much detail. Since the style of discussion adopted here avoids reference to individual products or environments, you will not find detailed answers to product questions. The main purpose of these discussions is to introduce the subject and to provide some pointers for further investigation. I would invite you to read this with one eye on your current requirements, one on the characteristics of your software and hardware, and one on the evolution you anticipate in your business. Although this makes a total of three eyes, which might prove somewhat demanding for some, this combination of aspects will hopefully provide sufficient background information to see where and how TUXEDO can fit into the specific cases you may be thinking of.

8.1 Business modelling

One of the challenges facing virtually all types of business is the need to be focused and efficient in the current marketplace, but ready to quickly adapt to changing conditions. Only the combination of focus on the current business activities and rapid evolution allows companies to keep up with the competition and, if possible, establish an edge.

Computer systems and software applications play a delicate role in this respect. Without computer systems, most businesses these days would not even survive. So, because of the extaordinary role that software plays in the prosperity of a business, increasing attention is being paid to the capabilities that software platforms like TUXEDO provide to support the combination of focus, efficiency, and evolution. The ability to assist with these requirements is a major challenge for applications, because it requires the reconciliation of three separate aspects of the business: the existing business characteristics (i.e. the fixed aspects of the business), the business conditions (i.e. the variable trading conditions), and the future characteristics (i.e. the future aspects of the business). The ability to model these three components within an application or an application environment is, roughly speaking, what goes under the name of business modelling.

8.1.1 Business characteristics

The existing characteristics of a business are mainly static components, in the sense that they are known at the time the application is designed, vary only over a relatively long period of time, and are typically fixed at any moment in time. For example, if in a banking environment the procedure for opening an account includes verifying the identity of the applicant, storing personal details, and assigning an account number, the application can be programmed to perform exactly such a set of operations. The modelling of these characteristics within an application is an easy task, since the necessary information is available in advance and can be translated into a program.

Different products provide different features and programming techniques for translating business characteristics into applications, so certain products are more suitable than others. In this respect, TUXEDO makes available a set of features that can save a lot of programming and can add a degree of flexibility to the application; as we have seen in the previous chapters, prioritisation, data-dependent routing, synchronous, asynchronous and conversational paradigms, batch requests, load balancing, etc., are among these.

Modelling the known characteristics of the business is, however, only one of the aspects to take into consideration, and, in a way, not the critical one as far as business modelling is concerned. After all, we take for granted that the application will be able to execute the operations required by the business. In terms of business modelling, a more important aspect is the ability to capture the volatile aspects of the application environment, i.e. what is determined by the changing business conditions and by the future business characteristics. If, for example, the trading is very high one day, the application will need extra performance; if a service is to be made available only when the bank manager is in the office, the application will have to make the service unavailable when he/she is out; if the procedure for opening a bank account changes, say, because of modifications to the law, the application will have to incorporate these changes. These aspects cannot be statically coded in the application, because they are not known in advance and vary at different times over the lifetime of an application. Still, an ability to react to such changes is vital to maintain a competitive position. This is an area in which software platforms can play a substantial role, and this is where TUXEDO provides specific capabilities.

8.1.2 Changing business conditions

As we said, business conditions are those aspects of the business that vary because of different external conditions during a certain period of time, typically during the day. Of course there are many different types of conditions that may vary during a day, many of which are specific to the type of business, so a general examination can only be conducted on a sufficiently high level of abstraction. In order to see what capabilities TUXEDO can offer, let's focus on a generic set of volatile conditions common to many business environments; these would probably include:

- The workload, for example during peak hours. While the services requested are the same, the volume might become suddenly higher; in order to adapt to it, a boost of performance is required.

- The availability of services, for example opening a bank account. Although this service is generally available, its availability might have to be restricted to certain times of the day, for instance during front-office hours, say from 9 am to 2 pm; in order to adapt to this, the service should be disabled outside that timeframe.

- The type of customer, for example customers who are going to spend or invest large sums. While the procedures and services are the same, these might have to be given a special treatment as a privilege and incentive. In order to adapt to it, priorities must be defined and privileges must be taken into considerations.

- The type of service, for example services available only to certain levels of management for security reasons. While these services must be available at all times, their use must be restricted; in order to adapt to this, forms of authorisation must be defined.

- Different trading timeframes, for example offices that open only in the morning. While the services are the same, they must be made available to other offices only in the morning instead of all day; in order to adapt to this, specific locations must be disabled at certain times and enabled at others.

The list could probably continue and could include other not so general conditions for some specific environments. In general, the possibility to model such aspects should not be left to the pure application code. If this were the case, these conditions would be treated like fixed characteristics, and any change would have to be reflected in the application. A product like TUXEDO, capable of controlling the various application entities, is very handy for controlling these changing conditions and integrating this level of modelling in the applicative environment.

In the case of higher workload, for example, additional performance can be obtained through the addition of new application servers, possibly on different machines. This can be done either manually by the administrator or via automatic procedures triggered by configurable parameters. Because no change to the application is required, this can occur whenever the conditions require; the end result is that the customers do not suffer from application overload when peak hours occur, for example the lunch hour, or peak periods, for example the start of the summer sales. In certain cases, stored requests and batch processing can also be used instead of, or in conjunction with, runtime processing; again, the activation of these can be set via automatic procedures.

In the case of services restricted to certain hours of the day, manual or dynamic advertisement of services can be implemented. Again, this can be triggered by configurable parameters, and is transparent to the application code. The same can be implemented for conditions other than times, for instance whenever the branch manager or his/her deputy are not logged onto the system. In addition, unsolicited messages can be used to warn the users automatically of the availability/unavailability of such services, thus making the whole environment aware of the changes of conditions as they occur.

In the case of privileged customers, prioritisation of service requests can be implemented. Either special services can be configured with higher priority and used when special conditions are verified, or priorities can be dynamically changed to accommodate special conditions as they occur. The end result is that particularly important customers can be offered a better service.

In the case of restricted types of services, security features can be implemented to guarantee that such services are only executed by the authorised people. Through the use of the application authentication key returned to individual users, access control lists can be implemented under the control of the administrator, with the possibility to change criteria as the need arises; most of this can be made transparent to the application programming.

In the case of different trading timeframes, for example the case of stores which do Sunday trading, advertisement and unadvertisement of services can be implemented. Data-dependent routing can be used to route service requests to the open locations while disabling the unavailable ones. This is also transparent to the application code, with the result that at any one moment application services are only available where trading is available. Unsolicited messages can also be used to inform about these changes as they occur.

All of this makes it possible to adapt the behaviour of the application to the business conditions with little or no programming, and, quite importantly, to keep dynamic control over such behaviour.

8.1.3 Future business characteristics

While fixed business characteristics are modelled in an application via appropriate coding, and changing conditions are modelled through the use of features transparent to the coding, activated when conditions change, the modelling of future characteristics is a vague task. In the absence of details not yet available, future characteristics can be taken into consideration via a flexible architecture. If, for example, the procedure for opening a bank account change because of modifications in the law, such changes should be implemented with the least impact possible on the rest of the application. This implies avoiding large modifications to the code and delays in the deployment. In general, it needs to be done as cheaply as possible. If new services must be made available, their addition must not affect the existing portions of the application, so that the cost of integration and the necessary coding are reduced. If new systems must be made available, their addition should not have to be reflected in the existing code, as this would make the process more lengthy and expensive.

These characteristics are usually not handled very well in monolithic applications, even when such applications operate in client/server environments. On the contrary, with a flexible architecture like the one provided by TUXEDO they can be more easily taken into consideration. Because the application code itself is divided into clients and servers, there are a set of modular units which can be addressed separately. Changes to existing modules affect only one module, not the entire code. Addition of new code can be done, for example, with the introduction of a new server, thus isolating all the programming from the rest of the application.

Because of this structure, new or modified services can be integrated with the old application without affecting other portions of the application. The modification of services because of changes in the law, for example, can be left to specialised companies that can provide an update package with one or two new application servers. With the use of /DOMAINS, further degrees of expansion can be implemented without having to modify existing portions of the application.

Moreover, when changes occur, dynamic administration and configuration can be used; services, components, machines, locations, can be added or changed with no impact to the portions of application not directly involved, and without having to make them unavailable. This makes it possible to undertake changes in the application in a modular fashion, by introducing new or better services while phasing out old ones in an almost continuous process.

8.2 High application availability

One of the issues traditionally important in the area of OLTP is that of high application availability. That is, the need to guarantee that certain applications, usually defined as *mission-critical*, run continuously or at the worst with minimal interruptions. Given the nature of traditional OLTP environments, banks, airline reservation systems, etc., this requirement is hardly surprising; the unavailability of the application would cause inefficiencies, delays, complaints, and, ultimately, loss of money, so no wonder a lot of emphasis has been put on ways to address this issue.

The reasons which lie behind the unavailability of an application are of multiple nature, typically hardware faults (CPU, memory, disks, network), but also software problems (programming errors, lack of operating system resources) and maintenance operations. Hardware faults are clearly the major cause of unexpected and lasting interruptions of the application, but the others might play a role in certain circumstances. Software problems can be reduced by a thorough testing of the application before going live, but in certain cases such thorough testing is not possible because of lack of resources or time. Maintenance operations can be scheduled, but the frequency and duration can have a significant impact on the availability of the application.

Since the major cause of application interruption is hardware faults, the subject of high application availability is generally related to the subject of hardware fault tolerance. Because from a theoretical point of view the provision of fault tolerance is an irresolvable task since one would have to have an infinite number of equivalent hardware and software resources available at all times (if my system has, for instance, three CPUs in case one or two become unavailable, what happens if a failure to the third CPU occurs while the other two are broken?), the problem is not so much about the provision of total fault tolerance, but about the narrowing of the window within which problems can lead to the unavailability of the application.

The most widely used solution for narrowing this window is the use of so-called fault-tolerant systems, i.e. machines that through separate CPUs, multiple memory segments, multiple disks, disk mirroring, etc., guarantee that failures in those components do not affect the behaviour of the system and the availability of the application (unless of course all components of the same type became unavailable at the same time, a highly unlikely event). This approach has been the most popular for one fundamental reason; in traditional OLTP, applications and data are typically located on one mainframe system, and because the single major reason for application unavailability would be the unavailability of the mainframe, strengthening the mainframe system would therefore strengthen the availability of the application.

This approach has proven effective with only one significant drawback: the cost. Fault-tolerant hardware is expensive, with the result that fault-tolerance, as well as OLTP, has been available only to companies or organisations that could justify and afford that type of investment because of the value of the business. With the advent of Open OLTP, however, and the adoption of OLTP techniques in environments other than the ones mentioned above, the subject of high application availability is becoming a generalised issue. After all, everyone is interested to avoid losing business because of failures in their computing and application environments.

The way in which TUXEDO can help with the creation of highly available applications has become a subject of general interest in conjunction with this product. Moreover, while the use of fault-tolerant systems is still the most obvious solution in this area, it is clear that the availability of such systems is primarily based on financial considerations more than technical ones. The issues about high application availability are moving away from the technical merits of fault-tolerant hardware, and are now becoming much more related to cheaper ways of achieving fault tolerance, i.e. ways for narrowing the window to an acceptable level without having to go for expensive investments in hardware. Actually, in many cases the window might not even have to be very small; as long as interruptions are not too long, performance does not deteriorate too much, etc., the situation could still be up to a satisfactory level.

This is the area in which an open OLTP monitor like TUXEDO can be of great help. Of course if TUXEDO is coupled with fault-tolerant hardware there is one more option to play with. TUXEDO runs on fault-tolerant hardware and, through features like server replication and server migration it supports disk mirroring and disk sharing as a matter of setup. In the absence of these, however, or alongside these, it is important that the system can offer cheap options. Many of TUXEDO's features can be used to achieve various degrees of fault tolerance and consequently of application availability. In order to examine them, let's split the causes of application unavailability in three areas: hardware faults, software faults, and maintenance operations.

8.2.1 Hardware faults

Hardware faults can happen at any time and there is obviously nothing a layer of software can do to prevent them. What the software can do, though, is to try and ensure that the effects of hardware faults are not too extensive, and that when possible, alternative options are made available. In general, the amount of help that can be given by TUXEDO depends first of all on the number of System/T machines in the configuration; if there is only one and this crashes or it cannot be used for any other reason, then there is very little TUXEDO can do - fault-tolerant hardware is the only viable solution. If there is more than one, however, as may well be the case in a distributed environment, then there are several options that TUXEDO makes available.

First, to prevent the effect of a hardware fault from being totally disruptive, distribution of functionality across machines is generally helpful, since the application is not forced to rely on one single machine. For example, resources like queue spaces can be configured on more than one machine. This not only makes performance better for the specific functionality, but also creates a more robust environment altogether. Even when one machine is central to the application, say because this is where a central database resides, the hard disks of other machines can be used for data replication via multiple server groups and batch processing, thus making the data available without having to use disk-mirroring and disk-sharing hardware. Assuming this is possible, distribution of application servers can also be useful, as it allows for the provision of services at all times on multiple machines. In general, distribution is a good ingredient for high application availability. It is also cheaper than dedicated hardware, because it can make use of hardware resources which would be there anyway for other purposes.

To examine how this applies to TUXEDO environments, let's split the discussion further into several different areas: (a) faults that cause a machine to crash (e.g. CPU, or memory, or disk fault); (b) faults that cause a machine to become partially unusable (e.g. failures in write to disk, but not in read); (c) faults that cause a machine to become unreachable over the network (e.g. failures in the network board); (d) faults that cause all machines to become unreachable (e.g. a fault in the network cables); (e) finally, faults that cause a peripheral to be unusable (e.g. a printer):

- (a) In the case of machine crash, usually two different types of problems occur: the users logged on that machine, or connected to that machine over a network cannot access the application any more; the application servers and the data on that machine are no longer available. As far as the users are concerned, if they are PC users, alternative connections can be specified, so that the application client can automatically try to connect to another machine. This makes the crash of the machine immediately recoverable, in the sense that after a certain timeout, probably in the order of a few tens of seconds, the user can connect to another machine and gain access to the application again.

  As far as the application servers are concerned, these may be available also on other machines, in which case TUXEDO will route the requests only to the available ones. If they are not available anywhere else, TUXEDO allows them to be migrated to another machine as a matter of administration, so that this can be executed immediately. One difficulty, of course, is that data might not be available on the other machines if one doesn't have disk mirroring or disk sharing. If this is the case, for all services that can have a delayed processing, requests can be stored in a queue on another machine while the broken one is being repaired, thus allowing operations still to be executed. The loss in this case is related to the services that cannot be delayed or that need to access data only available on the broken machine. The other cases can be looked after through migration coupled with batch processing. The actual migration of users and servers can be executed at runtime while the rest of the application is still running. Also, if the crashed machine cannot be repaired, dynamic reconfiguration allows the administrator to add a new machine without having to stop the remaining portions of the application. Basically, there is the possibility to keep as much as possible of the application alive by using the other machines, and the code of the application is not affected by the changes needed to restore the system's functionality.

If the crashed machine is the TUXEDO master machine (presumably also the one where the administrator performs all the functions), the configuration of a backup master allows the master functionalities to be migrated at runtime without having to stop the application. The backup master can be any one of the other System/T machines, and therefore the functionality can be restored within seconds.

- (b) In the case when one machine is partially usable, problems might be similar to those of the previous case, but something more might be saved. If the application clients are not affected by the fault, they might not need to be migrated to other machines, and will still be able to request services wherever these are available. If some services are not affected by the fault, these can still be available, while those affected can be unadvertised. Unsolicited notifications in the application servers can also be useful at this point, to notify users of the unavailability of certain services and to notify the administrator that certain actions are necessary. As a result, there is the possibility to focus the scope of corrective actions and keep alive as much as possible of the application.

- (c) In the case where one machine becomes isolated from the rest of the network because of a failure in its network board, there are problems from two different perspectives: from the portion of the application on the isolated machine (clients, servers, data), and from the portion of the application external to the isolated machine. As far as the external portion is concerned, this case is no different from the one where one machine crashes, and all the same actions can be applied in order to avoid using that machine. As far as the isolated machine is concerned, there are several things that could happen; users connected to it can be migrated to another if they are PC users; servers and services can be migrated under the same conditions as for the crashed machine; the combination of these is equivalent to abandoning the machine. If some of these actions are impossible, since the machine is still alive and the local portion of the application is still available, the local users can store their requests on the isolated machine, so that they are executed when the connection is back; this helps the local users to use at least part of the application. Once the network is available again, TUXEDO reconnects the isolated machine and propagates a new version of the Bulletin Board, so that the local users can again access all portions of the applications, including all changes that may have taken place in the meantime. This usually does not require a restart of the application for the local users.

- (d) In the case where the machines cannot access one another because of a complete network failure, each machine finds itself in the case described above, and roughly the same capabilities can be used. If possible, users and application servers could be migrated to the TUXEDO master machine, then migrated back when the network is restored. If not, each machine can keep on using local services and store requests for external ones. When the network is re-established, the machines can be reconnected either via administrative commands, or automatically when the requests can be routed again via the network.

- (e) In the case of failure of a peripheral, assuming there is more than one in the environment, the services accessing such peripheral can be unadvertised, manually or automatically. TUXEDO routes requests automatically to other peripherals without the application having to be affected.

In general, because TUXEDO controls entities like application servers and machines over the entire network, because it can dynamically update the configuration and the contents of the Bulletin Board, and because it allows the use of disk queues alongside memory ones, backup machines and backup functionality can be configured and activated in a sufficiently simple and inexpensive way. To make use of backup functionality, a TUXEDO application can make use of resources that were already available, whilst the addition of only a small amount of backup hardware can greatly improve the effectiveness of the environment. Backup hardware does not have to have particular features in terms of hardware fault tolerance. In several cases, an acceptable degree of high application availability can be achieved without expensive or sophisticated hardware.

8.2.2 Software faults and maintenance operations

Software faults can typically occur in case of programming errors, and the impact they have with respect to the availability of the application depends on where and when they occur. Apart from the faults in the operating system and in software packages used by the application, which are outside TUXEDO's control, there are two critical areas for a TUXEDO application:

the application servers, because they make available the services to the application, and the Bulletin Board, because it contains information necessary for the functioning of the entire application. Programming errors that cause the unavailability of the application servers or the Bulletin Board can therefore therefore have an impact on the stability and availability of the application.

- *Unavailability of one or more application servers because of software faults* is a fairly remote possibility, but because not all the real conditions can be fully tested prior to the application going live, there can always be the slight risk that at a certain point one application server will die because of programming errors like divisions by zero or similar. When this happens, the services offered by such server are no longer available, and obviously the entire application can suffer in terms of functionality and performance.

  In order to strengthen the application in this area, there are several things TUXEDO can offer. First of all, there can be multiple instances of the same server. The number of instances can be defined both in the configuration and at runtime, without having to program the servers for this specifically. The use of multiple instances protects the application from errors occurring in, say, one particular service with a certain particular input, thus not losing services that work as expected. This doesn't protect from the loss of performance due to the loss of one server, but to resolve this problem a new instance of the server can be started.

  Another possibility is the activation of the automatic server restart. If the fault is not too serious, it can be acceptable to restart the server at least a certain number of times over a certain period of time, for example a day, before deciding that the server is unusable. This again can be done in the configuration and doesn't need special programming. Automatic server restart protects from isolated programming errors as well as the loss of performance, because it restores the functionality of all services provided by the server except the one which fails.

  Unadvertisement of the faulty service within a server can also be executed, so that the possibility of hitting the same problem is reduced while all services except the faulty one are still available. This operation can be done manually by the administrator, or under certain conditions by the server itself through the use of the ATMI for service advertising/unadvertising.

  Finally, another possibility is to replace the faulty server with a fixed one as soon as it is available. This can be done dynamically by stopping the server, but without having to stop any other portions of the application. Although this causes a temporary unavailability of some services, the time to replace the server is minimal and therefore the unavailability might not be very noticeable. If there is room in the Bulletin Board, the fixed server could actually be started before stopping the faulty one, thus avoiding such temporary unavailability.

- *Unavailability of the Bulletin Board* because of programming errors is an extremely remote possibility. This would occur mainly as a result of a wrong pointer assignment; because the Bulletin Board is part of each process's virtual address space, a write starting from a wrong address might end up overwriting the contents of the Bulletin Board, thus making it unusable. In order to protect the Bulletin Board from unintentional corruption, TUXEDO makes available a parameter that forces all processes to attach to the Bulletin Board only when they execute ATMI functions, i.e. only within "trusted" code. Outside the code of the ATMI, processes are not attached to the Bulletin Board, so errors cannot corrupt it. The price to pay for this is slower execution. Unless the application is in its first stages and not properly tested, this protection should probably not be used in a production environment.

- *Maintenance operations* are not normally a threat to application availability, since they can be scheduled and carried out when this causes less disruption to the environment. However, if we consider mission critical applications, where services must be available 24 hours a day, then every stoppage of the application might have an impact. If this happens every time functionality is added or changed, every time a new machine is added, etc., then in the long run this could cause inefficiencies. TUXEDO allows both dynamic administration and dynamic reconfiguration, so in the vast majority of cases the existing portions of the application will not be affected while adding/changing other portions.

In general, because application servers are separate from clients, and because TUXEDO controls the availability of servers, users can carry on with most of their work at all times, and in the worst case only the individual faulty piece of the application will not be available. Because little or no programming is required to look after these conditions, and several automatic actions can be set up, several cheap, acceptable solutions to application availability can be designed for problems deriving from faults in the application software.

All in all, through the combined use of distribution and other features for dynamically handling the unavailability of certain application components, it is possible to reduce the window when the application is unavailable and to try and limit the disruption caused by various faults. This can be set up not just for large OLTP environments but also for smaller types of business, even when only a limited number of small, inexpensive machines are available.

8.3 Can TUXEDO be useful in my environment?

Although the subject of debate for some time, distributed computing and Open OLTP have risen to the forefront of the IT industry only in the last few years, fuelled by the efforts of many manufacturers and by the appearance on the market of several products in this area. The combination of increasing pressure from manufacturers and growing popularity has led many companies to reconsider their computing requirements in the light of distributed computing techniques. However, whilst this process of reconsideration has been seen as a useful exercise, it has also underlined some common elements of difficulty. Due to the fact that Open OLTP and distributed computing are still relatively young, due to the fact that different products put emphasis on different aspects of distributed computing and OLTP, and due to different, sometimes conflicting, types of messages put across by different manufacturers, many companies find it complicated to clearly see how a distributed computing approach can be effective for their environment, and find it very difficult to identify which product would be the best candidate for their computing environment.

Gathering information, talking to different suppliers, attending shows, demonstrations, etc., is usually useful to start with, but the amount of information obtainable at that level does not usually go into sufficient detail. A more effective approach is actually to evaluate different products, but due to the intrinsic complexity of evaluating technology rather than products, this process is often expensive and lengthy. In many cases companies are reluctant to invest money and resources without knowing in advance that there are good chances that a type of technology could be the right choice. So, a very genuine question is often: "If I am in this particular situation, and I want to move towards this other situation, could TUXEDO be useful?". From a consultancy perspective, an equivalent question is also: "Given a customer in a certain situation, should I offer TUXEDO as a solution?". Unfortunately very little information is available to answer these questions. Only experience determines a correct answer, but due to the relative novelty of the product in the commercial arena, such experience is not yet widely available.

Although generic answers to these questions do not exist, some indications can be obtained by observing a set of environments and conditions for which TUXEDO is known to be suitable. By comparing these with the specific details of each individual case, we should hopefully be able to determine whether TUXEDO is a product to be taken into consideration.

The purpose of this section is to provide some general comments about this subject. Comments are ordered by type of environment, in the sense that the starting point is the environment that a company might already have. Comments relate to the areas in which TUXEDO is helpful. Information relevant to this subject can also be found in Chapter 2, in the section about the industry's perspective on TUXEDO (Section 2.5).

8.3.1 Environments

The environments considered in this list are quite generic, so that a set of common characteristics can be identified. Many of them relate to a situation where some type of UNIX system is already present, but non UNIX environments are also included in the list. Evolution plans, i.e. plans to make changes in the environment as opposed to keeping the same hardware and software, are also a distinguishing factor.

1. *UNIX only - Single hardware supplier - No significant evolution plans*
   This would appear to be a case where TUXEDO cannot play a significant role. If you are in this sort of "static" situation, the existing application, for example a pure DBMS application, might already provide a sufficient set of features, with additional features being provided by newer versions of the DBMS. However, there might still be reasons why you might want to use TUXEDO in addition to the existing DBMS.
   A typical case is if you are interested in improving the performance of your application; the split of the application into clients and servers, the possibility to locate servers on different machines, the possibility to sequentialise simultaneous accesses to the database, the use of load balancing and MSSQ, the use of different queuing mechanisms, the multiplexing of many users among a low number of servers, all this contributes to making the environment more efficient and to supporting more users without having to upgrade the hardware.
   Another case could be if you are interested in business modelling, as described an earlier section. If you want additional flexibility, or the ability to address changing business conditions, or a more integrated administration for the application, TUXEDO's features help to create an environment that a pure DBMS solution might not allow.
   If you have a distributed environment with several UNIX systems, TUXEDO could also be useful to add degrees of robustness to the application, by helping with the implementation of some levels of high application availability in addition to those provided by the DBMS.
   Importantly, the use of an open OLTP monitor allows an application

to be structured in a way that even if no evolution is expected, future changes in the plans might still be taken into consideration. In certain cases, this might be a good reason by itself for using TUXEDO, even if no specific advantages are seen for the existing environment.

2. *UNIX only - Single hardware supplier - Evolution plans*
    In this case, the same considerations apply as the previous case, but there might be additional aspects to take into consideration; if the evolution plans encompass the use of other machines, TUXEDO helps to integrate both PCs and other UNIX systems within the same application, by offering a consistent environment between the old and new machines. In addition, it would allow integration to occur over a period of time as a matter of configuration rather than application update.
    If the plans encompass the use of additional resources, be they databases or something else, TUXEDO helps to integrate these new resources with the existing ones, without them having to be of the same type or nature. If the use of additional resources leads to distributed transaction processing, TUXEDO supports global transactions across homogeneous and heterogeneous types of resources, as long as these are XA-compliant.
    If the plans encompass expansion of the business, TUXEDO can help to integrate other applications or other environments within the existing one. These do not have to be of the same type and do not have to run on the same type of systems as the existing ones. Again, if this leads to transaction processing across applications, TUXEDO supports it over homogeneous and heterogeneous applications.

3. *UNIX only - Multivendor environment - No significant evolution plans*
    This case is similar to the first one and the same considerations apply. Because TUXEDO provides a consistent set of interfaces and tools across many platforms, because it performs automatic encoding and decoding of data, and because it is independent of the implementation of the networking software, all such platforms can be seen as if they were a homogeneous one; therefore, from an application point of view, a multivendor environment can be seen as single vendor one. The possibility to maintain this approach over a number of different existing and future hardware and software systems makes TUXEDO an effective software platform for multivendor environments.

4. *UNIX only - Multivendor environment - Evolution plans*
    Here the combination of comments for all previous cases applies. If you are looking for better performance, business modelling, application availability, distributed transaction processing, integration of new

hardware and software, interoperability with other applications, or any combination of these, TUXEDO can be the right platform.

5. *UNIX plus PCs - No significant evolution plans*
    This case is similar to the first and third case, and the same comments apply. Because TUXEDO provides the same libraries and interfaces on PCs (UNIX, DOS, WINDOWS, OS/2, Apple Macintosh), the advantages of using TUXEDO for performance, business modelling, application availability, etc., apply also to PC users. In fact, in case of performance issues, the use of TUXEDO can prove beneficial because the separation of the application into clients and servers makes it possible to locate the database operations (services) directly where the database resides, thus avoiding the overhead of excessive data flow between the PCs and the server machine(s). See also Chapter 3 for a discussion about this subject.

6. *UNIX plus PCs - Evolution plans*
    This case is similar to cases two and four, so again all comments apply here. Because of the separation between client and servers, any plans for integration of new hardware, software, resources, etc., can encompass the use of PCs. As far as PC clients are concerned, new systems are made transparently available by TUXEDO, no reconfiguration of the PCs is necessary, and probably no additional software either.

7. *Non UNIX mainframes only - No significant evolution plans*
    This case is not suitable for TUXEDO. TUXEDO is not a traditional mainframe product, and its core components do not run on mainframes. The various features like load balancing, data-dependent routing, prioritisation, etc., are not applicable. The System/HOST extension cannot be used independently of System/T, and this is not available on non UNIX mainframes.

8. *Non UNIX mainframes only - Evolution plans*
    This case is more suitable than the previous one. If the plans encompass moving towards open systems and gradually replacing the existing mainframe applications with client/server applications in an open environment, TUXEDO can provide a suitable environment for undertaking the migration. In particular, System/HOST and System/DOMAINS can be used to design migration paths from the mainframe configuration to an open one. Instantiations of System/HOST allow the integration of specific mainframe environments (MVS/CICS, DEC ACMS, etc.) from within a TUXEDO-based application on UNIX systems. More details about this are provided in Chapter 7.

9. *UNIX plus mainframe - No significant evolution plans*
   In this case TUXEDO can be useful for all that concerns the UNIX side, and all comments made in cases one, three and five are applicable. If the existing connection with the mainframe can be implemented via System/HOST, then the benefits discussed in those points can be taken into consideration.

10. *UNIX plus mainframe - Evolution plans*
    In this case TUXEDO can be useful for all the reasons discussed in cases one to six, and also those related to migration in point eight.

11. *Three tiers architectures - UNIX plus mainframe plus PC*
    In this case TUXEDO can be useful for all the reasons mentioned in the previous points.

Regardless of the environments, another way of looking at TUXEDO is to consider the areas which are best addressed by the product. These include:

- Performance
- Hardware interoperability
- Software interoperability
- Standards
- Distributed transaction processing
- Application availability
- Business modelling
- Client/server architecture
- Changing business conditions
- Expanding/changing locations.

If the reasons why you are looking for change to the environment include any of the above, the chances are that TUXEDO would be able to help. At a first glance there seem to be a lot of areas addressed by TUXEDO, but this is in fact the truth. Although TUXEDO does not provide solutions to all distributed and/or OLTP environments, this product is in many ways in a unique position in the market. Given its availability on many different software and hardware platforms, it is a very effective interoperability platform. Because of its features for OLTP, it is very effective for flexibility, robustness, and performance. Finally, given its features in terms of standards, it is very effective for integration of current and future environments.

All these reasons make people use TUXEDO as a safe choice, to help invest, and protect investments, in an evolving market. This is reinforced by TUXEDO being produced by a software company rather than a hardware manufacturer (like IBM's CICS, or NCR's TopEnd or SNI's UTM), and also by not being dependent on specific software platforms (like Transarc's Encina with respect to OSF's DCE).

8.4 Migration towards TUXEDO

Once people have taken the decision that TUXEDO could provide a suitable platform for their business, the next step is usually related to the question: "How can I migrate from my current environment, and how difficult or expensive is this?". Yet again there is no general answer to this question: it depends on the existing environment, on the aspirations, on type of hardware, software, human resources, etc. We all know that every case has to be treated differently, so describing one case instead of another would not be very helpful. What might be interesting to discuss, though, is a set of general points related to the subject of migration towards TUXEDO, to see what are the considerations that often play a role in it.

In a migration process towards TUXEDO, the first important aspect to consider is of course the starting point, i.e. the type of environment and application you may already have. Again, there are millions of different cases, but in general we can identify some common categories: pure mainframe environments, pure PC environments, mixed mini and PCs, mixed mini and mainframes, three tiers. As far as the application is concerned, its structure can be monolithic or client/server, and the data can be centralised on a single server machine, or distributed across multiple server machines. The starting point clearly has an impact on the migration process, and depending on the different cases, the difficulties to move towards TUXEDO vary significantly, in terms of code reuse or rewriting, in terms of architectural design, and, not to be underestimated, in terms of attitude to computing. Needless to say, if we start from a pure mainframe environment with large monolithic applications and centralised data, the migration path will be more dramatic than the case when we start from a client/server environment on minis and PCs.

Another important aspect is the direction you want to take. Again there can be different options, for example implementing the same application over a different hardware platform, or changing the application architecture, or changing functionality and environment altogether. Obviously this aspect has an impact too, in the sense that the perception of difficulty for the migration varies significantly, depending on the goals. A seemingly simple task of reimplementing an application with TUXEDO might be perceived as difficult if we wanted to adapt TUXEDO to the logic and programming of the existing application. In contrast, a seemingly difficult task of integrating different hardware, software, and resources in an application might be perceived as simple, given the features provided by the product.

In general, migration towards TUXEDO encompasses two separate types of actions: migration of environment and migration of applications. These are almost independent of each other. The former is not related to any material action, but rather to the adoption of a philosophy of open application architecture. It doesn't mean migration of code, but migration of approach, and applies even in the case when a brand new application is to be developed. The latter is related to the actual migration of an existing application, and is more related to the technical difficulties of using existing code or programming techniques within a TUXEDO application.

8.4.1 Migrating towards a TUXEDO environment

Migrating to a TUXEDO environment means migrating to a client/server environment, and, more specifically, to an environment where the applications are split into clients and servers, each of them having independent lives. Accepting this type of client/server architecture is straightforward in certain cases and very difficult in others, since it means reconsidering aspects such as the role of existing components of the environment and the ownership of resources. Experience suggests that we must address all the issues with an open mind, decide what would be the optimal choice in TUXEDO terms, and then see how far we are from it.

An example of this type of migration could be in the area of data security. If you are working with a DBMS environment, it is usually possible to assign permissions to each user and have the DMBS engine verify at runtime whether the user is allowed to access certain portions of data. This is possible because in such an environment each user is known to the database, and his/her access rights are declared when the connection with the DBMS is established. However, when you use TUXEDO's client/server architecture for the application, the user might not be known to the DBMS because the user does not connect to the database. The entity that connects to the database is an application server, which is allowed to execute a certain type of operation on all the relevant data for all the users that might request such operations.

Security on data access is therefore applied at a different level. The user is authenticated by the system, and then the user's request is authorised by the server for each individual service at the time the service is executed. Security might not be applied at SQL level, but that doesn't mean that it is less secure; in the end, the user is only allowed to execute the operations he/she is supposed to, only the verification is done at a different stage. Is this a case where the migration is complicated? The answer is yes if you want to implement the security in the same way as in a pure DBMS environment, the answer is no if you look at the end result. In such a case an open approach is needed, and the final result must be taken into consideration rather than an individual aspect *perse*.

Another issue related to migration of environment is about the preservation of existing skills. Everyone wishes to preserve existing expertise, skills, and investments in code. If, for example, I have expert CICS programmers, I might want to preserve their skills in the new environment. Of course this is a correct approach, however, again, we must have an open mind on these matters. Thinking about it, there is no point into being interested in Open OLTP and looking at its benefits but expecting things to be exactly like they were before. Obviously we want to preserve the skills and investments, but even more to be in the position to be able to grasp the changes in the technology, today and in the future.

So, what might it really mean to preserve existing skills in a new environment? If I have expert CICS programmers, what I might want to preserve is not really the pure CICS expertise, but rather the experience gained through years of CICS programming. One aspect, for instance, could be COBOL programming, in order to maintain productivity, but whether that includes CICS verbs or TUXEDO verbs might be irrelevant. Another aspect is the experience in designing OLTP applications. Given the experience with the existing environment, and, perhaps, with its limitations, experienced people can probably find better solutions with new technology rather than with old ones. While it might require more initial training (retraining, in fact), the productivity might be boosted by new technology, and the whole environment might benefit from a totally different approach. The investment in skills might be preserved simply by the historical memory of limitations in previous environments, and by the ability to use the same programming language.

At this point you could say: "Well, isn't this just a never-ending story, since I might just as well abandon CICS on mainframe and use TUXEDO on UNIX, but will I not run into the same problem again once newer technology is available and I want to move away from TUXEDO to a new environment for exactly the same reasons?". The answer here is that this is much less likely to happen. Once we move not just to open systems, but to an open application architecture, additions and changes to the applications do not occur via complete rewriting and replacement. They occur via interoperation with new application components, perhaps developed using new technology. This is the conceptual difference between a closed architecture, even if on open systems, and an open application architecture. The migration to this architecture and the standards it embodies is the first aspect of the migration process towards TUXEDO.

8.4.2 Migrating an application to TUXEDO

Migrating an existing application to TUXEDO essentially means adapting its architecture to TUXEDO's client/server model, and using TUXEDO interfaces to accomplish the results. Therefore, the migration of an application to a TUXEDO environment requires a certain number of code changes, and, most probably, a certain amount of redesign. It must be clear that no application can be moved to TUXEDO without partial rewriting, however, the amount of code rewriting varies depending on the type of application we have in the first place. The purpose of this section is to consider some of the more frequent cases, and to discuss in general what could be the difficulties.

- *From a traditional mainframe environment - Monolithic application - Centralised data.*
  In a case like this, a complete migration of the application requires redesign and rewriting. From the programming point of view, this should probably be regarded as the most effective approach. However, because such a complete migration could be extremely expensive in one step, an alternative approach consists of a staggered migration via interoperation with System/HOST.

  In this case the migration of front-end functionalities can occur first, and some of the rest later. The migration of front-end functionalities requires the rewriting of masks and screens using new tools and interfaces, but this can be made easier by 4GL tools or specific compatibility tools. The programs on the mainframe can stay there, but might require adaptation for being used with TUXEDO's gateways. In general, these modifications are not extensive, and are confined at the beginning of the program for reading the input, and at the end for returning the results.

  The second step can be the migration of certain programs and data. If possible, programs and data should be migrated together, by isolating from the central database the data relevant to a family of programs, and moving such data along with the programs. The migration of the code can be reasonably easy or very difficult. If the program provides an individual functionality, it can probably be converted into an application server with no major modifications provided that data access is possible through the same interfaces (e.g. SQL). The gathering of input data must be converted to TUXEDO's service interface, and the return must be converted in TUXEDO's ATMI; the body of the program could, however, be roughly similar. If the program calls other programs, the way in which this is achieved must be converted into the request/response or conversational paradigms. This might involve more extensive changes.

Chances are that a redesign and rewrite would be more effective.

If the program requires interaction with the user at different stages, or it directly performs input/output operations towards the user, these operations should be moved to the client side and a conversational paradigm should be used. However, redesign and rewrite would probably be more effective at this point.

For these environments, it is expected that the use of OLTP application generators that support TUXEDO, for example Magna X®, will make the process increasingly easier.

- *From a UNIX environment - RDBMS - Centralised data*
In this case the original application is probably monolithic, in the sense that front-end and back-end functionality are all bundled in the same executable. This means that the application does both screen handling and SQL work. The application might be running on the UNIX machine or on a PC via networking implementations of SQL. In this case redesign is necessary; the front-end operations should be extracted and packaged separately in a client program, while the SQL work should be isolated into services and packaged in one or more application servers.

If the application is already structured in a way that each screen invokes functions to execute sequences of SQL statements, then the identification of services can be reasonably straightforward. So could be the replacement of the invocation of functions with the invocation of services via TUXEDO's ATMI. The connection with the database engine must be placed in the server's initialisation phase; input and output for the services must be translated into TUXEDO's service interface and ATMI. If SQL code is intermixed with screen handling, probably a rewrite is more effective.

- *From a UNIX environment - RDBMS - Distributed data*
In this case the same situation as the previous case applies, but, in addition, there might be the case of distributed transaction processing. If transactions involve data on different machines, transaction demarcation can be provided using TUXEDO's semantics, and transactions can be coordinated by TUXEDO. In order to achieve this, statements like "SET TRANSACTION LEVEL" and "EXEC COMMIT WORK" must be replaced by TUXEDO's ATMI or X/Open's TX interface.

8.5 DBMS non XA-compliant

(This section is almost entirely copied from Section 5.2.3. It is repeated here for the benefit of those readers who are only interested in a high-level reading of the book. A more extensive examination of DTP in a TUXEDO environment is provided in

Chapter 5).

Although most of today's popular DBMSs provide XA-compliant interfaces, a recurrent question is usually whether non XA-compliant DBMS systems can also be used in a TUXEDO application. Actually, the question is typically split into two further questions: (a) if non XA-compliant resources can be used with TUXEDO; and (b) if they can participate in a global transaction.

A quick answer to this is yes and no. Saying that a resource is non XA-compliant means that it cannot support the DTP interface specified by X/Open and implemented by TUXEDO. In other words, the DTP capabilities of TUXEDO cannot be used in conjunction with such resources. Consequently, a non XA-compliant resource cannot take part in a global transaction coordinated by TUXEDO. However, there are a number of other capabilities that do not involve DTP. In particular, all features used for distributed processing are still applicable. TUXEDO applications can use servers that open and access non XA-compliant resources. Such servers are still accessed through the ATMI communication paradigms, and features like load balancing, prioritisation, and data-dependent routing still apply. In many environments, especially in those where there is one single database, this is sufficient. These features alone can provide the desired level of flexibility and performance.

When resources do not support the XA interface, service calls are always made in non transactional mode. The implementation of transactions in these services occurs by specifying the transaction boundaries through the native resource interface (i.e. SET TRANSACTION LEVEL and COMMIT WORK). Of course this does not allow for DTP, unless the resource supports it via its native interface.

8.6 Summary

In this final chapter we have seen some of the popular topics in conjunction with TUXEDO. The subject of business modelling is important because businesses are forced to address the problem of changing business conditions in the application. Several features of the TUXEDO System are helpful in this area, both to handle changing conditions over a specific timeframe, and to adapt the application to future characteristics.

High application availability is becoming a critical issue in distributed environments, even for applications which are not historically linked to mission-critical operations. An increasingly important role for an OLTP monitor is to provide features to achieve a sufficient level of high availability without having to invest in fault-tolerant hardware. TUXEDO's features in this area allow the user to build a more robust environment in case of hardware and software failures, and also to reduce the impact of maintenance operations.

The possibility to quickly understand if a product like TUXEDO can be useful in a specific environment is also becoming increasingly important. TUXEDO is known to be suitable for resolving various problems in many environments. A list of the most frequent conditions and environments has been provided.

Finally, the process of migration towards TUXEDO is often subject of interest. Migration towards TUXEDO does not simply include the technical difficulties of adapting existing application to TUXEDO's programming interfaces and architecture. It also involves accepting an open application architecture and being prepared to look at the set of final benefits, rather than trying to adapt TUXEDO's framework towards other approaches to application design.

Appendix A: Simple case study

The purpose of this appendix is to show what a TUXEDO application might look like. The most straightforward way of achieving this would have probably been to include a real application, but I believe that this approach would have not been effective for the purpose of this book. Unfortunately real applications are complex; the code is long and not easily readable over book pages; TUXEDO-related portions of the code are difficult to isolate from the rest; purpose and context need to be explained.

Instead, I used a simplified application, one that executes a set of operations likely to be found in any TUXEDO application, but that does not require much programming. In order to "visualise" this application, you could think of a PC at the Reception of a hospital, used to record information when a new patient is admitted. Personal details, date, and information about the expected treatment are recorded in the hospital's database, for the patient's record. Some of the patient's details, and the date of admission are also recorded in a Health Authority regional data centre, for administrative purposes.

The physical configuration could be the one presented in Figure 98. A UNIX mini, located in the hospital, hosts the local database and a set of application servers. The servers could be used by different hospital units to store and retrieve various categories of data. As a minimum, there will be one or two instances of a server offering a service for entering patient data into the database. In a real environment there would probably be several other servers providing different types of services, but for this example we assume that only one type of server is available. System/T is installed on this machine.

In every hospital unit, one or more PCs are connected to the UNIX mini (the local server machine) over a LAN. The connection is handled by

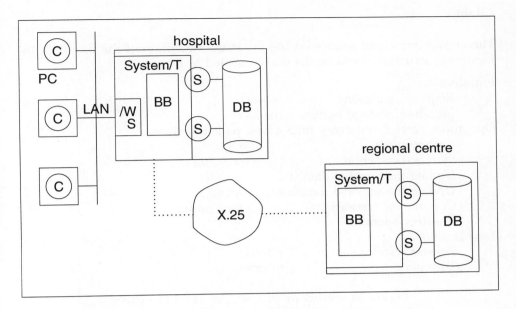

Figure 98. Sample application: physical configuration

System/WS, through the libraries installed on the PCs and the workstation handlers installed on the UNIX mini. In the figure, only the portion on the mini is shown.

The regional centre is also a UNIX system and is connected to the local server machine via an X.25 line. The system runs System/T, and hosts the Health Authority regional database. Also hosted on this system are a set of application servers for updating the regional database. As a minimum, there will be one or two instances of a server offering a service for updating the patient data.

Both databases are XA-compliant, and therefore can support a two-phase commit protocol coordinated by TUXEDO. The databases do not have to be of the same type, for example in the hospital there could be an INFORMIX OnLine, while in the regional centre there could be a TUXEDO System/D. In the following pages the client, the server in the hospital, and the configuration file are shown.

Client

The application client resides on the PC at the Reception of the hospital. Its high-level structure could be the one presented in Figure 99.

Initialisation
        Register as a client   - tpinit()
        Initialise message buffers - tpalloc()
Operations carried out every time a new patient arrives
        Gather input
        Start a transaction   - tpbegin()
        Update the hospital database   - tpcall()
        Update the regional database   - tpcall()
        Commit the transaction   - tpcommit()
        Confirm operation
Termination
        Release resources   - tpfree()
        Terminate   - tpterm()

Figure 99. Structure of a simple TUXEDO client

Of course this is not the only possible one; for example, asynchronous calls could be used, thus increasing the parallelism of execution for the database updates. Also, a real client program would probably be able to perform other operations, e.g. enquiries. Depending on the environment and programming style, it might make use of conversations, unsolicited modification, etc. However, I think this client is real enough to give a feeling of TUXEDO programming, and, as a side advantage, it can have roughly the same structure in different languages.

In order to focus on the TUXEDO-related code and to make the code as compact as possible, one further simplification has been applied: the procedures for gathering input, displaying output, and handling errors have been coded as a one-line function, but the actual code has been omitted. The generic names for these functions are *input()*, *display()*, and *error()*, and ideally correspond to any functions one may wish to implement for that purpose. Also, the actual structure of the request buffers is not shown, and we can simply assume that it is suitable to contain sufficient data in the appropriate format. Typically, the buffer will be a VIEW structure with a certain number of fields, or a generic STRING of characters.

This client is shown in several programming languages: C, COBOL, Windowing Korn Shell (WKSH®), VisualBasic, and INFORMIX 4GL. This selection should hopefully cover the most popular programming styles. TUXEDO programming is shown in bold.

Client: C

In this C client two separate VIEW buffers are used for the two database updates. These are allocated once and for all in the initialisation phase, and then reused each time.

```
#include "atmi.h"          /* TUXEDO Header File */
#include "hospital.h"      /* VIEW Header File - view hospital */
#include "natins.h"        /* VIEW Header File - view natins */

main()
{
        long vnatlen, vhosplen;
        struct hospital *vhospital;
        struct natins *vnatins;
        int in_use;

        /* Initialisation */
        if (tpinit((TPINIT *) NULL) == -1) {
                error();
                exit(1);
        }

        if((vhospital = (struct hospital *)tpalloc("VIEW", "hospital",
                        sizeof(struct hospital)) == NULL) {
                error();
                tpterm();
                exit(1);
        }

        if((vnatins = (struct natins *)tpalloc("VIEW", "natins",
                        sizeof(struct natins)) == NULL) {
                error();
                tpterm();
                exit(1);
        }

        in_use = 1;

        /* Client's loop */
        while (in_use)
        {

                /* get input */
                input(vhospital, vnatins, in_use);
```

```
        /* Start Transaction */
        if (tpbegin(30, 0) == -1) {
                error();



        }

        /* Make first service call */
        if(tpcall("HOSPUPD", (char *)vhospital,
                            sizeof(struct hospital),
                            (char *)&vhospital, &vhosplen,
                            TPSIGRSTRT) == -1) {
                tpabort(0);
                error();
        }

        /* Make second service call */
        if(tpcall("NIUPD", (char *)vnatins,
                            sizeof(struct natins),
                            (char *)&vnatins, &vnatlen,
                            TPSIGRSTRT) == -1) {
                tpabort(0);
                error();
        }

        /* Commit Transaction */
        if (tpcommit(0) == -1) {
                error();
        }

        /* Confirm Operation */
        display();

    }

    /* Termination */
    (void)tpfree((char *)vhospital);
    (void)tpfree((char *)vnatins);
    tpterm();
}
```

Client: COBOL

In this COBOL client, the same VIEW buffers as the C example are used. However, buffer allocation is missing from the initialisation phase because this is not necessary for the COBOL ATMI. Due to the impossibility of handling buffer pointers in COBOL, buffer allocation and handling are automatically done by the function performing the service request (TPCALL).

```
        IDENTIFICATION DIVISION.
        PROGRAM-ID. CLIENT.
        AUTHOR. FULVIO.
        ENVIRONMENT DIVISION.
        CONFIGURATION SECTION.
        WORKING-STORAGE SECTION.
******************************************************
* Tuxedo definitions
******************************************************
        01  TPTYPE-REC.
        COPY TPTYPE.
*
        01  TPTRXDEF-REC.
        COPY TPTRXDEF.
*
        01 TPSTATUS-REC.
        COPY TPSTATUS.
*
        01  TPSVCDEF-REC.
        COPY TPSVCDEF.
*
        01  TPINFDEF-REC.
        COPY TPINFDEF.
******************************************************
* Application data
******************************************************
        01  HOSPITAL-REC.
        COPY HOSPITAL.
*
        01  NATINS-REC.
        COPY NATINS.
*
        01  IN-USE     PIC 9.
*
```

249

```
PROCEDURE DIVISION.
******************************************************
* Initialisation
******************************************************

START-CLIENT.
*
    MOVE SPACES TO USRNAME.
    MOVE SPACES TO CLTNAME.
    MOVE SPACES TO PASSWD.
    MOVE SPACES TO GRPNAME.
    MOVE ZERO TO DATALEN.
    SET TPU-DIP TO TRUE.
*
    CALL "TPINITIALIZE" USING TPINFDEF-REC
            USER-DATA-REC
            TPSTATUS-REC.
    IF NOT TPOK PERFORM ERROR.
*
    MOVE 1 TO IN-USE.
*
******************************************************
* Client's Loop
******************************************************
CLIENT-LOOP.
    IF IN-USE = 0 GOTO TERMINATION.
*
******************************************************
* Get input
******************************************************
    PERFORM INPUT.
*
******************************************************
* Start Transaction
******************************************************
    MOVE 30 TO T-OUT.
    CALL "TPBEGIN" USING
            TPTRXDEF-REC
            TPSTATUS-REC.
    IF NOT TPOK PERFORM ERROR.
******************************************************
* Make first service call
******************************************************
    MOVE "VIEW" TO REC-TYPE.
    MOVE "hospital" TO REC-SUBTYPE.
    MOVE "HOSPUPD" TO SERVICE-NAME.
    SET TPSIGRSTRT TO TRUE.
```

```
        CALL "TPCALL" USING TPSVCDEF-REC
                TPTYPE-REC
                HOSPITAL-REC
                TPTYPE-REC
                HOSPITAL-REC
                TPSTATUS-REC.

        IF NOT TPOK
                CALL "TPABORT" USING
                        TPTRXDEF-REC
                        TPSTATUS-REC.
                PERFORM ERROR.
        END-IF.
*****************************************************
* Make second service call
*****************************************************
        MOVE "natins" TO REC-SUBTYPE.
        MOVE "NIUPD" TO SERVICE-NAME.
*
        CALL "TPCALL" USING TPSVCDEF-REC
                TPTYPE-REC
                NATINS-REC
                TPTYPE-REC
                NATINS-REC
                TPSTATUS-REC.
        IF NOT TPOK
                CALL "TPABORT" USING
                        TPTRXDEF-REC
                        TPSTATUS-REC.
                PERFORM ERROR.
        END-IF.
*****************************************************
* Commit Transaction
*****************************************************
        CALL "TPCOMMIT" USING
                TPTRXDEF-REC
                TPSTATUS-REC.
        IF NOT TPOK PERFORM ERROR.
*****************************************************
* Confirm Operation
*****************************************************
        PERFORM DISPLAY.
        GOTO CLIENT-LOOP.
```

```
****************************************************
* Termination
****************************************************
 TERMINATION.
*
     CALL "TPTERM" USING TPSTATUS-REC.
     IF NOT TPOK PERFORM ERROR.
*
     STOP RUN.
```

Client: Windowing Korn Shell

This is a non graphical version of a WKSH client. It is assumed that the data are passed in one environment variable used as a STRING buffer. A STRING buffer is used because there is no straightforward representation of VIEW buffers in shell programming. The server reading the request will probably have to manipulate the data in order to extract the individual values. Also in this case the buffer handling is done internally, so no allocation needs be done. This is example was contributed by Steve Pendegrast of USL.

```
#!/usr/bin/wksh
. $WKSHLIBDIR/libtux/tuxinit.sh
integer IN_USE=1
tpinit || exit 1
# Client's loop
while ((IN_USE))
do
        # get input
        input VHOSPITAL VNATINS IN_USE

        # Start Transaction
        tpbegin 30 || error

        # Make first service call
        tpcall -s HOSPUPD "$VHOSPITAL"  || {
                tpabort
                error
        }
        # Make second service call
        tpcall -s NIUPD "$VNATINS" || {
                tpabort
                error
        }

        # Commit Transaction
        tpcommit || error

        # Confirm Operation
        display
done
# termination
tpterm
```

Client: VisualBasic

The code of this client is limited to three subroutines, one to perform TUXEDO initialisation while loading the initial form (Form_load), one for the execution of service requests (Button1_Click), and one to perform TUXEDO termination (Form_unload). Not included are the (probably many) subroutines to define and handle the graphics on screen and the mouse clicking. These are not significant, as far as TUXEDO programming is concerned. As in the case of WKSH, this client uses STRING buffers.

```
Dim TuxDir As String
Dim vhospital As tuxbuf
Dim vnatins As tuxbuf

'Errors from ATMI
Const TPMINVAL = 0
Const TPEABORT = 1
Const TPEBADDESC = 2
Const TPEBLOCK = 3
Const TPEINVAL = 4
Const TPELIMIT = 5
Const TPENOENT = 6
Const TPEOS = 7
Const TPEPERM = 8
Const TPEPROTO = 9
Const TPESVCERR = 10
Const TPESVCFAIL = 11
Const TPESYSTEM = 12
Const TPETIME = 13
Const TPETRAN = 14
Const TPGOTSIG = 15
Const TPERMERR = 16
Const TPEITYPE = 17
Const TPEOTYPE = 18
Const TPERELEASE = 19
Const TPEHAZARD = 20
Const TPEHEURISTIC = 21
Const TPEEVENT = 22
Const TPEMATCH = 23
Const TPEDIAGNOSTIC = 24
Const TPMAXVAL = 25
```

```
´ Initialization

Sub Form_load()
    TuxDir$ = Environ$("ROOTDIR")
    slot.picture = LoadPicture(input$)
    ret% = TPINIT(ByVal 0&)
    If ret% < 0 Then
        Error ()
        Exit Sub
    End If
    vhospital.bufptr = TPALLOC("STRING", "", 100)
    If vhospital.bufptr = 0 Then
        Error ()
        Exit Sub
    End If
    vnatins.bufptr = TPALLOC("STRING", "", 100)
    If vnatins.bufptr = 0 Then
        Error ()
        Exit Sub
    End If
End Sub

´ Client's loop

Sub Button1_Click ()
    Static retlen As tuxbuf

´ Get Input
    vhospital.bufptr = Input(Readout.Caption)
    vnatins.bufptr = Input(Readout.Caption)

´ Start Transaction
    ret% = TPBEGIN(30, 0)
    If ret% = -1 Then
        Error ()
        Exit Sub
    End If

´ Make first service call
    ret% = TPCALL("HOSPUPD", vhospital.bufptr, 0, vhospital, retlen, 0)
    If ret% = -1 Then
        ret% = TPABORT(0)
        Error()
        Exit Sub
    End If
```

```
´ Make second  service call
     ret% = TPCALL("NIUPD", vnatins.bufptr, 0, vnatins, retlen, 0)
     If ret% = -1 Then
       ret% = TPABORT(0)
       Error()
       Exit Sub
     End If

´ Commit Transaction
     ret% = TPCOMMIT(0)
     If ret% = -1 Then
       Error()
       Exit Sub
     End If

´ Confirm Operation
     Display()

End Sub

´ Termination

Sub Form_unload(Cancel As Integer)
     ret% = TPFREE(vhospital.bufptr)
     ret% = TPFREE(vnatins.bufptr)
     ret% = TPTERM()
     If ret% < 0 Then
          Error ()
     End If
End Sub
```

Client: INFORMIX 4GL

This client has the same structure as the others but, because with INFORMIX 4GL all TUXEDO function calls are handled by the INFORMIX software, buffer handling is totally transparent to the application. Instead of using buffers, the application provides input to service calls through variables, like for any other function call. The buffers internally used by this client have an INFORMIX-defined structure, and can be used only in conjunction with servers written with INFORMIX 4GL (see example in the next section). It is expected that this limitation will be removed in future releases of INFORMIX 4GL, thus making clients produced with INFORMIX 4GL usable with servers coded in other languages. This example was contributed by Rainer Lutz of INFORMIX.

```
main
        define  in_use          integer
        define  ret             integer
        define  vhospital       char(80)
        define  vnatins         char(80)

## Initialisation
        if ftpinit() = -1 then
                error()
                exit program 1
        end if

        let in_use = 1

## Client's loop
        while in_use = 1

## Get input
                call input(vhospital, vnatins, in_use)

## Start transaction
                if ftpbegin(30) = -1 then
                        error()
                end if
```

```
##  Make first service call
              call fptpcall("HOSPUPD", vhospital,
                            TPSIGRSTRT, 2)
                      returning ret
              if ret = -1 then
                      call ftpabort()
                      error()
              end if

##  Make second service call
              call fptpcall("HIUPD", vnatins,
                            TPSIGRSTRT, 2)
                      returning ret
              if ret = -1 then
                      call ftpabort()
                      error()
              end if

##  Commit transaction
              if ftpcommit() = -1 then
                      error()
              end if

      end while

##  Termination
      if ftpterm() = -1 then
              error()
              exit program 1
      end if

      exit program 0

end
```

Server

This server is located on the UNIX mini where the hospital's database resides, and is used to update the patients' records. Using the same criteria as for the client, the server presented here is a simplified version of an application server, in which only the TUXEDO programming is emphasised.

Because the server's main is provided by TUXEDO (as a reminder, the server's main is the portion of the server's code which initialises the program, dequeues requests, invokes service routines, and delivers replies), the programming involves only the service routines. In our simplified version, we assume that the server offers only one service (HOSPUPD), although, in a real application, it would probably offer more. As far as TUXEDO programming is concerned, there is no real difference, as every service is a separate function.

```
receive input
if buffer is not a VIEW              - tptypes()
        move data to a VIEW
        if this is impossible
                return error  - tpreturn()
verify input
if input not valid
        return error         - tpreturn()
update database
if update fails
        return error         - tpreturn()
return success               - tpreturn()
```

Figure 100. Structure of the HOSPUPD service

The structure of service HOSPUPD is shown in Figure 100. The server always works with VIEWS. Because the service could be called by clients using STRING buffers, a conversion is necessary. Like in the case of the client, the code for converting the data into a VIEW, verifying the input, and updating the database has been omitted. The functions used for these operations are *convert()*, *verify()*, and *dbupdate()*. In particular, function *dbupdate()* is assumed to contain all SQL statements necessary to update the patient's data, for example the fields in a table named *patients*. The way in which this is done is independent of TUXEDO programming, and, if the data are not stored in a DBMS, it might not even occur via SQL statements (e.g. in case of an ISAM file). Whichever the way, the coding of the service is the same, only function *dbupdate()* will be different. Note that this service doesn't have to explicitly start a transaction, as this has already been done by the client. Finally, the service returns success or failure, but doesn't return data. This would be different for an enquiry service, in which a reply buffer would be filled and sent to the client via tpreturn().

The programming languages presented here are C, COBOL, and INFORMIX 4GL. Tools like WKSH and VisualBasic are only used for front-ends (clients), so they are unusable here.

Server: C

In a C service, the input is received directly in a TPSVCINFO structure (see Chapter 4). The data field contains the application data sent by the client. The type of the received buffer is obtained via function tptypes().

```
#include "atmi.h"        /* TUXEDO Header File */
#include "hospital.h"     /* VIEW Header File - view hospital*/

/* Service HOSPUPD */

HOSPUPD(TPSVCINFO *input)
{
        struct hospital *hospital;
        char *buftype, *bufstype;

        if (tptypes(input->data, buftype, bufstype) == -1) {
                error()
                tpreturn(TPFAIL, 0, NULL, 0L, 0);
        }
        if (strncmp(buftype,"VIEW",4) != 0) {
                /* Convert input */
                if (convert(input->data, hospital) == -1) {
                        error()
                        tpreturn(TPFAIL, 0, NULL, 0L, 0);
        } else {
                hospital = (struct hospital *)input->data;
        }

        /* Verify input */
        if (verify(hospital) == -1) {
                error()
                tpreturn(TPFAIL, 0, NULL, 0L, 0);
        }

        /* Execute update */
        if (dbupdate(hospital) == -1) {
                error()
                tpreturn(TPFAIL, 0, NULL, 0L, 0);
        }

        /* Return
        tpreturn(TPSUCCESS, 0, NULL, 0L, 0);
}
```

Server: COBOL

In a COBOL service, the input must be obtained through a call to function TPSVCSTART. This returns the data sent by the client in a user record, and the type of buffer in a TUXEDO-defined record. Therefore the type of buffer is available in a field and there is no need to invoke function tptypes().

```
        IDENTIFICATION DIVISION.
        PROGRAM-ID. HOSPUPD.
        AUTHOR. FULVIO.
        ENVIRONMENT DIVISION.
        CONFIGURATION SECTION.

        WORKING-STORAGE SECTION.
 *********************************************************
 * Tuxedo definitions
 *********************************************************
        01  TPSVCRET-REC.
        COPY TPSVCRET.
 *
        01  TPTYPE-REC.
        COPY TPTYPE.
 *
        01 TPSTATUS-REC.
        COPY TPSTATUS.
 *
        01  TPSVCDEF-REC.
        COPY TPSVCDEF.
 *********************************************************
 * Application data
 *********************************************************
        01 INPUT-REC.
        COPY INPUT.
 *
        01 HOSPITAL-REC.
        COPY HOSPITAL.
 *
        05 STATUS              PIC S9(9) COMP-5.
             88 OK                 VALUE 0.
             88 NOK                   VALUE 1.
 *
```

```
        PROCEDURE DIVISION.
*
    MOVE LENGTH OF INPUT-REC to LEN.

        CALL "TPSVCSTART" USING TPSVCDEF-REC
                    TPTYPE-REC
                    INPUT-REC
                    TPSTATUS-REC.
        IF NOT TPOK
              PERFORM ERROR.
              SET TPFAIL TO TRUE.
              COPY TPRETURN REPLACING
                    DATA-REC BY INPUT-REC.
        END-IF
****************************************************
* Convert
****************************************************
        IF REC-TYPE NOT = "VIEW"
              PERFORM CONVERT.
              IF NOT OK
                    PERFORM ERROR.
                    SET TPFAIL TO TRUE.
                    COPY TPRETURN REPLACING
                          DATA-REC BY INPUT-REC.
              END-IF
        ELSE
                    MOVE INPUT-REC TO HOSPITAL-REC.
        END-IF.
****************************************************
* Verify
****************************************************
        PERFORM VERIFY.
        IF NOT OK
              PERFORM ERROR.
              SET TPFAIL TO TRUE.
              COPY TPRETURN REPLACING
                    DATA-REC BY INPUT-REC.
        END-IF
****************************************************
* Execute update
****************************************************
        PERFORM DBUPDATE.
        IF NOT OK
              PERFORM ERROR.
              SET TPFAIL TO TRUE.
              COPY TPRETURN REPLACING
                    DATA-REC BY INPUT-REC.
        END-IF
```

```
*******************************************************
* Return
*******************************************************
       SET TPSUCCESS TO TRUE.
       COPY TPRETURN REPLACING
            DATA-REC BY INPUT-REC.
```

Server: INFORMIX 4GL

The structure of this service is similar to the others, but because the buffer handling is done internally by the INFORMIX software, a conversion is never necessary. However, this also means that the client must send the data in the proper format, and this is only done by clients produced with INFORMIX-4GL. As said, this limitation is expected to be removed in future versions of the product. Also, function *dbupdate()* will have to contain INFORMIX-4GL code and will only allow updates to an INFORMIX OnLine database.

```
globals "SVRGLOB.4gl"

function locserv()
        WHENEVER ERROR CALL svrlogerr
end function

##  service HOSPUPD

function HOSPUPD(hospital, flags)
        define  hospital        char(80)
        define  flags           char(64)
        define  ret             integer

##  Verify
        if verify(hospital) = -1 then
                error()
                call ftpreturn("TPFAIL", 0, "", 0, 0)
        end if

        let in_use = 1

##  Execute update
        call dbupdate(hospital) returning ret
        if ret = -1 then
                error()
                call ftpreturn("TPFAIL", 0, "", 0, 0)
        end if

##  Return
        call ftpreturn("TPSUCCESS", 0, "", 0, 0)

end function
```

Configuration file

The configuration file for an application is usually located on the master machine. In this example, we assume that the master is the UNIX mini at the hospital. The UBBCONFIG contains information about the two UNIX systems with System/T on board, and also about the network, the Workstation Handlers, the servers, and the services (see also Chapter 6). No specific information about the PCs is necessary in the UBBCONFIG; each PC communicates sufficient information at the time it connects to the application via System/WS.

The open string for the databases and the appropriate transaction manager servers are also listed in the configuration file. The open string and the name of the transaction manager server are the only necessary pieces of information as far as the databases are concerned. The databases do not have to be of the same type, for example in the hospital there is an INFORMIX OnLine, while in the regional centre there is a TUXEDO System/D.

A number of parameters, especially those in the RESOURCES sections, define the maximum number of entities handled by this TUXEDO application. For our example, we can have a total maximum of 50 application servers, 100 services, and 80 PCs simultaneously connected to the application. Following is the entire UBBCONFIG file for the application.

Configuration file: UBBCONFIG

```
*RESOURCES
IPCKEY              52220
MASTER              SITE1
UID           410
GID           600
PERM          0660
MAXACCESSERS        150
MAXGTT              100
MAXSERVERS 50
MAXSERVICES100
MAXWSCLIENTS        80
MAXCONV             10
MODEL               MP
LDBAL         Y
OPTIONS             LAN
CMTRET              COMPLETE
MAXBUFTYPE 16
MAXBUFSTYPE         32
SCANUNIT      10
SANITYSCAN 12
DBBLWAIT      6
BBLQUERY      180
BLOCKTIME     6
NOTIFY              DIPIN
SYSTEM_ACCESS       FASTPATH
USIGNAL             SIGUSR2

*MACHINES
local   LMID=SITE1
        TUXCONFIG="/u/admin/application/tux"
        ROOTDIR="/u/admin/tuxbin"
        APPDIR="/u/admin/application"
        TLOGNAME="TLOG"
        TLOGSIZE=100
region  LMID=SITE2
        TUXCONFIG="/home/admin/application/tux"
        ROOTDIR="/home/admin/tuxbin"
        APPDIR="/home/admin/application"
        TLOGNAME="TLOG"
        TLOGSIZE=100
```

Appendix A: Simple case study

```
*NETWORK
SITE1
        NADDR="0x0002cbfcc009c1ca"
        BRIDGE="/dev/tcp"
        NLSADDR="0x00021234c009c1ca"
SITE2
        NADDR="0x0002cbfcc009c1c8"
        BRIDGE="/dev/inet/tcp"
        NLSADDR="0x00021234c009c1c8"
*GROUPS
WSGRPLMID=SITE1    GRPNO=1
LOGRP        LMID=SITE1    GRPNO=2
             TMSNAME=TMS_INF
             TMSCOUNT=3
             OPENINFO="INFORMIX-ONLINE:hospdb:INFORMIXDIR=/usr/informix:
                  SQLEXEC=/usr/informix/lib/sqlturbo"
REGRP        LMID=SITE2    GRPNO=3
             TMSNAME=TMS_SQL
             TMSCOUNT=3
             OPENINFO="TUXEDO/SQL:/u/tuxedo/myapp/appd1:appdb:readwrite"

*SERVERS
WSL          SRVGRP=WSGRP        SRVID=100
             CLOPT="-A -- -d /dev/tcp -n0x00021234c009c1ca -m1 -x20 -wWSH"
             GRACE=0             RESTART=Y
locserv      SRVGRP=LOGRP        SRVID=1
             CLOPT="-A"
             RQPERM=0660 REPLYQ=N     RPPERM=0660
             MIN=2 MAX=4CONV=N
             SYSTEM_ACCESS=FASTPATH
             MAXGEN=3    GRACE=86400 RESTART=Y
regserv      SRVGRP=REGRP        SRVID=1
             CLOPT="-A"
             RQPERM=0660 REPLYQ=N     RPPERM=0660
             MIN=2 MAX=4CONV=N
             SYSTEM_ACCESS=FASTPATH
             MAXGEN=3    GRACE=86400 RESTART=Y
*SERVICES
HOSPUPD     LOAD=200    PRIO=60
       BUFTYPES="STRING;VIEW:hospital"
       AUTOTRAN=Y
NIUPD LOAD=150      PRIO=50
       BUFTYPES="STRING;VIEW:natins"
       AUTOTRAN=Y
```

Appendix B: Platforms

As mentioned several times, System/T is available on multiple hardware and software platforms. Following is a list of the platforms I know of, just to give you an indication.

Hardware	Software
Alpha AXP	DEC™ OSF/1™
Amdhal 5370/390	UTS
AviiON®	DG/UX
AT&T 3B2	SVR3.2
Bull DPX/2/20	BOS
HP 9000	HP/UX
IBM® RS/6000™	AIX™
ICL DRS®	SVR4
NCR	SVR4
Olivetti LSX®	SVR4 & DC/OSX
Sequent Symmetry	DYNIX/ptx™
SUN Sparc™	SunOS™ & Solaris™
Tandem Integrity	Nonstop/UX
Unisys U6000	SVR3.2 & SVR4
i386/486™ based PCs	SCO™ ODT, SVR4, SVR4.2, UnixWare®

New platforms are regularly added by Novell and by TUXEDO source code licensees. For an up-to-date list, the best bet is to contact Novell.

/WS is available on most of the above hardware platforms, plus MS/DOS®, MS/WINDOWS®, OS/2®, and Apple Macintosh®. At the time of going to press, I understand that Unisys have ported /WS to WindowsNT®. Netware® connectivity is also expected to be made available.

/HOST is available for MVS™/CICS™ on IBM® 308x/309x/43xx and Amdhal 5370/390, for GCOS7-TDS on Bull, and for OpenVMS®/ACMS on DEC™.

Glossary

Most of the technical terms used in this book are commonly used in the areas of OLTP and distributed computing, so there shouldn't be any ambiguity as far as their meaning is concerned. However, a few of them have a specific meaning in the context of the TUXEDO System, and some refer to specific features and components of TUXEDO and other products. For your reference, following is a summary; this is mostly based on the glossary provided with TUXEDO's documentation, with the permission of Novell, Inc.

Abort

The action of terminating a transaction so that all protected resources, such as database records, have the same value they had at the beginning of the transaction.

Access machine

The processor within the administrative domain of an application at which a client first accesses the system. For native clients, this is the machine on which they are running. For workstation clients, this is the site where they contact the application.

Administration

In a TUXEDO environment, the act of monitoring and administering a TUXEDO application via tools and automatic functions. Also the act of setting up the environment for an application. Complementary to *System programming*.

Administrative domain

That portion of an application that is actively administered at runtime by a DBBL process. This does not include workstations or host processors.

Application

The collection of client and server processes which use the TUXEDO System to communicate with each other. From a TUXEDO-specific point of view, the collection of servers, services, and associated RMs described in a single UBBCONFIG or TUXCONFIG configuration file.

Application domain

The collection of processes, machines, resources, and configuration files that constitute an individual TUXEDO application. Virtually synonymous to *Application*, this term is used in the context of *System/DOMAINS*.

Application Program Interface (API)

The verbs and environment that exist at the application level to support a particular system software product.

Application Transaction Monitor Interface (ATMI)

This is the application programming interface for the TUXEDO System, and includes transaction routines, buffer management routines, service interface routines, and communication routines.

Backup

The act of an RM in using a log to restore a resource or resources to some predetermined state by applying log entries sequentially to the resource until the desired state has been achieved; also, the act of an RM to restore logically a resource or resources to a pretransaction state by not applying the resource state changes requested by the transaction.

Backup master

The machine defined in the UBBCONFIG which can undertake the role of the *master machine*, should this become unavailable.

BDMCONFIG

The binary configuration file for interdomain communication. This is used in conjunction with *System/DOMAINS* and is created from the

DMCONFIG ASCII file.

BRIDGE

Internal process that maintains virtual circuits to other nodes participating in an application for the purpose of transferring application messages between the nodes.

Buffer types

An abstract name for a message type. The TUXEDO System provides seven predefined types for message communication: FML, CARRAY, STRING, VIEW, X_COMMON, X_C_TYPE, X_OCTET. These buffer types are transparently encoded and decoded across a network of heterogeneous machines. Applications can define additional buffer types.

Bulletin Board

A collection of shared data structures designed to keep track of a running application. It contains information about servers, services, clients, and transactions pertaining to a TUXEDO application. The Bulletin Board is replicated on each *System/T* machine in the application.

Bulletin Board Liaison (BBL)

An internal administrative process responsible for maintaining a copy of the Bulletin Board on a particular node. When the system is running, one BBL process runs continuously on each logical machine in the application.

CARRAY buffer

A data structure that is an array of characters any of which can be the null character. The interpretation of the array is entirely application dependent.

CICS

Customer Information Control System - one of IBM's OLTP systems.

Client

An application process which registers with TUXEDO and subsequently communicates with TUXEDO-registered servers. Clients can run on *System/T* machines or on PC and workstations connected to one of such machines via the *System/WS* extension.

Client/server model

A processing model by which certain entities (servers) offer a set of services for carrying out operations, and other entities (clients) request such services instead of directly executing the operations. In a TUXEDO environment, an application is split into client and server processes.

Commit

The act of completing a transaction so that changes to the database are recorded and stable. Protected resources are released.

Connection

A half-duplex communication channel between processes.

Conversation

A dialog (send/receive information) over a connection.

Conversational

The attribute of communication that is described by sending data to and receiving data from another component in an iterative fashion without return to the OLTP monitor until the whole application thought is completed; the salient feature of this form of execution is that each "receive" after the first puts the process in a state of suspension until the component being addressed responds.

Conversational server

A server that offers services that require a connection to have a conversation with the requester. The conversation follows an application-established protocol. A conversational service must conform to the startup and termination rules of TUXEDO services.

Data-dependent routing

Routing that directs a request to be processed by a particular group of application servers based on the value in a data field of the message.

Data transfer protocol

A set of rules for transforming data of a particular buffer type from one representation into another.

Data Base Management System (DBMS)

A software system that provides an application with access to shared data.

Distinguished Bulletin Board Liaison (DBBL)

An internal administrative process that runs on the *MASTER* node of the application and communicates with *BBLs* to coordinate updates to each Bulletin Board.

Distributed Processing

In a TUXEDO environment this term identifies the set of capabilities provided by the system in support to distributed computing among different applicative entities and heterogeneous types of systems.

Distributed Transaction Processing (DTP)

Coordination of transactions among application servers residing on separate nodes and/or using different RMs. DTP implies the capability to coordinate multiple, autonomous actions as a single logical unit of work.

DMCONFIG

An ASCII configuration file used in conjunction with *System/DOMAINS* for describing the characteristics of interdomain communication.

dmloadcf

An administrative tool to convert a *DMCONFIG* file into a binary *BDMCONFIG*.

dmunloadcf

An administrative tool to extract an ASCII representation of a *BDMCONFIG* file.

Domain

See *Application domain* and *Application*.

DTP model

The reference model for distributed transaction processing in a TUXEDO environment. This includes different components (application, transaction manager, and RMs) and different interfaces (noticeably the *ATMI* and the *XA*). TUXEDO's DTP model has been adopted with some changes by X/Open.

Event

An indication to a TUXEDO process of the occurrence of a particular state or condition, for example disconnection, transaction request mode, connection request, and so forth.

External Data Representation (XDR)

A canonical data format defined by SUN Microsystems and used to transfer data between heterogeneous hardware nodes, using a neutral data format.

Field table

A file of FML field names and their identifiers. The field table enables users to refer to fields by logical names rather than by the system field identifier.

FML buffer

A buffer of self-describing data items accessed through the field manipulation language API.

Foreign node

A node in the network that does not have access to the configuration's Bulletin Board, or which cannot execute the full complement of TUXEDO software. A node is considered to be foreign if and only if it is not considered to be *native*.

Form

A template to guide a user entering data into the system or to display data on the user's terminal.

Gateway

Communication mechanism between different environments (for example, between native and foreign nodes, or between autonomous applications).

Gateway server

A server process that is resident on a *native* node, that communicates with one or more foreign machines.

Global transaction

A commonly accepted name for a transaction that uses multiple servers and/or multiple RM interfaces and is coordinated as an atomic unit of work.

Global Transaction Identifier (GTRID)

A data structure whose value uniquely identifies a global transaction.

Group

A collection of servers and/or services on a machine, optionally associated with an RM. A group is an administrative unit used for booting, shut down, and migration of servers and services.

Handler

See *Workstation Handler*.

Host

A foreign node having services that can be made available to a TUXEDO application running on one or more native nodes.

/Host

See *System/HOST*.

/Host Instantiation

The set of software that enables a System/T application to access services of a *particular* host environment via one or more communications mechanisms. Some of this software runs on native System/T nodes, and some may run on host nodes. /Host instantiations must conform to requirements mandated by the generic /Host capability.

Internationalisation

A mechanism that allows customisation of a system's text messages and date formats into an application's language and format of choice.

Inter Process Communication (IPC)

This is typically achieved through the uses of resources made available by the operating system's kernel, for example message queues, semaphores, and shared memory segments.

Indexed Sequential Access Method (ISAM)

The predecessor to VSAM KSDS; more restrictive than KSDS, harder to use, and, in most instances, slower.

LAN

Local area network.

LAN partition

The failure of a LAN connecting the machines of an application resulting in a loss of message communication between the machines. A partitioned site is one that no longer has access to the master node.

Lazy connection

A network connection not brought up until needed.

LINK

A CICS application function that allows one program to call another program that lives in the same region. It also provides for an argument-parameter communication between the two programs. Its operation is synchronous: the "calling" program suspends execution while the "called" program is executing.

Listener

See *Workstation listener* or *tlisten*.

Local domain

The set of services made available by a TUXEDO applicative domain to external applicative domains. This term is used in the context of *System/DOMAINS*.

Local machine

The machine on which the process or resource is located.

Local transaction

A local RM transaction that is active on behalf of a global transaction.

Logical machine (LMID)

A processing element used in a TUXEDO application and given a logical name in the configuration file.

LU

A port through which an end user accesses a SNA network in order to communicate with another end user and through which the end user accesses the functions provided by system services control points.

LU6.2

An IBM-defined set of protocols, procedures, and environment descriptions that define a method of region-to-region or machine-to-machine communication; defining features are program-to-program communication and network-wide resource recoverability; the protocol inherent in CICS.

Machine

A generic processing element, typically a minicomputer. In a more specific TUXEDO context, one of the System/T nodes configured in the UBBCONFIG. A binary version of a form, generally containing fields into which users enter data.

Master node

The MASTER node for an application as designated in the RESOURCES section of the configuration file. It contains the master copy of the TUXCONFIG binary configuration file. Administration of the running system is done from the MASTER node.

Message

In a TUXEDO environment, the data exchanged between processes. A message is constituted of TUXEDO-defined headers and application data. See also *Buffer Types*.

Message catalogue

With respect to internationalisation, a file or storage area containing program messages, command prompts, and responses to prompts for a particular native language, territory, and codeset.

MP model

A type of application configuration that runs on more than one machine.

Multiple Virtual Storage (MVS)

One of IBM's principal mainframe operating systems.

Name server

A software component of System/T that transparently maps service names to physical addresses so that users can communicate with services by name rather than by internal identifier. Although not strictly true, the Bulletin Board is often referred to as the name server.

Native System/T node

A node in a particular System/T configuration that contains the full complement of System/T software, and which has access to the same

Bulletin Board as all other native nodes in the configuration (that is, it is part of the administrative domain of the application). A node is considered to be native if and only if not considered to be *foreign*.

Network address

A unique network identifier assigned to each network connection made. This unique identifier may either be assigned randomly by the provider or a specific identifier may be requested by the process establishing the connection. The format of the network address is provider-specific.

Network provider

Identifies the protocol used at the transport level and below to communicate data across a network. Network providers are typically accessed from programs through a transport interface. Examples of network providers are TCP/IP and StarLAN.

Node

A point on a network. The term is also used to refer to a computer (for example, a single instantiation of the operating system) that participates in a System/T application.

Non-master node

Any node of a System/T application that is not designated to be the MASTER node.

Non-partitioned

A term used to identify portions of a partitioned network that continue to be able to communicate with the DBBL on the master node.

On-Line Transaction Processing (OLTP)

Execution of units of work in an environment that appears to the user as immediate; real-time; usually having internal recoverability, history-keeping, and consistency-assurance features.

Open OLTP

Same as OLTP, but in "open" environments; additional features include vendor independence, interoperability of multiple software products, and compliance to standards.

Out-of-band communication

Data delivered by System/T outside the normal client/server

communications channels supported by System/T. See also *unsolicited messages*.

Partition

A state where some active nodes of a networked application are unable to contact other active nodes (e.g. due to a LAN failure).

Pier-to-Pier

One of the interfaces between the application and the communication RM in X/Open's DTP model.

Provider

The communications product supplying networking facilities through level 4 of the OSI communications protocol.

Recover

A request from a coordinator or a participant to complete an identified transaction.

Recovery

The act of restoring a resource in a consistent state after a failure during the commitment of a transaction.

Region

A subdivision of memory under MVS in which a separate task under the operating system can run, such as CICS, IMS, DB2, etc.

Remote domain

The set of services made available by an external applicative domain. This term is used in the context of *System/DOMAIN*. See also *Local domain*.

Remote Procedure Call (RPC)

A form of communication, similar to a procedure call, where a requester specifies a System/T service to be performed and passes data along with its request. An application server offering the service dispatches an application routine along with the caller's data; in the host environment, the application service routine is invoked. When the service is finished, a reply is sent back to the caller.

Remote Transaction Execution

The shipping of a request by one system to another system with the intent of having a transaction executed on the remote system, without notification of success or failure, and possibly no return of results, to the requesting system.

Request/response server

A server that offers request/response services. A service of type request/response is handled like a procedure and has the following properties: it is executed until completion, it does not have any dialogue with the requester, and it sends back a return value to the requester. For a requester, the execution of a request/response service can be synchronous or asynchronous.

Resource manager (RM)

An interface and associated software providing access to a collection of information and/or processes, for example a DBMS. Resource managers provide transaction capabilities and permanence of actions, and are the entities accessed and controlled within a global transaction.

Resource manager instance

A particular instance or occurrence of an RM (e.g. the EMPLOYEE database). There may be many occurrences or instances of the same or different RMs within a global transaction, each managing different data. Each RM instance is considered to be autonomous, in full control of local access (for both local and global transactions), administration, and so forth.

Rollback

Completion of a global transaction with the release of protected resources in their initial state. In our context, synonymous to *abort*.

RPC server

A server that offers RPC services. A service of type RPC is handled like a procedure and has the following properties: it is executed until completion, it does not have any dialogue with the requester, and it sends back a return value to the requester. For a requester, the execution of an RPC service can be synchronous or asynchronous.

Server

A process which registers with TUXEDO and subsequently receives service requests from a requester (that is, a client or another server) and dispatches the service routine that acts on the request. In the process of executing the service routine, it can exchange messages with the requester in a conversational fashion.

Server abstraction

Applications combine their service routines with a TUXEDO-provided main() in building a server process. System/T's main() provides server initialisation and termination as well as receiving incoming requests and dispatching them to service routines. All of this processing is transparent to applications.

Server group

See *group*.

Service

A module of application code that carries out a service request.

Service request

A request initiated by a requester process that asks for the invocation of a service.

SHM model

A TUXEDO application configuration that runs entirely on a single machine.

System Network Architecture (SNA)

A set of protocols, procedures, and environment descriptions that define a method of network management; used by CICS and IMS to do program-to-program communication through VTAM; 5-level protocol similar to 7-level OSI for data communications.

Socket

An endpoint of communication to which a name may be bound. The socket interface is one of the network access methods supported by TUXEDO.

STARLAN

An AT&T LAN product.

STRING buffer

A data structure that is an array of non NULL characters terminated by the NULL character. It is a self-describing buffer.

Structured Query Language (SQL)

A non procedural language for defining and accessing relational databases. SQL has become the industry standard database language.

Syncpoint

The act of completing a logical unit of work; syncpoint rollback means to reset all recoverable resources to the state they were in at the time of the most recent syncpoint, or the beginning of the transaction, whichever is nearer in time.

System administration

The preparation of an instance of a system for use in a particular setting or installation; also, changing the system as the installation changes. This term is often used in a way that subsumes system operations as well.

System programming

In a TUXEDO environment, the act of defining and programming the characteristics of a TUXEDO application in a UBBCONFIG configuration file.

System operations

Tasks that need to be performed regularly for a system. Examples are backup and restoration of data and logs, monitoring the system for error conditions, and so forth.

System/DOMAINS

A component of TUXEDO that enables a TUXEDO application (domain) to exchange information with a separate application, either under the control of TUXEDO or under the control of an OSI/TP-compliant TP monitor.

System/HOST

A component of TUXEDO that enables a System/T application to access host services.

System/Q

A component of TUXEDO that provides recoverable disk queues for delayed or batch processing.

System/T

The core component of TUXEDO. It provides distributed processing and distributed transaction processing capabilities to a distributed application, as well as administration functions.

System/WS

A component of TUXEDO designed to allow remote workstations and personal computers to participate in System/T applications without requiring the resources necessary to support servers on the workstation.

Transmission Control Protocol/Internet Protocol (TCP/IP)

A network provider that is supported by the transport layer interface.

Tele-Processing

In a TUXEDO environment, an equivalent term to *distributed processing*.

Transport Layer Interface (TLI)

The standard user level interface to data communications features as defined by level 4 of the OSI communications protocol.

tlisten

A network-independent listener process that runs as a daemon process and provides remote service connections for other processes.

TLOG

The System/T transaction log that keeps track of global transactions.

Transaction Manager Server (TMS)

A System/T server process that manages the two-phase commit protocol and recovery for global transactions.

tmadmin

An administrative tool to perform various actions, including browsing into the application, changing application parameters, and dynamically altering the behaviour of an application.

tmboot

An administrative tool to start up an entire application or portions of it.

tmconfig

An administrative tool to reconfigure a running application dynamically.

tmloadcf

An administrative tool to convert a *UBBCONFIG* file into a binary *TUXCONFIG*.

TMQUEUE

An internal process provided by *System/Q* to enable message enqueuing and dequeuing in disk queues.

TMQFORWARD

An internal process provided by *System/Q* to submit requests and enqueue replies.

tmshutdown

An administrative tool to stop an entire application or portions of it.

tmunloadcf

An administrative tool to extract an ASCII representation of a *TUXCONFIG* file.

Transport interface

The programming interface used to access a network provider. Transport interfaces are typically network provider independent to an extent.

Transport provider

See *network provider*.

TUXCONFIG

The binary configuration file for a TUXEDO application. This file is accessed by all System/T processes for all configuration information.

Two-phase commit

The protocol used for global transactions, in which each participating RM indicates a readiness to commit and then waits for the coordinating process to give permission to commit.

Typed buffer

A buffer for message communication involving data of a specific data type. See *buffer types*.

TX

The interface between the application and the transaction manager in X/Open's DTP model. This interface is directly derived from TUXEDO's *ATMI*.

TxRPC

One of the interfaces between the application and the communication RM in X/Open's DTP model.

UBBCONFIG

ASCII application configuration file. This is the ASCII representation of the TUXCONFIG file.

ULOG

The User Log file for a TUXEDO application. Each System/T node has one, to contain applicative or administrative messages or errors. An application process can write in the local ULOG through the use of function *userlog()*.

Unsolicited messages

Messages delivered to application clients outside the RPC-like or conversational communication paradigms. Unsolicited messages are sent by application clients, servers, and by the application administrator. Clients receive this type of messages through a message-handling function.

Unsolicited notification

A communication method by which an application process sends messages to one or multiple application clients outside the standard request/response or conversational paradigms.

VIEW buffer

A data structure similar to a C structure. As part of defining this buffer type, a view description file is created. It is a self-describing buffer.

Virtual Sequential Access Method (VSAM)

An IBM file management system; contains three file types: entry-sequenced (ESDS), key-sequenced (KSDS), and relative-record (RRDS); used in part as the underlying access method for other database management systems, such as IMS.

Workstation handler (WSH)

The System/T-supplied surrogate client responsible for managing a set of workstation client connections. These handlers are started dynamically by the workstation listener. The handler may be customised if necessary. This process resides within the administrative domain of the application.

Workstation listener (WSL)

The System/T supplied process responsible for acting as the single point of contact for workstation clients. The workstation listener also handles the distribution of workstation connections to workstation handlers, starting new handlers as necessary. This process resides within the administrative domain of the application.

/WS

See *System/WS*

XA

The interface between the transaction manager and resource manager in both TUXEDO's and X/Open's DTP model.

XATMI

One of the interfaces between the application and the communication RM in the X/Open's DTP model. The XATMI is derived directly from TUXEDO's *ATMI*.

XCTL

A CICS application function that allows one program to terminate and transfer control to another one.

XDR

See *external data representation*.

X_COMMON

One of the standard buffer types provided by the *XATMI* interface. It typically corresponds to a VIEW buffer for COBOL applications.

X_C_TYPE

Another standard buffer type provided by the *XATMI* interface. It typically corresponds to a VIEW buffer for C applications.

X_OCTET
The third standard buffer type provided by the *XATMI* interface. It typically corresponds to a STRING or CARRAY buffer.

Bibliography

- **"Building the TUXEDO® Transaction Processing System"** - White paper - UNIX System Laboratories, 1992

- **"On-Line Transaction Processing in Open Systems"** - White paper - UNIX System Laboratories, 1992

- **"The TUXEDO System - Product Overview"** - Decision Support, 1993

- **"The TUXEDO System - /T Reference Manual"** - Decision Support, 1993

- **"The TUXEDO System - /T Programmer's Guide"** - Decision Support, 1993

- **"The TUXEDO System - /T Administrator's Guide"** - Decision Support, 1993

- **"The TUXEDO System - Application Development Guide"** - Decision Support, 1993

- **"The TUXEDO System - FML Programmer's Guide"** - Decision Support, 1993

- **"The TUXEDO System - /Workstation Guide"** - Decision Support, 1993

- **"The TUXEDO System - /HOST Guide"** - Decision Support, 1993

- "**The TUXEDO System - /Q Guide**" - Decision Support, 1993
- "**Distributed TP: Reference Model, Version 2**" - X/Open Publications, 1993
- "**Distributed TP: The XA Specification**" - X/Open Publications, 1993
- "**Distributed TP: The TX SPecification**" - X/Open Publications, 1993
- "**Distributed TP: The XATMI Specification**" - X/Open Publications, 1993

Index

TRADEMARKS LIST